WITHDRAWN

P9-CEN-470

LIZZIE BORDEN

WITHDRAWN

LIZZIE BORDEN:

A Case Book of Family and Crime in the 1890s

Edited by:

Joyce G. Williams
J. Eric Smithburn
M. Jeanne Peterson

1980 Copyright © by M. Jeanne Peterson, J. Eric Smithburn and
Joyce G. Williams
All Rights Reserved
Printed in the United States of America

ISBN 0-89917-302-0

Reproduced by photo offset from typeset manuscript.
For information, write T.I.S. Publications Division, P.O. Box 1998,
Bloomington, Indiana 47402.

364.1523
L789

Table of Contents

36055

Diagrams and Illustrations

Cover cartoon from the Boston *Daily Globe,* June 21, 1893

Preface

Nearly every child in America has heard, if not learned, the grisly jingle that perpetuates Lizzie Borden's fame and clearly declares her guilt:

> Lizzie Borden took an axe,
> And gave her mother forty whacks.
> When she saw what she had done,
> She gave her father forty-one.

This little rhyme testifies to the continuing interest the Borden case holds -- as do the books, dances, films, and other presentations of the case produced in the last eighty-five years. But the poem gives no clue as to the reasons for our fascination with the Borden case. Lizzie and her family held no significant political position in 1890s America; the crime, in all its bloody brutality, would seem to offer little understanding of the normal, ordinary, everyday lives of Americans in those years. It would seem an aberration, a momentary derangement in the orderly flow of Victorian American life.

This book exists because the editors believe that the Borden case brings together many major themes and topics of late nineteenth-century American social and legal history. Fall River, the scene of the crimes, was fully in the mainstream of American history, with its growing industries and its growing immigrant population. The Borden family itself represents one of the phenomena of American history -- growing prosperity and the problems and expectations of social mobility. Life style, family relations, and the position of women in American society can all be examined through the prism of the Bordens' habits and experience. And the sources of information about the case that are published here -- legal records, newspapers, police documents, and private papers -- open a window on the workings of the press and the law and reveal the depth of social influence on these major institutions. These materials are published to provide an opportunity to explore at first hand the records of the case. From these records, readers may draw their own conclusions, not only about the crime itself, but about the society in which the crime, investigation, and trial took place.

Many individuals and institutions have helped us in the preparation of this book and they deserve our deepest thanks. The Fall River Historical Society made many Borden materials available to us, and the generous cooperation of Mrs. Florence Brigham was of enormous help. Other materials came to us from the Fall River Public Library, the New Bedford Free Public Library, the Boston Public Library, and the Providence Public Library, and we want to thank Hilding Hedberg and Eileen Stafieji of Fall River and Mary Cabral of New Bedford for their help. Special thanks go to Chief Justice James P. Lynch, Jr., of the Superior Court, Commonwealth of Massachusetts for permission to reproduce Judge Dewey's charge to the jury.

Many people connected with Fall River or the Borden case gave us generous assistance and took the time to share their knowledge and views with us. For this we thank Russell Lake, William Thurber, Frank Silvia, Jr., Mrs. Vida Turner, Mrs. Marion Durfee Holman, Mrs. Rosanne Sullivan, and Harold Hudner.

Very special thanks must go to Mr. and Mrs. Ellis Waring, Mrs. Edith Coolidge Hart, and Mrs. Florence Brigham for their extensive and supportive assistance. They gave more than we could have hoped for, and they helped us with grace and enthusiasm.

Those people who themselves have an interest in writing about Lizzie Borden and who generously shared their materials with us deserve a special note, for they understand the value of knowledge shared: hence, out thanks to Edward Sullivan and Tom Covel.

The skillful secretarial help the editors received made this book possible. Marilyn Van Deventer lived with the Borden materials and all their difficulties for years, and her skill and enthusiasm have been notable. Lori Bell, Debra Chase, Libby Gitlitz, Barbara Lariviere, Peter Leach, and Connie Strange also gave ably and generously of their time in the preparation of the manuscript.

Margaret Myers provided us with able research assistance, and Sylvia Hoffert lent her expertise in reading a portion of the manuscript. The diagrams of the Borden house are the product of Barbara DeWitz's talent. Kyu-Sun Rhee prepared photographs for use in this volume, and Anne Lee Bain gave us the benefit of her sound advice on a variety of editorial matters.

Finally, our students in Indiana University's Continuing Studies Program and the summer "Mini-University" encouraged us with their enthusiasm and interest. The book is done for them.

I

The Social Environment of the Crime

The rise of industry, the growth of cities, and the expansion of the population were the three great developments of late nineteenth-century American history. As new, larger, steam-powered factories became a feature of the American landscape in the East, they transformed farm hands into industrial laborers, and provided jobs for a rising tide of immigrants. With industry came urbanization -- the growth of large cities (like Fall River, Massachusetts, where the Bordens lived) which became the centers of production as well as of commerce and trade.

At the same time, the American population was growing at a rapid rate. In 1900 the population was seventy-six million, double what it had been only thirty-five years earlier. . In addition to natural increase, part of the population growth came from massive immigration. Between 1865 and 1900, over twelve million immigrants entered the United States. They came from Britain (including Ireland), Germany, and Eastern and Southern Europe. Sizable numbers of Roman Catholics and Jews often seemed a kind of invasion to a predominantly white, northern European, Anglo-Saxon Protestant society. Immigrants comprised half of the population of Fall River in 1890. Poor immigrants, crowding into the cities of the eastern seaboard and taking jobs as factory hands and servants, seemed to threaten the security and stability of the "WASP" community, many of whom felt the need to cling more closely than ever to their Anglo-Saxon and Protestant identity.

In our own day, Americans think of their society as essentially middle class. Only the very poor and the very rich seem to fall outside the middle class. But fine gradations of rank defined American society in an earlier era. The nineteenth-century ideal of equality was just that - - an ideal. And the principle was often ignored when it came to immigrants, particularly those from Southern and Eastern Europe and Ireland, and was frequently irrelevant even within Protestant and Anglo-Saxon society. People lived by, and observed in others, the distinctions of rank and wealth. This was especially true in a town like Fall River.

How did people assess and declare their position in society? Certainly money provided one base line by which social prestige could be judged and demonstrated. But patterns of consumption were as critical as the money itself in defining a family's social standing. The location and size of one's house, its furnishings, the possession of carriage and horses, the number and type of servants, the clothing, speech, and manners, the cultural and charitable activities of the family, and the

1

exercise of economic and political power in the community all bore witness to social rank. For example, in Fall River, the working classes lived in the city center, while the upper orders usually lived in the northerly section known as "The Hill." Names themselves mattered. Bridget was clearly an Irish name and indicated an immigrant background. A name like Elizabeth did not. Borden was an Anglo-Saxon name, a social advantage in Fall River.

The middle class in the 1880s deserves a closer look since this is the class to which the Bordens belonged. We can divide the middle class into two segments. The new middle class included professional men, white-collar workers, and all varieties of businessmen and manufacturers. Great and small gradations existed among these people on the basis of their wealth (or lack of it). For example, there was considerable social distance between the small shopkeeper and the wholesale merchant. The second major segment of the middle class was the old middle class. These people might also be businessmen or professionals, but unlike recent arrivals to prosperity, they were not new to America or to the middle class. They were an elite by virtue of a long history of life in America. Because of their long-established ties in New England, the Borden clan belonged to the old middle class.

One distinguishing feature of middle-class Americans was the system of values and attitudes by which they lived and looked at life, work, success, and the family. Nineteenth-century men were reared to value the idea of hard work. Idleness and laziness were thought to be positively dangerous. They led to vice, degradation, and finally personal disaster. It was a hard ethic, and the clergy of the nineteenth century made the rules very clear. Henry Ward Beecher, the famous mid-nineteenth-century parson, articulated the American ideal in *Seven Lectures to Young Men*: "Satisfaction is not the product of excess, or of indolence, or of riches; but of industry, temperance, and usefulness." He went on to say, "A good character, good habits, and iron industry are impregnable to the assaults of all the ill luck that fools ever dreamed of." The watchwords were truthfulness, frugality, modesty, and hard work. Developing such good character was the responsibility of each individual. Self-discipline and self-control formed the core of the "New Puritanism of Victorian America." From the pulpits, clergymen preached this secular ideal of hard work, morality, and prudence as the foundations for success, for the silk hat and the fat wallet.

But there was an ambivalence about success itself. Prudence led to success, but wealth made indulgence possible. Americans thought that success was dangerous, for it could lead to the very flaws of character that a man had avoided to begin with. Fathers warned their sons to "be on your guard against the dangers . . . of success & prosperity . . . the danger of immoderate elation, of too great self dependence or of an over estimate of our powers, attainments and goodness . . . ." There was a tension between those sober habits of self-denial and the opportunities for comfort and self-indulgence available to those who succeeded.

Servants were, of course, a part of the ease provided by success. One by-product of the mass immigration of the nineteenth century was the increased pool of servants available for work in prosperous American households, where the well-to-do might have a cook and one or two housemaids. Newly-arrived Irish girls commonly took posts as housemaids, but they soon found their way into factories, where they had more freedom and better pay. Inexperienced help and turnover among servants were, therefore, constant problems for the middle-class housewife. But when servants were available, they allowed for increased leisure and reduced physical labor for the women of the household.

The middle class idealized the home as a safeguard for morality and a haven from the pressures of work and the drive for success. The wife was to be a source of sustained and renewed piety and virtue for her husband -- never a competitor with him. She created a Christian environment and an orderly setting for domestic life -- a place where her husband could get away from the pressures of the world. In 1850 the anonymous author of *Reveries of a Bachelor* wrote: "A home! . . . *there* at least you are beloved; . . . there you are understood; . . . there all your errors will meet ever with gentlest forgiveness; . . . there your troubles will be smiled away . . . ." But home was not a place of intellectual discourse. Nor was it always openly affectionate. A French visitor noted this when he wrote:

> [The American husband] asks for his dinner, and
> offers not a word more; his wife and children do not
> tear the American away from the practical world, and
> he so rarely shows them a sign of tenderness and
> affection that a nickname has been made for those
> households where the husband, after an absence,
> kisses his wife and children--they are called "kissing
> families." In the American's eyes, the wife is not a
> companion; she is a partner who helps him spend for
> his well-being and comfort the money he earns in
> business.

Men who espoused "iron industry" and disciplined their feelings often became incapable of emotional openness. They had been socialized away from the tender side of family life. As one writer in 1860 noted: "The pressure upon a multitude of business and professional men is really frightful; . . . it produces little short of an absolute separation from their families." Lizzie Borden's father was no stranger to this aspect of the male ethos.

3

Late nineteenth-century American men earned a living, but middle-class women's lives centered on the home. Until marriage -- sometimes after -- working-class women labored in factories or domestic service. Middle-class women stayed in the parental home until they married and established homes of their own. Marriage was the only norm. Three-fourths of all American women married between the ages of nineteen and twenty-five; by age twenty-seven nearly all women were married. In this respect the Borden daughters were exceptional since neither of them married.

In conformity with society's norms for their adult lives, the education of men and women differed markedly. While middle-class men prepared themselves, at school and university, for future careers, women's education was designed to meet the standards of their future lives; they rarely enjoyed higher education. Girls were often taught reading and writing, as well as domestic skills, by their mothers; sometimes their fathers taught them or tutors came into the home. A ladies' seminary might provide a finishing touch. Beyond the basic curriculum of reading, writing, religion, and character-building, the girl might learn a bit of music and dancing, the elegant accomplishments of the lady. But she avoided serious intellectual activity, which was regarded as "unfeminine."

A Victorian girl's reading went on under careful supervision. Many families forbade novels. History, however, was considered proper, because it revealed (some said) the "depravity of the human heart." Religious biography gave the girl examples of piety she might emulate.

The purpose of female education was ordinarily not to prepare women for work or career. Women might be teachers, nurses, or homemakers -- but prime qualifications for such work were the womanly qualities of high character that were prerequisites for marriage and motherhood. The single woman's purpose in life was also service -- social and religious -- within her family and within the larger community. Charity and good works in a town like Fall River were the extension, for the single woman, of her religious and social duties in a family.

Doctors and clergy alike advised parents on a girl's health regimen. To prepare and protect her health for motherhood, American girls should have plenty of fresh air and moderate exercise. She should avoid corsets, soft down beds, liquor, and other stimulants. Young girls should avoid strong emotions, especially anger, since high levels of emotional life could, some believed, endanger their physical and mental health.

From an early age, a young woman learned the norms of male-female relations. Man, she was told, was "woman's superior by God's appointment, if not in intellectual dowry, at least by official decree." A woman's submission to men -- even inferior men -- preserved the social

4

order and the divine order. Brides were admonished to "Reverence his *wishes* even when you do not [reverence] his *opinions*."

Science and religion alike provided the intellectual and moral justification for women's submission. A physician, Dr. John Wiltbank, explained the influence of female anatomy: her reproductive organs, he said, "exercise a controlling influence upon her entire system . . . . They are the source of her peculiarities, the centre of her sympathies." In 1878 Ralph Waldo Emerson drew the conclusion more pithily when he wrote: Woman is "more vulnerable, more infirm, more mortal than man." Perhaps physical size explained it all, as one doctor thought: "Woman had a head almost too small for intellect -- but just big enough for love."

Physical differences had their counterpart in female personality: "True feminine genius is ever timid, doubtful, and clingingly dependent; a perpetual childhood." Perhaps because of their physical and intellectual weakness, women were considered "naturally religious." A woman's "confiding nature leads her more readily than men to accept the proffered grace of the Gospel." This natural obedience to God had its analog in her submission to her father and later to her husband. Both, of course, had their origins in Biblical commands. *The Young Lady's Book* made the point very clear: "In whatever situation of life a woman is placed from her cradle to her grave, a spirit of obedience and submission, pliability of temper, and humility of mind are required of her."

All this suggests women's powerlessness. But obviously women had influence in the home, at least over their children and their physical environment. Some even saw power in women's weakness: "The empire of the woman is an empire of softness . . . her commands are caresses, her menaces are tears."

What happened when a woman did not find her place in a marriage, as a wife, a mother, a person of influence in the domestic sphere? Some tried to console spinsters that single life was better than a selfish or unhappy marriage. A few even dared hint that such a woman could have real freedom. But the single woman was an anomaly, a failure in a society where marriage and the nuclear family were the core of the social order.

Many women managed to make satisfactory lives for themselves within the Victorian norms. Whether naturally pious or not, they went to church and served God, husband, and family. They enjoyed the fruits of their husbands' successes in the ease, sometimes luxury, of booming American economic life. One can only speculate about what a woman like Lizzie Borden must have felt as the spinster daughter of a successful man who refused to his wife and daughters many of the normal benefits of their social position.

Not all women accepted the standards of the majority for them, and late nineteenth-century America saw the beginnings of new ideas about women's abilities and proper place in society. Frustration with the limits of their lives may have led some women to campaign for the vote, to seek a place in the professions, to assert the possibility of women's independence. Others may have felt equally rebellious, but rather than warring against their position, they either retreated into religion or they turned their anger inward, directing it toward their families or themselves.

The world of clearly defined social standards, of man's place, and woman's place -- this was the Bordens' world. The police, the journalists, the citizenry of Fall River, the courts, and the public shared the assumptions and values of the society. And those ideals and standards shaped the Borden case from beginning to end.

Recollections of Fall River at the Turn of the Century

Mrs. Edith Coolidge Hart was born in the early 1890s and lived in Fall River for eighty years. The following excerpts from Mrs. Hart's correspondence recall life in Lizzie Borden's home town around the turn of the century.

Source: Letters from Mrs. Edith C. Hart to Joyce G. Williams, July 19 and September 1, 1979. Quoted by permission of the author.

"You have visited Fall River, and you must have judged what a beautiful city it could have been physically. There was the 'hill' on which lived the so-called aristocracy. Below the hill and scattered throughout the city were various ghettos; the English, French, Polish, Jewish, and Portuguese had their own areas and their own churches. Fall River is a city of many beautiful Catholic churches, built on the contributions extracted from the poor mill workers. There were some horses and carriages on the hill. Few workers could even afford the five cent fare to ride on the trolley cars. . . . .

"The hill population of the so-called elite had the beautiful Central Congregational [Church] and later the First. At that time in the Protestant churches families rented pews. In the First Baptist and the Baptist Temple that was also so. When the First Congregational was built to house the most elite, Mr. Borden rented a pew; Lizzie would not join him there but continued in the Central. It might have been just to be obstinate. However, the ministers of the Central were devoted to her in a maudlin way, and that may have been the influence. . . . .

"There was a strong antipathy of the Protestants to the Catholics until almost the mid-1900s. I would say after World War II. . . . It was well into the 1900s before Catholics lived in the hill district. Even as late as the 1940s a Catholic priest could not even be a guest speaker in a Protestant church. In fact, an Irish Catholic family lived next door to [the Bordens]. The maids talked over the fence, but the Bordens would not even speak to the Kellys. . . . .

"It was a bigoted atmosphere not only in the town but in each church. The minister in my Baptist Church was fired because his son was a member of the dramatic group at Brown University. . . . . No stores were open on Sunday, no games, no theatre. In fact, a pall seemed to swoop down on the city when Sunday arrived. If you lost a button on Sunday, it was not repaired until Monday. Food for Sunday was cooked on Saturday. In Protestant churches there were at least four services each Sunday. . . .

"It is difficult to transmit that deadening atmosphere of bigotry to this generation. . . ."

II
The Family and the Murders

The house is still there on Second Street. It still has a look of narrowness, of confinement, and, to knowing viewers, of mystery.

The Borden family moved there in 1871. Formerly a fashionable address, the neighborhood had deteriorated, but some large, once-attractive homes testified to the past prosperity of the street. The Borden house was not one of them. The house stood very close to the sidewalk, with no porch to soften the entrance. It was extremely narrow -- about twenty feet wide -- and unadorned clapboards emphasized its sharp angular look. It had been built as a two-family home, which accounted for the strange arrangement of rooms. There were no halls, so that to go from front to back one had to walk through succeeding rooms. Two stairways, one at the front and one at the back, divided the upstairs bedrooms into two zones. The front stairway led to a guest bedroom and to the separate rooms of the daughters of the family. The steep stairway off the kitchen led to Mr. and Mrs. Borden's bedroom and to a small connecting room next to it. A locked door between the larger front bedroom and the back bedroom gave the final punctuation to this division of the house.

Although Mr. Borden had modernized the house, the only convenience was a furnace. There were two cold-water faucets in the house, one in a tiny sinkroom off the kitchen and the other in a cellar washroom. Toilet facilities were provided by a water closet in the cellar, where old newspapers were kept for sanitary purposes. As a matter of necessity slop pails were placed in each bedroom. The house was not connected with the gas main that brought light to other houses on the street. Mr. Borden used kerosene lamps and frequently sat in the dark to save fuel.

At the back of the deep lot on which the house stood was a grape arbor, a few pear trees, and a small stable which the Bordens called the barn. Andrew Borden had disposed of his horse, considering it an unnecessary expense, and in 1892 the building was used for storage only.

The house did not accurately reflect the social standing of the family. The Borden name had been identified for two hundred years with the development and prosperity of the state of Massachusetts. The Bordens were leading citizens of the town, and their name, as author Edwin Porter says, meant "open sesame" to the best society.

Some Bordens were richer and more successful than others. Andrew Borden had had to work harder and save more diligently than did his ancestors to acquire wealth. He began at the lower end of the socio-economic scale by peddling fish in the streets. He next became an undertaker. By being unusually perspicacious in this profession,

Andrew amassed a small fortune, which he then turned into a larger one by investing in farmland and in rental property.

The accumulation of money became Andrew Borden's all-absorbing passion. By the time he was seventy, he was worth half a million dollars. In 1892 he owned mills, a bank, city houses, and farms, but such were his life-time habits of thrift that he could still be seen on occasion carrying a basket of eggs from one of his farms to sell in the market. And he looked the part of a miser, especially one who had once been an undertaker. He was lean and tall, his eyes were hard, and his mouth was grim. He dressed year round in severe black garments of heavy cloth.

While Andrew Borden may have been a model of industry, thrift, and frugality, his virtues were not conducive to domestic harmony. No believer in conspicuous consumption, he imposed a stern economy on the household. And he even stopped attending church because one of the wardens happened to be a tax collector, and Borden's property taxes had been raised. His reputation in the town was that of a charmless and compassionless man who connived for and guarded every cent. Andrew Borden did not choose to spend money to live on "The Hill" where the prominent families of the city lived.

In 1845, Andrew Borden married Sarah J. Morse. A rare picture shows Sarah to be sharp-featured, with alert eyes and an elaborate coiffure. She suffered from severe migraines and spells of unexplained rage; no one knows whether these attacks had a physical or a psychological source. Three children were born to this couple at intervals of five years: first Emma, in 1849; five years later, another daughter, Alice, who did not survive; and after a third five years, Lizzie Andrew Borden, in 1860. Her second name hints that Mr. Borden had hoped for a son.

Sarah Borden died in 1862, when Emma was twelve years old and Lizzie was two. Andrew waited two years before marrying again. His second wife was Abby Durfee Gray, a thirty-seven-year-old spinster whose middle name linked her, but only in a distant way, with the prominent Durfees of Fall River. The stepchild of a tin peddler, Abby had a half-sister, Sarah, who was only one year old at the time of Abby's marriage.

Abby no doubt had resigned herself to spinsterhood when Andrew Borden walked her home from church one day and shortly afterward proposed marriage. It seemed to be a marriage of convenience. Andrew needed a housekeeper for four-year-old Lizzie and fourteen-year-old Emma. Abby, slightly over five feet in height, overweight, and long past marrying age, may have felt content simply to have a husband. There were no children from this marriage. Over the years of their marriage, Abby grew heavier, and by 1892 she weighed over 200 pounds. A docile, soft-spoken woman, she seemed no match for a dominant husband and difficult daughters.

Stepmothers were not unusual in this era when women died young, and the two Borden girls grew up with no discernible signs of maladjustment. Abby was not noticeably unkind, and if the two Borden girls seemed to depend on each other to the exclusion of their stepmother, Abby could lavish her maternal feelings on her half-sister, who became her sole friend and companion.

In 1892 Emma was forty-one years old and a stereotypical spinster of the era: small, almost frail, and self-effacing. She had a few close women friends who seemed exceptionally devoted to her. Her activities were limited almost entirely to visiting these friends. Her attitude toward her younger sister seemed not so much affectionate as appropriate -- not openly warm, but friendly, with dutiful letters written when the two were apart.

Lizzie, at thirty-two, had developed quite differently. She was a Borden -- Bordens were rich -- and Bordens were noticed. Lizzie wanted to be noticed. She was very active in the only area open to her in that society, the area of good works. She attended church regularly, taught a Sunday school class of Chinese children, the sons and daughters of Fall River laundrymen, and was secretary-treasurer of the Christian Endeavor. She also belonged to the Women's Christian Temperance Union. These eminently respectable activities earned her the staunch support of two ministers of the Central Congregational Church, the Reverends W. Walter Jubb and E. A. Buck.

Lizzie liked stylish clothes. She favored blue. She liked to have her picture taken. Many pictures of Lizzie survive while few of Emma exist. Lizzie's red hair was always carefully dressed, crimped in the fashion of the day. Her face was full, and her large eyes were an unusual shade of gray, almost transparent. Indeed, her eyes were unusual enough to cause comment. There were those who described her eyes as colorless and empty. Some would say expressionless. She liked to stare steadily at people, and most wavered under her prolonged gaze. Some of Lizzie's acquaintances thought she tried to stare people down in order to control them.

But Lizzie could not control the person she most wanted to control -- her father, keeper of the Borden money. Like her father in many ways, stubborn, determined, and independent, she continually challenged him in the area of most importance to her: her economic rights as a Borden. She wanted money, but, unlike her father, she wanted the comforts that money could buy. One can imagine the constant dissension between the two over money for a new dress, the expense of repainting the house, possible remodelling of the house. This agitation may have prompted Emma, the older sister, suddenly to give up her larger bedroom -- one she had occupied for twenty years -- to Lizzie for the sake of peace.

This less than united family, headed by a grim-faced man with a monomania for saving money, became completely divided emotionally as Emma and Lizzie became women. The daughters had never been close to either their father or their stepmother. Some students of the Borden family have made much of the fact that Lizzie gave her father her gold high school ring, suggesting that this gift shows her devotion to him. With like devotion, some say, Andrew Borden gave Lizzie a sealskin cape and a trip to Europe for her thirtieth birthday. But an occasional gift need not mean devotion: it may be an attempt to buy loyalty or to purchase peace. A more revealing aspect of the relationship of father and daughters was the fact that in 1892 both Emma and Lizzie (aged forty-one and thirty-two respectively) were completely dependent on their father. He gave them a weekly allowance of four dollars each.

The occupants of 92 Second Street pursued solitary paths, according to their interests, until five years before the murders, when an incident occurred which threw the family into an unhappy imbroglio. Abby's half-sister, for whom she felt real affection, had not married well, and in 1887 she and her family faced eviction from their comfortable home. Abby no doubt appealed to Andrew, who bought the half-house in which Sarah Whitehead lived. In 1887 Andrew deeded the house, for which he had paid about $1,500, to Abby, with the understanding that Abby's sister could live there rent-free.

The daughters learned of the transaction, although it had been done surreptitiously. Lizzie and Emma felt that the financial transaction was treachery. Although the $1,500 house was the only property Abby ever owned, the stepdaughters saw the gift as evidence of Andrew's partiality to Abby and an infringement of their rights. They also believed that their Uncle John, Sarah's brother, had connived with Andrew secretly to deprive them of a share of the Borden property.

Lizzie talked of this injustice to several people. She argued that what her father had done for Abby he should also do for his own blood relations. As a consequence, Andrew gave the sisters a piece of property worth about $3,000. This gift did not appease the sisters, who gradually withdrew from any contact with their father and stepmother, eating most of their meals at a second serving and no longer speaking to Abby except to answer direct questions. To everyone they made it plain that Abby was their *step*mother, and sometimes they said more. Lizzie, when talking to her seamstress, referred to Abby as a "mean old thing."

From 1887 to 1892, members of this family indulged in a cold war. The peculiar arrangement of the house fostered the alienation of the family members. This house, devoid of luxury, divided within, had always been kept locked -- the doors to the outside, for example, were always triply locked. Beginning in 1887, however, the habit spread throughout the house. Doors to the bedrooms were locked by their

12

occupants. Windows, closets, and bureau drawers were kept locked. A heavy bureau was placed against the locked door between Lizzie's room and the Bordens' bedroom. The maids, first Maggie, and then in 1889, Bridget, lived in a small cubicle on the third floor of the house and apparently went along with the bizarre behavior of the family, unlocking the doors and then relocking them immediately.

In the early summer of 1892, the Borden house was robbed. Abby, who seldom left the house, had gone with Andrew to visit one of his farms in Swansea, and the house had been locked with dedicated thoroughness. Emma, Lizzie, and Bridget remained at home. Someone presumably invaded the fortress, going straight to Mrs. Borden's bedroom and making off with her modest supply of jewelry and $30 or $40 from a small desk. This daring burglary took place in daylight in a neighborhood where houses were close together. To get inside the house and inside the desk required the unlocking of at least four locks. The women inside had to be avoided. Yet no one saw a stranger.

The burglary was not discovered until the parents returned home. At this point, Mr. Borden sent for the police. Lizzie was eager to answer questions, volunteering that she had found a large nail stuck in a keyhole. Mr. Borden suddenly asked that the investigation be dropped. Although Bridget was Irish, and thus liable to suspicion in late nineteenth-century Massachusetts, and, although she had been in the house at the time of the theft, no one suggested that she had done it.

Thereafter, Mr. Borden locked his bedroom door, but he placed the key in plain sight on the mantle during the daytime. Such an act may have been done for the convenience of Mrs. Borden. But it may also have been a defiant gesture, affirming his trust in the maid Bridget.

This daylight theft, a miniature crime when compared with the one to come, could be viewed in several ways. Perhaps it was simply an unsolved burglary. Perhaps it was the work of someone in the household, a petty act of greed or revenge. Perhaps it was a subtle act of terror or a test of the family's loyalties. Later Lizzie, when discussing the case, denied that her father stopped the investigation. She claimed that the family's silence on the matter covered the detectives' continuing investigation. The crime was never solved.

The theft frightened Abby more noticeably than anyone else. And it heightened the atmosphere of tension in the house.

The air was far from soothing in the first week of August, 1892. A heat wave, some said the hottest ever in Fall River, caused the straw hats on the horses to have a boiled and droopy look. The dry goods store downtown was like an oven. The few women out shopping walked slowly. Children played listlessly.

The heat seemed to be responsible for troubles in the house on Second Street. On Tuesday and Wednesday, August 2 and 3, Mr. and Mrs. Borden and their maid Bridget suffered severe nausea. Emma was away on a vacation, but Lizzie, who had remained at home, complained of a queasy stomach, too. A joint of mutton, prepared the preceding Sunday, had made up the major portion of the meals served on Monday, Tuesday, and Wednesday. Without refrigeration, the meat could have spoiled rapidly in the extreme heat and caused family illness.

Abby Borden didn't believe the heat was responsible for her illness. She thought she was being poisoned. She also felt that she knew who was responsible: her stepdaughter Lizzie. Despite her weight and the resultant difficulty of movement, on Wednesday morning she laboriously walked across the street to tell her fears to Dr. Seabury Bowen. Dr. Bowen, a neighbor and a family friend, reassured her, sensibly suggesting it was something she ate that had made her sick, and he accompanied Abby back across the street, offering to examine Mr. Borden. Mr. Borden responded with extraordinary anger and ordered the doctor out of the house, indicating that he didn't intend to pay him for his services.

That Wednesday afternoon Uncle John Vinnicum Morse, brother of the first Mrs. Borden, arrived for a visit. As a relative and an experienced farmer, he sometimes advised Andrew Borden on business matters. On his visits he slept in the spare bedroom and ate his meals with the family. Although he was a frequent visitor in the Borden home, Lizzie did not seem to like him. On the evening of August 3, she did not join the family at mealtime, but remained in her room. In the evening she visited a friend, Miss Alice Russell, thus successfully avoiding seeing her uncle at all. That evening at Miss Russell's, Lizzie painted a picture of doom and gloom, speaking of vague threats made against her father from unknown enemies, dwelling on her father's irascible behavior in general, and in particular discussing his treatment of Dr. Bowen earlier that day. Lizzie also told Miss Russell that she was afraid the milk had been poisoned and that she feared something dreadful was about to happen. She thoroughly depressed Alice Russell, whose reassurances became weaker. Lizzie then went home and directly to her bedroom, without stopping in the sitting room where her uncle and parents were sitting.

Like Mrs. Borden and Lizzie, the usually taciturn Andrew Borden had expressed apprehension about the family's situation. Earlier in the week he had spoken to some of his business acquaintances, telling them there was trouble in his household.

As the sun rose on that Thursday, it seemed to promise the hottest day of the lingering heat wave of the year. Uncle John joined Mr. and Mrs. Borden for an early breakfast. The ubiquitous mutton made another appearance as hot mutton broth. Along with this choice item were served overripe bananas, johnnycake, bread, coffee, and cookies. Emma was away at Fairhaven visiting friends, and Lizzie did not come down for breakfast.

The ailing Bridget had pulled herself together to build a fire and to serve the remarkable breakfast. Soon after, Uncle John left to visit a nephew and niece in Weybosset Street. Andrew unlocked the door to let him out and, as he relocked it, Mrs. Borden called to John, inviting him to come back for the noon meal.

With the departure of Uncle John, the remaining members of the Borden household quickly re-established their usual routines. Emma, of course, was absent. Lizzie came downstairs and ate a scant breakfast of coffee and cookies (probable time: 8:40). At this time Bridget, who had felt sick earlier, went into the backyard and threw up. Mr. and Mrs. Borden went about their usual morning tasks. Mr. Borden emptied slop jars, brushed his teeth in the kitchen, and departed for work. Mrs. Borden flicked a feather duster around in the dining room and told Bridget, who had spent ten or fifteen minutes in the yard vomiting, to wash the windows on the lower floor inside and out. After closing the downstairs windows, Bridget went directly to the cellar and out to the barn for pails, brushes, and a ladder. Only Lizzie and her stepmother remained inside the house. Mrs. Borden went to the spare guest room to tidy up after Uncle John and to put fresh pillow slips on the bed.

No one was absolutely certain where Lizzie was between 8:50 and 9:30. Bridget said that Lizzie appeared at the side screen door sometime during this interval and that Lizzie gave her confusing instructions about locking or unlocking the back door. Bridget assumed that Lizzie wanted the door kept locked and that she wanted her to get the water for window washing and rinsing from the barn rather than the kitchen faucet. This is just what Bridget did. And, on one of her trips from the south-side yard to the barn, she had a friendly chat with the Kelly's maid on the southeast side of the house.

Between 9:00 and 9:30 Abby Borden was assaulted and killed with an axe in the spare bedroom. She received nineteen blows on the head and back. Her skull was shattered. One blow penetrated five inches. A large flap of flesh was detached from her back from a particularly damaging blow. She fell to the floor between the bed and bureau.

Bridget continued to wash the windows outside, seeing no one in the downstairs rooms, in the yard, or at the back entrance.

At 10:40 Mrs. Kelly left her house for a dental appointment. As she passed the Borden home she saw Mr. Borden coming around the house from the side entrance and fumbling with some keys. At 10:42, Mr. Borden was trying unsuccessfully to unlock the front door. They exchanged morning greetings: Mrs. Kelly's sprightly "Good morning. It's another hot day," was answered tersely by the frustrated seventy-year-old man, wilting in the heat, unable to get into his house.

Bridget, now washing windows in the dining room, heard Mr. Borden's attempts to get in and rushed to the front door to help him. She found the door not only double locked but bolted from the inside, an unusual procedure at this time of day. Bridget had trouble pulling the bolt back, muttered something under her breath, and as Mr. Borden entered the house at 10:45, he complained that he had tried to get in the side entrance but had found that locked, too.

At this juncture, Lizzie, whom Bridget had not seen in over an hour, stood on the landing at the head of the stairs, and laughed.

The laugh startled Bridget. Mr. Borden, however, did not look up but went to the mantle piece, took the key, and climbed the back stairs to his room, where he stayed a very brief time before returning to the sitting room, unlocking and locking all the way.

Lizzie descended the stairway slowly and joined her father in the sitting room. Bridget, still washing windows in the dining room, heard Lizzie ask if there was any mail. Then, apparently in answer to a query about his wife, whom he had not seen either downstairs or in their bedroom, Lizzie told him that Mrs. Borden had received a note from a sick friend and had gone out to help.

Then, as was his noontime custom, Mr. Borden stretched out on the mahogany-framed upholstered couch along the wall to take a nap. Lizzie later said she helped him remove his congress boots. Bridget then heard Lizzie ask her father if she should leave the windows as they were for his nap. With her father made comfortable, Lizzie shut the door and joined Bridget in the dining room, setting up an ironing board on the dining room table. She ironed some handkerchiefs as Bridget finished the windows.

The two had a brief conversation. Lizzie encouraged Bridget to attend a sale on yard goods at a downtown store. Bridget displayed interest but also complained of feeling tired and sick. Having finished the windows, Bridget went upstairs to her third floor bedroom. The time was approximately 10:58.

Between 11:00 and 11:15 Andrew Borden was killed. Twelve blows by an axe mangled and disfigured his face. Half an eye hung on his cheek. Blood dripped from his head and from the sofa to the floor.

At 11:15 Lizzie called Bridget with these words: "Come down quick. Father's dead! Someone came in and killed him." Bridget hurried downstairs to be confronted by Lizzie, who was standing near the sitting room door. She told Bridget not to go in the room but to get a doctor. Bridget ran across the street to get Dr. Bowen. Mrs. Bowen said the doctor was out but would come as soon as possible. Bridget ran back and delivered her message to Lizzie, who then told her to go out to get her old friend, Alice Russell, so that Lizzie wouldn't have to be alone. At this point, Bridget asked for the first time the question which would be asked again and again: "Miss Lizzie, where were you when this happened?" Lizzie answered: "I was in the yard and heard a groan and came in and the screen door was wide open."

Bridget left again to fetch the frail Miss Russell and was observed by Mrs. Churchill, the Bordens' neighbor on the north side. The sight of Bridget running to and fro, gasping, led Mrs. Churchill, who saw Lizzie standing inside the screen door, to use her neighborly prerogative and ask if there was any trouble.

Lizzie's answer was remarkable. She made two or three comments about the heat, then said: "Do come over. Someone has killed Father."*

Mrs. Churchill hurried over. Lizzie was seated on the bottom step of the back stairs. Her neighbor, full of questions, asked Lizzie where her father was, and where she had been when it happened, and where her mother was.

Lizzie answered calmly that her father was in the sitting room. She had gone to the barn to get a piece of iron. She didn't know where her mother was; she had a note to go see someone who was sick, but she may have come back.

Mrs. Churchill took charge: she crossed the street to the stable and asked for help. One of the men, John Cunningham, telephoned for the police, who logged the time of the call as 11:15. Many in the police department were on their annual excursion, a picnic on the bay. Marshall Hilliard dispatched Officer George Allen to the house. Meanwhile, Mrs. Churchill had been joined by Miss Russell. The women did their charitable best to console Lizzie by chafing her wrists and rubbing her forehead.

Dr. Bowen had also received the message. When he arrived at the Borden home, Lizzie directed him to the sitting room where the body of his neighbor lay, still dripping blood. The doctor made certain he was dead. He noticed that Mr. Borden's coat was wedged in back above the pillow where his head rested, and he still had on his congress boots. There was no sign of a struggle. Dr. Bowen guessed that he had been asleep, had been killed with the first blow, and had been dead no more than twenty minutes. The time was approximately 11:30.

Dr. Bowen came out of the room considerably shaken. The women heard him say: "Murdered! He's been murdered." Then Lizzie was asked the same question for the third time: "Where were you?"

"In the barn, looking for some iron." This time Lizzie said nothing about being in the yard, about the groan, about the open screen door.

---

*Mrs. Churchill did not tell the police or the court of Lizzie's inconsequential prelude to the news of her father's death. Only after the trial did she tell the neighbor, Mrs. Kelly, these details.

It is not too much to say that of all the people in the house, Lizzie was most in control of herself. The women persisted in fluttering about her and in trying to apply known remedies for fainting. Lizzie was so far from fainting that when Alice Russell said at one point that she wished she had a fan, Lizzie informed them in a calm voice that there was one in the china closet.*

Among those present who displayed a great deal of agitated concern was Bridget. Bridget was apparently the first one to raise a question about Mrs. Borden. She asked Lizzie if she should try to find Mrs. Whitehead, who might know where Mrs. Borden was.

Lizzie then said that she was almost sure she had heard her come in and go up the front stairway. Bridget refused to go up alone. Together she and Mrs. Churchill slowly ascended the front stairs. From the turn of the stairs, where Lizzie had stood and laughed her strange laugh, the women could see the body of Mrs. Borden lying on the floor on the far side of the bedroom.

"Is there another?" someone asked. Mrs. Churchill answered, "There's another."

This time, there was no need to send for anyone. Dr. Bowen, who had left the house briefly to send a wire to Emma Borden in Fairhaven, had returned and went directly upstairs. He found Abby lying face down, almost filling the space between bed and bureau; her head had been battered. A switch of hair had been hacked off and lay on the floor beside her; a bloody kerchief lay nearby. The blood on and about the body was congealed. It was apparent that she had been killed much earlier than her husband -- an hour and a half to two hours earlier.

The time was 11:45 A.M. At this point, several police officers joined the scene.

Assistant Marshal Fleet's Notes of His Interview with Lizzie Borden, Bridget Sullivan, and John Morse

The only known records of the police investigations in these early days are the handwritten notes of Assistant Marshal John Fleet. He recorded his questioning of Lizzie, Bridget, and Uncle John on the day of the murders. Fleet's manuscript is printer here just as written, including spelling and punctuation errors and his abbreviations. Illegible manuscript is indicated by _____.

Source: Courtesy of Edward Sullivan.

Aug. 4, 1892. Went to the Borden house 2nd St., at about between 11:45 & 12M. found Mr. Borden dead on the lounge. Head badly cut. Dr. Dolan standing over him. Went up stairs, to found Mrs. Borden. Dead on the Floor betw bed and dressing case. Head badly

---

*Miss Russell told this story to a Boston *Post* reporter in 1929.

18

smashed face downward. Saw Lizzie A. Borden in bedroom on same floor. Was sitting with Minister Buck on lounge asked her what she knew of these murders. She said that she knew nothing further than her father came in about 10-30 or 10-45 and that he seemed to be quite feible and she helped him and advised him to lay down on the lounge which he did. I was ironing handk in the Dining room which I left and went in the barn upstairs and remained there for half an hour, Bridget had gone up stairs, and when I came back I found father dead on the lounge, and went to the back stair and called Bridget_____ down stairs told her that someone had killed father and told her to get Dr. Bowen. Did you see anyone around here? No. I haven't seen anyone in the house or yard. Who is this Mr. Morse? he is my uncle he came here last night and slept here but went away before 9 o'clock, a.m. and did not get back until after the murder He could not know any thing about the murder. Have you any idea who could have done this? No I do not know that my father had had trouble with anyone, but about 2 week ago a man called and they had some talk about a shop and father told him that he could not have it for that purpose. Man talked as though he was angry. didn't know who he was did not see him, could not tell all that he said. Man came here this morning about nine o'clock, I think he wanted to hire a store talked English did not see him, heard father shut the door and think the man went away.

Saw Lizzie 2 hours later, wanted to search her room, Dr. Bowen was in. She did not want to be bothered, would make her sick, told her that I must search on account of the murders, otherwise should not be doing my duty, She then allowed the search to go on. Could not find anything in the room which would show blood and found no Instruments that had been used for murder. She said that it was imposible for any o: to get in or throw anything in her room because she always kept it locked. Lizzie said that she had not seen Mrs. Borden since about 9 o'clock She thought_____ Bedroom when she was

_____

Had a conversation with Bridget Sullivan. Said she saw Mr. Borden come in the house about 10-40 A.M. Saw him come in the Dining room go to the window and look at some paper which he had in his hands. He then went in the sitting room. Sat down in the large chair near the window, and left Lizzie Ironing some handkerchiefs in the Dining room. Went up-stairs at 10:55 to fix up my room. After I had been in the room about 10 minutes Lizzie called me down-stairs saying that her father was dead some one has killed him, go and get Dr. Bowen and went for the Doctor he was not in and I went for a Miss Russell on Borden St. Did you see anyone that you think would or could had done the killing? No I did not. I was washing the windows outside & did not see anyone in the yard or go in the house and did not see anyone but Mr. Morse this morning and he went away before 9 o'clock, am very

19

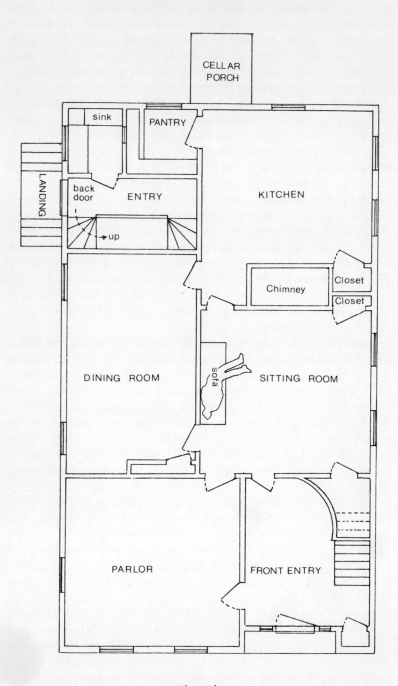

First Floor

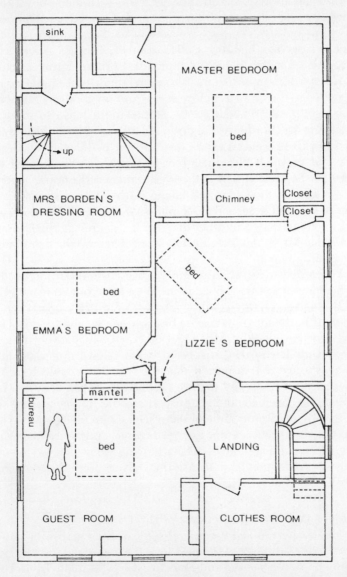

Second Floor

Adapted from: E. Porter, *Fall River Tragedy* (1893); V. Lincoln, *A Private Disgrace* (1967); and A. de Mille, *Lizzie Borden: A Dance of Death* (1968).

sure that I was not up stair more that 10 to 15 minutes. I did not here the door opened when I was up stairs nor did I see anyone from my window.

Conversed with John V. Morse at the A. J. Borden house. Said that he was A. J. Borden's Brother-in-law his sister was Mr. Borden's first wife, had always been on friendly terms with the family and had frequently made visits to his house, last night I stoped here and slept in the room where Mrs. Borden was found dead. I arrived here yesterday afternoon from New Bedford. Called upon Mr. Borden. Afterward got a carriage from Kirbys stable & went to Mr. Borden's farm. Arriving at the house again about 8-30 p.m. We sat up I think until about 10 o'clock went to bed in the room as before stated, got up about six o'clock this morning got breakfast about 7 a.m. Stoped in the house til about 8-40 a.m. leaving Mr. Borden at the door. Went to the Post office wrote a letter from there went as far as third St. on Bedford, from there to Pleasant St. through Pleasant Street to Weybosset St. arriving there about 9:30. Saw relatives from the West remain at the house from 9-30 to 11-20 A.M. I then soon left taking horse car and stopped at the corner of Pleasant & Second St. & got to Mr. Borden's house about or near 12 o'clock. Saw a number of _____ around the house and was told that Mr. & Mrs. Borden was killed That was the first I knew of their death.

Where do you live when at home? I live at South Dartmouth. Have been here about 2 years. I lived in the West for about 20 years. (Came back 2 years ago.) Have you any idea who did this? I can't see who could do this, do not know that he had any enemy in the world. Have you seen or have you heard Bridget or Lizzie say that they had seen anyone around who they suspected? No I have not. Mr. Morse afterwards asked if I suspected that the Murderer could have been concealed in the house last night? I replied that I did not, then I said that he might have been in the house, but could not see how he could have been there without some of them seeing him. He said it was very strange that this should be done in the daytime, and right in the heart of the city. It put him in mind of the Nathan murder which was twenty or twenty-five years ago. In that case they never found the murderer.

J. Fleet

Fall River Daily Herald Reports of the Crime

Newspapers in Fall River, and soon in cities across the country, carried frequent reports of the murders, the investigations, and public reaction. However neutral and objective the press might have claimed to be, their stories reflect the individual reporters' views of the case and, often, the biases of the larger society. The Fall River *Daily Herald* accounts show clear marks of late nineteenth-century values and ideas - - about immigrants, servants, strangers, women, men, wealth, social standing, and a host of other issues. The case itself receives varying treatment, and the views of the press and the public alike changed as the case developed.

A Note on the Text: The typographical errors in the original news accounts have been removed for this edition, but grammatical and factual errors have been left standing (e.g., Bridget Sullivan mis-identified as Lizzie Corrigan).

Source: Fall River Public Library files; Fall River *Daily Herald,* August 4, 5, 6, and 8, 1892.

August 4, 1892

SHOCKING CRIME

A Venerable Citizen and His Aged Wife

HACKED TO PIECES AT THEIR HOME

Mr. and Mrs. Andrew Borden Lose Their Lives

AT THE HANDS OF A DRUNKEN PARK HAND.

Police Searching Actively for the Fiendish Murderer.

The community was terribly shocked this morning to hear that an aged man and his wife had fallen victims to the thirst of a murderer, and that an atrocious deed had been committed. The news spread like wildfire and hundreds poured into Second street. The deed was committed at No. 62 Second street, where for years Andrew J. Borden and his wife had lived in happiness.

It is supposed that an axe was the instrument used, as the bodies of the victims are hacked almost beyond recognition. Since the discovery of the deed the street in front of the house has been blocked by an anxious throng, eagerly waiting for the news of the awful tragedy and vowing vengeance on the assassin.

"FATHER IS STABBED."

The first intimation the neighbors had of the awful crime was a groaning followed by a cry of "murder!" Mrs. Adelaide Churchill, who lives next door to the Bordens, ran over and heard Miss Borden cry: "Father is stabbed; run for the police!"

Mrs. Churchill hurried across the way to the livery stable to get the people there to summon the police. John Cunningham, who was passing, learned of the murder and telephoned to police headquarters, and Officer Allen was sent to investigate the case.

23

Meanwhile the story spread rapidly and a crowd gathered quickly. A HERALD reporter entered the house, and a terrible sight met his view. On the lounge in the cosy sitting room on the first floor of the building lay Andrew J. Borden, dead. His face presented a sickening sight. Over the left temple a wound six by four had been made as if the head had been pounded with the dull edge of an axe. The left eye had been dug out and a cut extended the length of the nose. The face was hacked to pieces and the blood had covered the man's shirt and soaked into his clothing. Everything about the room was in order, and there were no signs of a scuffle of any kind.

SEVEN WOUNDS

Upstairs in a neat chamber in the northwest corner of the house, another terrible sight met the view. On the floor between the bed and the dressing case lay Mrs. Borden, stretched full length, one arm extended and her face resting upon it. Over the left temple the skull was fractured and no less than seven wounds were found about the head. She had died, evidently where she had been struck, for her life blood formed a ghastly clot on the carpet.

Dr. Bowen was the first physician to arrive, but life was extinct, and from the nature of the wounds it is probable that the suffering of both victims was very short. The police were promptly on hand and strangers were kept at a distance. Miss Borden was so overcome by the awful circumstances that she could not be seen, and kind friends led her away and cared for her.

A squad of police who had arrived conducted a careful hunt over the premises for trace of the assailant. No weapon was found and there was nothing about the house to indicate who the murderer might have been. A clue was obtained, however. A Portuguese whose name nobody around the house seemed to know, has been employed on one of the Swansey farms owned by Mr. Borden. He had a talk with his employer and asked for the wages due him. Mr. Borden told the man he had no money with him, to call later. If anything more passed between the men it cannot be learned. At length the Portuguese departed and Mr. Borden soon afterward started down town. His first call was to Peter Leduc's barber shop, where he was shaved about 9:30 o'clock. He then dropped into the Union bank to transact some business and talked with Mr. Hart, treasurer of the savings bank, of which Mr. Borden was president. As nearly as can be learned after that he went straight home. He took off his coat and composed himself comfortably on the lounge to sleep. It is presumed, from the easy attitude in which his body lay, that he was asleep when the deadly blow was struck. It is thought that Mrs. Borden was in the room at the time, but was so overcome by the assault that she had no strength to make an outcry. In her bewilderment, she rushed upstairs and went into her room. She must have been followed up the stairs by the murderer, and as she was retreating into the furthest corner of the room, she was felled by the deadly axe. Blow after blow must have been rained upon her head as she lay unconscious on the floor.

Hurriedly the murderer slipped down the stairs and rushed into the street, leaving a screen door wide open after him in his sudden flight. No sign of blood could be found on the carpet or on the stairs, nor could any weapon be discovered anywhere. Nobody can be found who saw the murderer depart, and it is safe to conclude that he carried so small a weapon that it could be concealed in his clothing. Had he carried a gory axe in his hand, somebody's attention would have been attracted to it.

Then the investigation began. People were at a loss what could have been the motive for such a deed. Mr. Borden's quiet disposition was well known, and, although, he was considered wealthy, yet his unpresuming ways were not such as to have invited robbery. In fact, his silver watch was in his pocket and his clothing was not in any way disturbed as to encourage the theory that the foul murder had been committed for gain.

MISS BORDEN ATTRACTED

The heavy fall and a subdued groaning attracted Miss Borden into the house. There the terrible sight which has been described met her gaze. She rushed to the staircase and called the servant, who was washing a window in her room on the third floor. So noiselessly had the deed been done that neither of them was aware of the bloody work going on so near them.

To a police officer, Miss Borden said she was at work in the barn about 10 o'clock. On her return she found her father in the sitting room with a horrible gash in the side of his head. He appeared at the time as though he had been hit while in a sitting posture. Giving the alarm, she rushed upstairs to find her mother, only to be more horrified to find that person lying between the dressing case and the bed sweltering in a pool of blood. It appeared as though Mrs. Borden had seen the man enter, and the man, knowing that his dastardly crime would be discovered, had followed her upstairs and finished his fiendish work. It was a well known fact that Mrs. Borden always left the room when her husband was talking business with anyone. A person knowing this fact could easily spring upon his victim without giving her a chance to make an outcry. Miss Borden had seen no person enter or leave the place. The man who had charge of her father's farm was held in the highest respect by Mr. Borden. His name was Alfred Johnson, and he trusted his employer so much that he left his bank book at Mr. Borden's house for safe keeping. The young lady had not the slightest suspicion of his being connected with the crime. As far as the Portuguese suspected of the crime was concerned, she knew nothing of him, as he might have been a man who was employed by the day in the busy season. What his motive could have been it is hard to tell, as Mr. Borden had always been kind to his help.

Another statement made by the police, and which though apparently light, would bear investigation, is the following: Some two weeks ago a man applied to Mr. Borden for the lease of a store on South Main street that was vacant. After a short time as Miss Borden was passing the room loud words were heard, her father making the remark, "I will not let it for that purpose." Quietness was restored in a short while and when the man departed her father said: "When you come to town next time I will let you know." This was two weeks ago, but in the meantime the store has been let to another. It was dark at the time of the calling and she did not recognize his features.

WENT TO SWANSEY.

At 12:45 o'clock Marshal Hilliard and Officers Doherty and Connors presented a carriage and drove over to the farm, hoping that the suspected man would return there in order to prove an alibi. The officers will arrive at the place some time before the man, as the distance is some ten miles, though it is hardly probable that he will return there. What makes it rather improbable that the man suspected is a Portuguese laborer is the statement of Charles Gifford of Swansey. Mr. Gifford says that the only Portuguese employed on the upper farm is Mr. Johnson, and he is confined to his bed by illness. Another man might be employed by Mr. Borden on the lower farm for a few days, but he does not believe it. An attempt was made to reach Swansey by telephone, but no answer was received.

A SIGNIFICANT INCIDENT.

Among the significant incidents revealed in the search through the premises was brought to light by John Donnelly, who with others searched through the barn to see if any trace of the fugitive could be found there. In the hay was seen the perfect outline of a man as if one had slept there over night. Besides this, it was evident that the sleeper was either restless or had been there before, because an imprint was found in another part of the hay that corresponded with the outline of the first impression. Somebody may have been in the habit of going there for a nap, but the imprint was that of a person of about five feet six inches tall, and was shorter than Mr. Borden. This has given rise to the suspicion that the murderer may have slept about the place and waited for an opportunity to accomplish his deed.

ANOTHER STORY.

Another sensational story is being told in connection with the murder. It appears that the members of the family have been ill for

26

some days and the symptoms were very similar to those of poison. In the light of subsequent events this sickness has been recalled. It has been the custom of the family to receive the supply of milk from the Swansey farm every morning, and the can was left out of doors until the servant opened the house in the morning. Ample opportunity was afforded, therefore, for anybody who had a foul design to tamper with the milk, and this circumstance will be carefully investigated by the police.

Medical Examiner Dolan, who promptly responded to the call for his presence, made a careful examination of the victims and reached the conclusion that the wounds were inflicted by a heavy, sharp weapon like an axe or hatchet. He found the skull fractured in both instances and concluded that death was instantaneous. As to the blow that killed Mrs. Borden he thought that it had been delivered by a tall man, who struck the woman from behind.

A BOGUS LETTER.

It is reported that Mrs. Borden received a letter this morning announcing the illness of a very dear friend and was preparing to go to see her. This letter has turned out to be a bogus one, evidently intended to draw her away from home. In this case it would look as if the assault had been carefully planned. A suspicious character was seen on Second street this morning who seemed to be on the lookout for somebody, and the police have a description of the man.

Marshal Hilliard, Officers Dowty and Connors went to Swansey this afternoon, but found the men at work on the upper farm who had been employed there of late. The lower farm will be visited at once. William Eddy has charge of this one.

At 2:10 o'clock a sturdy Portuguese named Antonio Auriel was arrested in a saloon on Columbia street and brought into the police station. The man protested his innocence and sent after Joseph Chaves, clerk for Talbot & Co., who recognized the man, and he was immediately released.

SKETCH OF MR. BORDEN.

Andrew J. Borden was born in this city 69 years ago. By perseverance and industry he accumulated a fortune. A short time since he boasted that he had yet to spend his first foolish dollar. Mr. Borden was married twice. His second wife was the daughter of Oliver Gray and was born on Rodman street. He had two children by his first wife, Emma and Elizabeth. The former is out of town on a visit and has not yet learned of the tragedy.

Mr. Borden was at the time of his death president of the Union saving's bank and director in the Durfee bank, Globe yarn, Merchants and Troy mill. He was interested in several big real estate deals, and was a very wealthy man.

27

A DEEP MYSTERY

Hundreds in Front of the Borden Homestead

DISCUSSING THE MURDER

Miss Borden Has Not the Least Suspicion of the Guilty Parties -- The Story of the Milk Verified -- Police Scouring the Town.

The excitement over the Borden murder grows intense. Hundreds block the street in front of the house, and are discussing the horrible circumstances. Dr. Dolan, assisted by a half dozen physicians, has been conducting an autopsy. There are no new details to be given to the public.

Further investigation shrouds the affair in deeper mystery. A HERALD reporter saw an intimate friend of the family who has been with Miss Borden ever since the terrible blow was struck. Miss Borden is anxious that any stories that connect the maid servant, Lizzie Corrigan, or of the men at the farms, with the deed be refuted. All of them have been in the family's employ for many years, and Mr. Eddy, the superintendent of one of the farms, is at present so ill that Miss Borden was anxious that the stories should not reach his ears that any of the old help were suspected of the deed. Miss Borden states that she has not the least clue to give the officers. When she went into the house from the barn and saw her father lying with dripping wounds, she was overcome and rushed to the staircase to call the servant and sent her for help. Mrs. Churchill, who saw the servant running, enquired the cause, and then went for Dr. Bowen. After Miss Borden had recovered from the first shock, she remembered that Mrs. Borden had not been seen, and she asked some of the friends who were with her to go and look for her. John Maude, a relative of the Bordens, and Mrs. Churchill proceeded through the house and at length found Mrs. Borden where she lay in the chamber upstairs.

The story relative to the suspected milk has been verified, and the doctors will take special pains to look for traces of poison at the autopsy. Even if any are found, it will be difficult to form a clue from this fact, since it has been the custom to leave the can on the doorstep, and anybody could have tampered with it.

The police are particularly vigilant and every stranger who excites the least suspicion is stopped and examined. Whether the murderer took advantage of a day when the majority of the police were out of town and could not be called out to hunt for the fugitive can only be conjectured. This is certainly a case that will furnish excellent opportunity for the detective talent of the force, although the clues that are afforded are of the most meager and unsatisfactory character.

August 5, 1892

THURSDAY'S AFFRAY

No Clue as Yet to Its Perpetrator.

Police Working Hard to Remove the Veil

Of Mystery That Envelops the Awful Tragedy.

A Postal Card That Would Serve As A Link.

Further investigation into the circumstances of the Borden murder shroud it with an impenetrable mystery. Nothing that has ever occurred in Fall River or vicinity has created such intense excitement. From the moment the story of the crime was first told to long after midnight Second Street was crowded with curious people anxious to hear some particulars that had not been told before.

Theories were advanced, some of them plausible enough, but not one could be formed against which some objection could not be offered from the circumstances surrounding the case. Everybody agreed that money was at the bottom of the foul murder, but in what measure and concerning what person could not be conceived. That a bloody deed such as that perpetrated in broad daylight, in a house on one of the busiest streets could have been so quickly and noiselessly accomplished and the murderer escape from the house without attracting attention is wonderful to a degree. Nobody was seen to enter the house by any of the occupants, although all of them except Mr. Borden were busy about the rooms or in the yard.

WAS HE CONCEALED?

Could it be that the murderer was concealed inside the dwelling and had awaited a favorable moment to carry out his nefarious plans? The more the circumstances are considered, the more probable becomes this view of the case. People who have carefully examined the ground believe that Mr. Borden was the first victim, and that the killing of Mrs. Borden was by no means unpremeditated. Having accomplished the bloody work downstairs, the murderer slipped stealthily into the rooms above in search of the wife and, finding her in the northwest chamber walking across the floor to the dressing case, had crept up behind her without attracting her attention and delivered the fatal blow.

The plausibility of this view lies in the fact that the fall of Mrs. Borden, who weighed very nearly 200 pounds, would certainly have jarred the building and awakened her husband, who could only have been sleeping lightly on the lounge, as it was but a few moments after his daughter had seen him quietly reading there that the deed was done. Further investigation confirms the belief that Mrs. Borden was not chased upstairs by the murderer because she was so near the end of the room that she would have been forced to turn and face her pursuer, and the cuts on the head would have been a different nature.

Twenty minutes were all the time the murderer had to finish his terrible work; conceal the weapon with which he accomplished his crime, and conceal it in such a way as to leave no traces of blood on the carpet or through the house that would reveal how he escaped; to pass out of the house by the side door within 15 feet of the barn where the daughter was engaged and a like distance from the Buffinton house on the north; pass the length of the house and disappear up or down Second street. John Cunningham was going down the street about that time, and he saw nobody pass him; and people who live below saw nobody. Had the man run through the orchard and jumped Dr. Chagnon's fence, escaping to Third Street, he would have had to pass the barn door, and would have been seen from the living rooms of the Chagnon abode. How the murderer could have done so much in so short a time and cover his tracks so successfully is not the least mysterious feature in the case.

BUT THE MOTIVE.

Certainly nobody who knew Mr. Borden or his wife can furnish any light upon this matter from the relationship with them in business or social circles. Beyond attributing it to money in the abstract, no theory can be advanced that is borne out by the facts thus far revealed. It was not robbery, because things were not overhauled. Mr. Borden had been the means of amassing a fortune of half a million dollars. Nevertheless he bore himself strictly honest, and if he had expected dollar for dollar and cent for cent he always offered the same to others. Whether he had at some time or other made an enemy in his dealings, one who would have been led by a desire for revenge to stain his hands with life blood, has never been suspected by those outside the family, and may or may not have been true. The only other motive must be laid at the doors of those who would profit by the death of the couple, but people who knew them refuse to accept such a view for a single instant.

TALKS WITH INMATES.

There are no new developments in the case to be gathered from the people in the house. Regarding the servant, Bridget Sullivan, a woman of about 25, it is pretty well established that at the time that Mr. Borden was assaulted she was in the attic of the house. Her statement to the police is as follows: "I was washing windows most all of the morning and passed in and out of the house continually. At the time Miss Lizzie

30

came down stairs I went to one of the upper rooms to finish the window washing. I remained there until Lizzie's cries attracted my attention; then I came down and went for Dr. Bowen; I never saw any one enter or leave the house."

Miss Borden made the following statement to Officer Harrington as soon as she was sufficiently composed to talk coherently of the affair. It differs in only one particular from the one she told Dr. Bowen, namely, the time in which she was out of the house and in the barn. She said she was about 20 minutes, and, upon being requested to be particular, insisted that it was not more than 20 minutes or less than that time. She said that her father enjoyed the most perfect confidence and friendship of his workmen across the river, and that she was in a position to know this, unless something unusual had happened within a few days. She told the story of the angry tenant, saying that the man came to her father twice about the matter, and that he persistently refused to let the store which he wanted for the purpose desired. The only vacant property of Mr. Borden was the room recently vacated by Baker Gadsby and it is thought that this is the place the man wanted to use. Mr. Borden told the man at the first visit to call again and he would let him know about the rental. It is supposed to be an out-of-town man and that he called and found that Jonathon Clegg had occupied the store. It is also thought that the tenant wanted to use the place as a rum shop; this Mr. Borden would not allow. It may be added that the police attach little importance to this latter matter.

MR. MORSE TALKS.

Visiting at the house on the day of the murder was John W. Morse; a brother of Mr. Borden's first wife. He is fully six feet in height with gray beard and hair. He was not adverse to talking, and said in response to questions:

"My sister Sarah A. Morse, married Andrew Borden in the city of Fall River when both were, as I remember it, in their 22nd year. That was 47 years ago. At that time Mr. Borden was in reduced circumstances and was just beginning to enter business. They lived for years on Ferry Street. They had three children, one of whom died when he was but three or four years old. The others, both girls, grew to womanhood and are now living; they are Emma L., aged 37, and Lizzie A., aged 32.

"Mr. Borden first went into the furniture business on Anawan street, where he remained for 30 years or more. My sister died 28 years ago. At that time Mr. Borden was worth fully $150,000, which amount he had invested largely in mill stocks, which were highly paying securities. He told me on one occasion that he had $78,000 in mill stocks alone. He afterwards invested heavily in a horsecar line, but now I am ahead of my story.

"About 20 years ago I went out west, and settled at Hastings Mills, Ia. On the 14th of April two years ago I returned home, and since last February I have been staying with a butcher by the name of Davis, in a little town of South Dartmouth, which is near New Bedford. Yes, I am a bachelor. I have a sister living in this city. She married Joseph Morse, a second cousin. I have also one brother whose name is William, who lives at Excelsior, Minn. He is 65 years of age.

"Wednesday I came here from New Bedford early in the afternoon. I left that city on the 12:35 train, which arrived here about 1:30 o'clock. I walked from the station up to the house and rang the front door bell. Mrs. Borden opened it. She welcomed me and I went in. Andrew was then reclining on the sofa in about the position he was found murdered. He looked up and laughed saying, 'Hullo, John, is that you? Have you been to dinner yet?' I replied in the negative. Mrs. Borden interrupted Mr. Borden, saying: 'Sit right down, we are just through and everything is hot on the stove. It won't cost us a mite of trouble.' They sat by my side through dinner, and then I told them I was going over to Kirby's stable and get a team to drive over to Luther's. I invited Andrew to go, but he declined, saying he didn't feel well enough. He asked me to bring him over some eggs from his farm which is there located. I returned from the ride about 8:30 o'clock and we sat up until about 10 o'clock. Then Mr. Borden showed me to my room, his wife having previously retired, and bade me good night. That was the last I saw of him until Thursday morning.

"It was about 6 o'clock when I got up, and had breakfast about an hour later. Then Andrew and I read the papers, and we chatted until about 9 o'clock. I am not positive as to the exact time, and it may have been only 8:45 o'clock. While at the table I asked Andrew why he did not buy Gould's yacht for $200,000, at which price it was advertised, and he laughed, saying what little good it would do him if he really did have it. We also talked about business. I had come to Fall River, for one reason, to buy a pair of oxen for Butcher Davis, with whom I lived. He had wanted them, and I had agreed to take them on a certain day, but had not done so. Andrew told me when I was ready to go after them to write him at the farm, which would save him bothering in the matter. When I left the house I started for the post office. I walked down Second Street, and, stopping in, got a postal card and wrote to William Vinnicum of South Swaney. I dropped it in the office and then went out of the north door of the building to Bedford street, and thence on to Third street, to Pleasant, to Weybosset street. I stopped there at the house of my cousin, David Emery, No. 4; I went there to see my nephew and niece, the former of whom I found away. There I remained until 11:30 or 11:45 and then I started back to Borden's, as I had been asked there for dinner. I hailed a car going by and rode to Second street and thence I walked to the house.

"When I entered the premises I did not go by the front door. On the contrary, I walked around behind the house and picked some pears. Then I went in the back door. Bridget then told me that Mr. and Mrs. Borden had been murdered. I opened the sitting-room door and found a number of people, including the doctors. I entered, but only glanced once at the body. No, I did not look closely enough to be able to describe it. Then I went upstairs and took a similar hasty view of the dead woman. Everything is confusion, however, and I recall very little of what took place."

THE MEDICAL EXAMINER.

Dr. Dolan was called upon after the autopsy, but he had no further facts to disclose. He described the wounds and said that death must have been almost instantaneous in both cases after the first blow. Acting upon the rumor about the poisoned milk, the doctor took samples of it and saved the soft spots of the body for further analysis. He was of the opinion that the wounds were inflicted by a hatchet or a cleaver, and by a person who could strike a blow heavy enough to crush in the skull. In the autopsy, Drs. Coughlin, Dedrick, Leary, Gunning, Dutra, Tourtellot, Peckham and Bowen assisted.

NOTES.

John J. Maher was on a street car on New Boston road Thursday afternoon rather under the influence of liquor. He was telling that when a reward was offered for the man he could find him in 15 minutes. When questioned by an officer as to what he really knew, Maher said that a boy had seen a small man with a dark moustache come out of the house at the time of the murder and, going down Second street, had turned up Pleasant. Maher was locked up on a charge of drunkenness.

Officers Doherty and Harrington have been on continuous duty since the case was reported.

It was rather warm for the officers who were detailed to hunt for the murderer's weapon in the loft of the barn, but they thoroughly examined every corner for the article.

Officers Dyson, Ferguson, Mayall and Hyde were detailed to watch the house of the victims until 1 o'clock, when they were relieved by Officers Doherty, Harrington, McCarthy and Reagan.

An effort has been made to obtain information relative to the condition of the property left by Abraham B. Borden, father of Andrew. A search at the probate office shows that no will was left by Abraham, and that Andrew J. was appointed administrator of the estate. Andrew J.'s mother left a will, but her property amounted to less than $3,000, and that was all willed to her brothers and nieces.

Officer Medley was one of the busiest men about town Wednesday night, and every remark or idea connected with the tragedy was thoroughly sifted by him.

When the news of the murder reached the people on the excursion it seemed too incredible, and a great many would not be convinced until they reached home.

If interest and hard work in the case were to land the perpetrator of the crime into custody Assistant Marshal Fleet would have the man behind the bars long before now.

Every morning paper in Boston had a representative in this city Thursday night, and as a result the telegraph operators were kept busy into the small hours of the morning.

The excitement attending the tragedy continued at blood heat throughout the night, and it required a number of officers to keep the street clear in front of the house up to midnight.

Among the many articles secured on the premises is a crowbar over three feet long and weighing about nine pounds. It was found in the shed by one of the officers. It appeared at first that there was blood on it, and a hasty investigation by two or three policemen convinced the finder that the substance with which it was spotted was blood. It was consequently brought to the police station, where it was found that the spots were nothing else than a few drops of paint and rust.

MORSE'S NIECE.

Mrs. Emery, upon whom Mr. Morse called, was disposed to talk freely to Officer Medley, who interviewed her Thursday night. She said in reply to questions that she had several callers during the day, and that one of them was John Morse.

"Was Morse the name we heard?" asked the officer of a companion.

"Yes," retorted Mrs. Emery quickly, "Morse was the man. He left here at 11:30 o'clock this morning."

"Then you noticed the time?" observed the officer.

"Oh, yes," was the reply, "I noticed the time."

"How did you fix it?" was the next question.

After some little hesitation, Mrs. Emery said that one of her family was sick, and that Dr. Bowen was her physician, "Dr. Bowen came in just as Mr. Morse left."

"Did they meet?" queried the officers.

"No, they did not," said Mrs. Emery.

At this point the niece in question entered the room and corroborated Mrs. Emery's statements, though both women finally fixed upon 11:20 as the exact time of Mr. Morse's departure.

Mrs. Emery volunteered information that Mr. Morse was well-to-do, at least she supposed he was comfortably off and that he had come

34

east to spend his money. She was not positive on this point, however. Morse's niece was asked if she had ever seen her uncle before, and replied that she had. She had met him when she was five years old, and three weeks ago he had taken her from the cars at Warren to the Borden farm, Swansey.

THE OLDEST DAUGHTER.

Miss Emma Borden, who had been visiting in Fairhaven, returned home Thursday evening, having been summoned by the news of the crime. The details of the murder had not been told to her, and she was overcome by the recital. She is the oldest daughter of Andrew Borden by his first wife. All through the early hours of the evening the street was crowded with people, none of whom was admitted to the premises until they had disclosed the nature of their business. A watch surrounded the house all night, and officers were on guard inside. No further developments were reported. The family retired soon after 10 o'clock and all was in darkness. Undertaker Winward had taken charge of the remains at the request of Miss Borden, and will prepare them for burial.

THE THEORIES DISCUSSED.

Today nothing but the murder was talked about on the streets, and the interest continues to be intense. The announcement that the family had offered a reward of $5,000 for the detection of the murderers was the only new item to be discussed.

The theories which were advanced by those who have been closely connected with the case agree in one thing, and that is that the murderer knew his ground and carried out his blood thirsty plan with a speed and surety that indicated a well matured plot. How quickly the report that was gathered about the premises five minutes after the deed was discovered that a Portuguese had done it was scattered abroad after the murder is looked on with suspicion. *[sic]*

Detective Seaver and other members of the state police force are assisting the local department in its work and the office of the city marshal is the busiest place in town. New clues are being reported every hour and officers are busy tracking the stories to earth.

Mr. Morse, the guest of the Bordens, is well known in this city where he was born and lived many years. People recall that he went west quite early in life and engaged in raising horses in Iowa. He was said to have had considerable success with his stock and to have gathered together considerable property. Nothing definite about his affairs was known other than that he had told friends that he had brought a train load of horses with him from Iowa to sell, and they were now at Fairhaven.

SIGNIFICANT DISAPPEARANCE.

That letter of which mention was made Thursday as having been sent to Mrs. Borden, announcing that a friend was sick, has since disappeared. The explanation that was given out was that after reading its contents, Mrs. Borden tore it up and threw the pieces in the fire. Bits of charred paper were found in the grate, but not enough to give any idea of the nature of the note. Nobody about the house seems to know where the letter could have come from, and since publicity has been given and considerable importance attached to it, it is considered probable that the writer will inform the family of the circumstances and thus remove suspicions.

Various rumors have been started, one of which was that Miss Borden had assured a friend last winter after a mysterious robbery at the house that her father had an enemy somewhere. A HERALD reporter interviewed a lady to whom it was said this story had been told, but she denied any knowledge of it. Another was that the axe had been found in the yard, but the police have not heard of it.

A TENANT THEORY.

Causes for the murder are arising so fast at the present time that it is nearly impossible to investigate them. Hardly any of them are of sufficient weight to put a person under the ban of suspicion, but all are being thoroughly investigated. The latest story is about a former tenant named Ryan. According to the information Ryan occupied the upper floor of a house belonging to Mr. Borden, and was so obnoxious that he ordered him to move. While notifying the people he was compelled to seek the lower floor to escape the torrent of abuse that was heaped on him, and when the family moved the remark was made that they would like to see him dead. There is nothing more than this in the matter, but as all acts or words in connection with Mr. Borden in the past are being looked into the affair was looked into and found to amount to nothing.

A MAN WITH A CLEAVER.

Griffiths Bros., the carpenters on Anawan street, tell a story which may have an important bearing upon the terrible tragedy. They were driving up Pleasant street about 11:00 o'clock Thursday morning, when their attention was drawn to a man who was proceeding rapidly along the sidewalk in front of Flint's building. Under his arm, with the handle down, he carried a cleaver entirely unlike anything they had ever seen. It was the size of the instrument that caused them to take more than a passing glance at it. To them it looked like a tool sometimes used by fish dealers. It had a rusty appearance, as if it had not been used for some time.

36

The man was dressed very poorly. He had no beard and was short in stature. As the weapon with which the deed was committed has not been found, the carpenters venture the opinion that the cleaver they saw was the means by which Mr. Borden and his wife were killed.

SOUTHARD H. MILLER,

one of the city's most venerable citizens, and Mr. Borden's intimate friends, was spoken to on the matter. He replied that as far as motive was concerned for the deed he could not answer. He had known Mr. Borden for over a half a century, and his dealings were such that nobody could take offence with him. Having learned the cabinet making business, Mr. Borden applied to him in 1844, when the city hall was building, for a situation as a carpenter, work at cabinet making being dull. Mr. Borden continued in Mr. Miller's employ for about two years. He was a generous, plain and simple man. The reason he went into the bank business was so that he could more handily manage the property of Thomas Borden, his uncle.

In all the time that he had been acquainted with Mr. Borden, and it was more than an intimate acquaintance, there was never a family quarrel that would, under any circumstances, lead to the perpetration of the act. When the servant girl came across the street and told of the affair he was dumbfounded and thought it was only a mistake. He immediately looked up and down the street, however, and while pedestrians traverse that thoroughfare in goodly numbers, at the time there was not a person to be seen. Under no circumstances could he form an idea of the cause of the murder. It was but a short while before that he accompanied Mr. Borden to the corner of South Main and Spring streets, at his request, and conversed with him regarding the construction of a large building on the northeast corner of those streets, and it was more than probable that if his life had not been cut off so shortly an edifice such as would have been a credit to the city would have been erected.

The building in which Mr. Borden was killed had been erected by Mr. Miller, and throughout all their transactions he had found him to be a man of his word. As far as Mr. Morse was concerned, Mr. Miller had known him but for about a year, and in that time he had seen nothing that would prejudice him against the man. Mr. Borden's daughters were ladies who had always conducted themselves so that the breath of scandal could never reach them.

As the reporter was leaving Mr. Miller's parlor, Mrs. Miller, who was present during the interview, said that she had lost, in Mrs. Borden, the best and most intimate neighbor she had ever met.

COLLECTED A CHAIN.

The police have followed the case with leads from a dozen standpoints and have collected a chain of circumstantial evidence which points in a certain direction with startling coincidences.

The statement that Miss Lizzie had changed her dress yesterday was denied this afternoon by the servant, who stated that the same garment was worn all day. The story told by Morse of his visit to Flint village has been examined and found to be correct with slight variations in time that are immaterial. There can be no doubt that he was away from the house when the crime was perpetrated.

The police have worked in other directions and have discovered things which bring them face to face with embarrassing difficulties. The poisoned milk theory has been investigated, and an unsuccessful attempt was found to have been made to purchase a drug at a South Main street store that may have had something to do with a subsequent development of the case. The police are carefully guarding these facts and others of an important nature which they possess, and a sensation is promised when the time comes to lay all the evidence before the public. The necessity of another thorough search of the premises for the sake of bringing to light the weapon with which the deed was done is being urged. This will furnish an important link in the chain of evidence, and until it has been found it is doubtful whether any definite movement will be made.

A physician who took part in the autopsy told a reporter that if the dead body could speak they would disclose the fact that no mysterious stranger had been around to rob them of life; that the person who committed the foul deed was at that moment not far from the scene and knew just where to lay hands on the weapon. When pressed for an explanation of these mysterious words, the doctor declined further to commit himself, saying that strong suspicions were not trustworthy as evidence.

A BOY'S STORY.

This afternoon Marshal Hilliard was informed that a boy named Kirousck, aged 12, who lives on Central street, had an important communication to make to him in relation to this mysterious affair. The boy was immediately sent for and said that time between 10 and 11 o'clock he was passing on Second street in company with an employe of Fish, the fruit dealer, and noticed a man who was in the act of jumping the fence which divides the Borden and the Chagnon properties. The man was tall and well built, wore a light soft hat, black suit and some kind of russet shoes. A few seconds later, as the horse was going slowly, the boy heard a noise around the house as if some one had shrieked for help. Although it attracted his attention, he did not mention it to the man who was with him.

At the time the affair took place there was nobody in Dr. Chagnon's house, every inmate being on their way to attend a wedding anniversary. Miss Collett, who was keeping the house, was on the piazza for some time, but was absent about the time of the murder.

NO CLEARER!

The Solution of the Borden Mystery Still Delayed.

POLICE WORKING ON CLUES AND THEORIES

That Might Lead to the Perpetration of the Crime.

BODIES OF THE VICTIMS CONVEYED
TO OAK GROVE CEMETERY.

Mr. Borden's Closeness in Handling His Money.

All day Thursday the people who have been interested in working up the Borden murder case were busily concerned in establishing theories to explain the circumstances, and then quickly abandoning those theories for some other that looked attractive at first sight. All this meant that nothing definite had been found, and only circumstantial evidence was at hand.

Upon this a host of theories have been builded. The poison feature spoken of in Friday's HERALD is being made prominent, but unless the authorities have kept to themselves important facts which the other workers on the case have not discovered, there is little satisfaction to be gained from what is known.

THE CROWD FOLLOWS MORSE

Interest still holds at fever heat and will not be satisfied until the impenetrable mystery which surrounds the case is pierced. Hundreds of people throng the street in front of the house and eye anybody who enters the premises with eagerness. An example of the popular curiosity was furnished about 8 o'clock Friday night. At that time Mr. Morse and the servant came out of the house and turned down Second street. Somebody in the crowd knew him and the word was passed along: "There's Morse." At once the crowd took it up and started down the street after the couple. People on Main street saw the commotion and gushed into Second street to see what was the matter. When Mr. Morse dropped a letter in the box fully 1000 people were standing around the postoffice corridors and crowding up the steps to see him do it. This shows the state of the popular mind wrought up to the intensest interest in the case.

THE POISON THEORY

Facts may develop that will show the importance of the poison episode, but as yet the facts are meager. It appears that Lizzie Borden was ill with the rest of the family, and Dr. Bowen was called to attend them. Lizzie had told a friend the day before the murder that she was afraid somebody had tampered with the milk which had been left at the house. She seemed very much disturbed about it and remarked: "I am afraid that father has an enemy." Little was thought of the matter then, but in the light of subsequent developments this may prove to be important.

Relative to the poisoning Dr. Bowen said: "On Wednesday morning last, about 9 o'clock, Mrs. Borden came across the shed, and, entering our house, commenced conversation with my wife. She said: 'I am afraid my husband and I were poisoned last night. We ate supper as usual, and had nothing out of the ordinary on the table. About 9 o'clock we were both taken sick with terrible fits of vomiting and pains in the stomach. We finally got easier and so did not send for the doctor in the night. I thought, however, I would come over and see him this morning.' Therewith she came into my presence, and I asked her in a general way her symptoms. I could not gather from her statements any particular opinion as to the cause of the illness, but at this time in the year such troubles are not infrequent, a condition due to many causes.

"A little later in the forenoon I went over to see Mr. Borden. I found him reclining on the sofa in the sitting-room. I asked him how he was and if he thought anything had poisoned him. He laughed and said he guessed there was not very much the matter with him. We sat talking some little time and then I went out. That was the last time I talked with him.

"That is the whole basis for the talk of poison," continued Dr. Bowen, "and, personally, I do not take any stock in the theory. That is, I see nothing, thus far, sufficiently strong to indicate it. It is a very serious matter to make reflections and insinuations against a woman of unstained character as some of the papers are doing in their reports of this case, as they relate to Lizzie Borden," continued the doctor. "I have known her for many years, and have seen her several times since the tragedy. I believe her absolutely innocent of even a guilty knowledge of the crime. I will not say there may not have been occasional family differences between Mr. Borden and the girls. That is a matter I was in a position to know little about, but so far as I ever observed the inter-family relations were cordial.

"There are two reasons why I believe Lizzie ought not be even suspected, or her position in the case questioned. First, she had no money, and secondly, her character is above reproach. She has always been a person of undisputed virtue and christian living. But if these reasons are not enough let me add another, greater than the rest. I do [not] believe a hardened man of the world, much less a gentle and refined woman, in her sober senses, devoid of sudden passion, could strike such a blow with such a weapon as was used on Mr. Borden and linger to survey the bloody deed.

"I am a surgeon, and have been in active practice for years, and the first view of the old man's body staggered me. I could not inflict upon a dead dog the additional 11 blows that with manifest precision and care were driven into the victim's head. I believe no human being in sane mind could perpetrate such a terrible work and then duplicate it on the floor above, taking a defenceless old woman as a victim. For this particular reason I do not believe it right to insinuate a word against so good a woman as Miss Lizzie. She possesses our confidence, and we believe in her. Nevertheless, as a citizen who realizes the demand and need of law, I want the mystery fully cleared up and the guilty party punished."

SHE SAW A MAN

Mrs. Chace, who lives over the store of Vernon Wade's grocery, the second house south of the scene of the tragedy, says that about 11 o'clock she was on the roof of a building east of her house hanging clothes. While there she could overlook Mr. Borden's yard. At the time a man was sitting on the fence filling his pockets with pears. He appeared to be a medium sized man, but as he was in a crouched position it was impossible for her to tell his height accurately. On looking up he noticed her watching him, and immediately jumped the fence and passed through the east end of Dr. Kelly's property to Third street.

A STARTLING THEORY

gained some believers Friday night who put more faith in the poisoning story than the evidence seems to warrant. Was it not possible that the victims had been rendered unconscious by poison before the butchery began? The attitude in which Mr. Borden was found may have given support to this theory, but it is not so easy to explain why Mrs. Borden was found stretched at length on the floor where she had been stricken down by the murderous blow. Had she felt the effects of the poison slowly creeping over her, as it could be supposed that her husband did, was it not possible that she would have sought a resting place?

The trouble with the idea is that Mr. Borden was seen on the street half an hour before the news of his death was flashed over the country. During that half hour, it is known that he walked from his block on Main street to his home on Second street, exchanged his street coat for a house coat and sat down to read a paper. If he took poison after his trip down town it must have been prussic acid, for nothing else would have produced death so quickly. Professionals contended that there was nothing to indicate a dose of poison heavy enough to cause death or drowsiness. Poisons do not compose people to sleep, as a rule, and if morphine had been administered there would have been traces of it in the physical appearance of the man and woman.

CLOSE IN MONEY MATTERS

Hiram Harrington, 40 Fourth street, is married to Laurana, Mr. Borden's only sister. A reporter who interviewed him gathered the following story: "My wife, being an only sister, was very fond of Mr. Borden and always subservient to his will, and by her intimacy with his affairs I have become acquainted with a good deal of the family history during years past. Mr. Borden was an exceedingly hard man concerning money matters, determined and stubborn, and when once he got an idea nothing could change him. He was too hard for me.

"When his father died some years ago he offered my wife the old homestead on Ferry street for a certain sum of money. My wife preferred to take the money, and after the agreements were all signed, to show how close he was, he wanted my wife to pay an additional $3 for water tax upon the homestead."

"What do you think was the motive for the crime?" asked the reporter.

"Money, unquestionably money," replied Mr. Harrington. "If Mr. Borden died, he would have left something over $500,000, and all I will say is that, in my opinion, that furnishes the only motive, and a sufficient one, for the double murder. I have heard so much now that I would not be surprised at the arrest any time of the person to whom in my opinion suspicion strongly points, although right down in my heart I could not say I believed the party guilty.

"Last evening I had a long interview with Lizzie Borden, who has refused to see anyone else. I questioned her very carefully as to her story of the crime. She was very composed, showed no signs of any emotion or were there any traces of grief upon her countenance. That did not surprise me, as she is not naturally emotional. I asked her what she knew of her father's death, and, after telling of the unimportant events of the early morning, she said her father came home about 10:30. She was in the kitchen at the time, she said, but went into the sitting room when her father arrived. She was very solicitous concerning him, and assisted him to remove his coat and put on his dressing-gown; asked concernedly how he felt, as he had been weak from a cholera morbus attack the day before. She told me she helped him to get a comfortable reclining position on the lounge, and asked him if he did not wish the blinds closed to keep out the sun, so he could

42

have a nice nap. She pressed him to allow her to place an afghan over him, but he said he did not need it. Then she asked him tenderly several times if he was perfectly comfortable, if there was anything she could do for him, and upon receiving assurance to the negative she withdrew. All these things showed a solicitude and a thoughtfulness that I never had heard was a part of her nature or custom before. She described these little acts of courtesy minutely.

"I then questioned her very carefully as to the time she left the house, and she told me positively that it was about 10:45. She said she saw her father on the lounge as she passed out. On leaving the house she says she went directly to the barn to obtain some lead. She informed me that it was her intention to go to Marion on a vacation, and she wanted the lead in the barn loft to make some sinkers. She was a very enthusiastic angler. I went over the ground several times, and she repeated the same story. She told me it was hard to place the exact time she was in the barn, as she was cutting the lead into sizable sinkers, but thought she was absent some 20 minutes. Then she thought again, and said it might have been 30 minutes. Then she entered the house and went to the sitting room, as she says she was anxious concerning her father's health. 'I discovered him dead,' she said, 'and cried for Bridget, who was upstairs in her room.'

" 'Did you go and look for your stepmother?' I asked. 'Who found her?' But she did not reply. I pressed her for some idea of the motive and the author of the act, and, after she had thought a moment, she said, calmly: 'A year ago last spring our house was broken into while father and mother were at Swansey, and a large amount of money stolen, together with diamonds. You never heard of it because father did not want it mentioned, so as to give the detectives a chance to recover the property. That may have some connection with the murder. Then I have seen strange men around the house. A few months ago I was coming through the back yard, and, as I approached the side door, I saw a man there examining the door and premises. I did not mention it to anyone. The other day I saw the same man hanging about the house, evidently watching us. I became frightened and told my parents about it. I also wrote to my sister at Fairhaven about it.' Miss Borden then gave it as her opinion that the strange man had a direct connection with the murder, but she could not see why the house was not robbed, and did not know of anyone who would desire revenge upon her father."

Mr. Harrington was asked if he knew whether or not there were dissensions in the Borden family. "Yes, there were, although it has been always kept very quiet. For nearly ten years there have been constant disputes between the daughters and their father and stepmother. Mr. Borden gave her some bank stock and the girls thought they ought to be treated as evenly as the mother. I guess Mr. Borden did try to do it, for he deeded to the daughters, Emma L. and Lizzie A., the homestead on Ferry street, an estate of 120 rods of land with a house and barn, all valued at $3000. This was in 1887.

"The trouble about money matters did not diminish, nor the acerbity of the family ruptures lessen, and Mr. Borden gave each girl ten shares in the Crystal Spring Bleachery company, which he paid $100 a share for. They sold them soon after for less than $40 per share. He also gave them some bank stock at various times, allowing them, of course, the entire income from them. In addition to this he gave them a weekly stipend, amounting to $200 a year.

"In spite of all this the dispute about their not being allowed enough went on with equal bitterness. Lizzie did most of the demonstrative contention, as Emma is very quiet and unassuming, and would feel very deeply any disparaging or angry word from her father. Lizzie, on the contrary, was haughty and domineering with the stubborn will of her father and bound to contest for her rights. There were many animated interviews between father and daughter on this point. Lizzie is of a repellant disposition, and after an unsuccessful passage with her father would become sulky and refuse to speak to him for days at a time. She moved in the best society in Fall River, was a member of the Congregational church, and is a brilliant conversationalist. She thought she ought to entertain as others did, and felt that with her father's wealth she was expected to hold her end up with others of her set. Her father's constant refusal to allow her to entertain lavishly angered her. I have heard many bitter things she has said of her father, and know she was deeply resentful of her father's maintained stand in this matter.

"This house on Ferry street was an old one, and was in constant need of repairs. There were two tenants paying $16.50 and $14 a month, but with taxes and repairs there was very little income from the property. It was a great deal of trouble for the girls to keep the house in repair, and a month or two ago they got disgusted and deeded the house back to their father."

AN INTERESTING LEGAL PHASE

of the case is involved in the question: Who was killed first? There is a diversity of opinion in this phase of the case, and there is little to show which side has taken the correct stand. The police at present are working on the theory that Mrs. Borden was killed first, and with that involved the only motive which can now be assigned for the crime -- that of gain.

Quite a tidy sum, about $100,000, is the issue in the case. The amount on the basis that Mr. Borden was worth in the vicinity of $200,000 represents the one-third of an estate termed the widow's dower. If the wife was killed first this would not be taken into

44

consideration, but if the murderer struck down the old gentleman in the beginning, the one-third share goes to the heirs of Mrs. Borden, even if she was a widow but five seconds. Under the latter case, the Misses Borden, who are not the heirs of Mrs. Borden, will be entitled, in the division of the property, to only two-thirds of the estate, and the $100,000 or so will go to the nearest kin of Mrs. Borden. If, however, it is decided the other way, that the wife died first, the entire estate will be distributed between the two daughters.

It may, however, be less difficult to prove that there was an hour or so between the time of the murder of Mrs. Borden and that of her husband. Her movements are not accounted for after 9 o'clock in the morning, at which time she went upstairs to arrange the apartment in which Mr. Morse slept the night before. How much time was required in this work cannot be estimated. It certainly was completed when the murder was committed, whether 15 minutes, an hour, or two hours after she went upstairs. It is believed by the police that in those two hours she would have more than completed the work and gone to another part of the house, or in any event to her own room, if alive, when really it is evident that she had not left the room she first entered. The analysis of the stomachs will probably show, by the amount of food digested, whether there was any material difference in the time of the fatal attacks. Of course, if the second murder was committed only a few minutes after the first the digestive organs will fail to show the difference, but if an hour or more elapsed it can be shown, provided that breakfast was eaten by the couple at the same time.

A TELL TALE HAIR

The story started from a "high police official" as usual that a hatchet had been found Friday in the cellar of the house that had been recently scoured. It was a lather's hatchet with a claw hammer end. Every trace of blood had been removed, but a tell tale hair clung to one of the claws. It was a hair from Mrs. Borden's head, although the horrible hatchery had hidden the place where it had been removed from the head.

The police authorities still maintain that the deadly weapon has not been discovered, and they persist in the belief that it was a long handled axe, although it may have been a hatchet. Search high and low has been made for it. The cellar has been scoured, the yard has been hunted through, search parties have turned the interior of the barn upside down, but have found nothing.

John V. Morse has been interested in the search. He wanted to hire somebody to bury the bloody clothes. Towards the close of the afternoon Morse grew irritable, and had quite an altercation with David P. Keefe, who hired a man to bury the blood-stained clothes and pieces of the skull for him. Keefe charged $5 for the work, and Morse pronounced it robbery. Keefe said he wouldn't do the job for $100, though under some circumstances he allowed that he might be glad to do it for nothing. Morse finally paid $3. Later he locked the barn when a couple of Boston newspaper men were inside and found considerable fault with the liberties people took with the premises. He was reminded that a reward of $5000 had been offered, and that everybody was intensely interested.

THE FUNERAL SERVICES

took place at 11 o'clock, and were strictly private. The bodies were laid out in the dining room, with their heads toward the east. The coffins were plain and covered with black broadcloth. A wreath of ivy lay on the casket containing the remains of Mr. Borden, while a bouquet of roses occupied a similar place on Mrs. Borden's. The services consisted of an invocation and reading of scripture by Dr. Adams of the First Congregational church, after which prayer was offered by the Rev. Mr. Buck.

Among the parties who were present and accompanied the remains to their final resting place were the following: Southard H. Miller and wife, Dr. Bowen and wife, Mrs. Adelaide Churchill, Miss Mary Ann Borden, of whose estate Mr. Borden was the guardian; Frank Miller, George Whitehead and wife, the latter being a half-sister to Mrs. Borden; Mrs. Oliver Gray and daughter, the former being the stepmother to Mrs. Borden; Mrs. J. L. Fish of Hartford, a sister of Mrs. Borden; Mrs. J. D. Burt, William Wilcox and wife, Mrs. Restcome Case, Mrs. John Durfee, Hiram Harrington, brother-in-law of Mr. Borden.

For the family Miss Lizzie was the first to appear, and, escorted by Undertaker Winward, she took her place in the coach. No veil covered her face, and she walked with a firm and steady step to her seat in the carriage. Nothing in her manner would indicate that the finger of suspicion was pointed toward her, although it was easy to see that the burden of grief she was carrying was heavy. Emma Borden followed, her step and carriage being much weaker than her sister. The remains of Mr. Borden were then placed in the hearse by Abram G. Hart, George W. Dean, Jerome C. Borden, Richard B. Borden, James M. Osborn and Andrew Borden as pallbearers. Mrs. Borden's remains followed, with James C. Eddy, Henry S. Buffington, Frank L. Almy, J. Henry Wells, Simeon B. Chace, and John H. Boone as bearers. Dr. Adams and the Rev. Mr. Buck followed, accompanied by Mr. Morse. On their appearance the latter was the target of all eyes. He appeared to realize the fact, but held his head high and walked firmly to his seat in the carriage. The funeral cortege then proceeded to the Oak Grove cemetery; when there the final interment took place. The services were read by Dr. Adams, after which benediction was offered by the Rev. Mr. Buck. A return to the house was then made, and the victims of the most puzzling tragedy in the history of this country were left to rest beneath the clay.

HAVE SEEN NO PAPERS

The house has been carefully guarded and orders were issued to admit nobody who had no business there. A relative, who came from Fairhaven, could not get into the house. Officer Hyde, who has stood guard over the side door, was the Cerebus who drove away inquisitive reporters. It appears that no newspapers have been received inside the house since the murder, and that up to the time of the funeral neither of the sisters suspected the cruel suspicions which the police had formed. The Misses Borden were beginning to feel the strain terribly. Besides the kind friends who have sacrificed their own comfort to relieve the stricken daughters, they have seen nobody to talk to since the murder. The newspaper stories have been kept from Lizzie, but will be broken to her after the funeral, either by friends or officers of the law. Up to the present, Marshal Hilliard has respected the feelings of the daughters, knowing that he would be able to find either of them when he wanted to interview her.

As soon as the funeral cortege passed out of sight of the house, Marshal Hilliard, Assistant Marshal Fleet and Detective Seaver entered by the side door and proceeded to examine all the inmates who had not gone to the grave. They were closeted with them for a long time.

TO DISCOVER A MOTIVE

An effort is being made to discover a motive in the family relations of the Bordens. Their friends admit that things were not as pleasant as they might have been in the house. Mrs. Borden was not the mother of the girls and the father was not over liberal with them. Some stories that have been written concerning these relations, however, are regarded as the grossest exaggeration. If all that has been written should prove on further investigation to be true, a person will fail to find in the family relations anything so strained as to encourage the perpetration of one of the most startling crimes in the history of the country.

It is difficult to follow the conclusions of the police without agreeing that the work was that of a maniac. Such cruelty can hardly be conceived to have been planned and carried out by a sane person, but appears rather to be the wonderful cunning of a deranged mind. A leading physician said at noon that he was fully convinced that the act was not done by a man, as all authorities agreed in saying that hacking is almost a positive sign of the deed of a woman who is unconscious of what she is doing.

The statement of the servant girl that Lizzie Borden wore the same dress all morning, and upon that garment there was not a spot of

47

blood, has been verified. The time when Mr. Borden was talking with Charles Horton on the postoffice steps and when the officers stood over his dead body must have been consumed in hiding a bloody garment or removing blood stains. These evidences could not have been carried far away from the house, had the deed been done by an inmate. That they cannot be discovered is admitted to be a weak point in the government's case thus far, and every effort will be directed to searching the house from top to bottom, now that the bodies of the victims have been buried.

STORY OF A DRUG CLERK

Hypolyte Martel, a clerk for Philias Martel, a druggist on Pleasant street, relates the following story. Last Monday he was approached in the store by a young lady, who wanted to buy arsenic from him and was willing to give any price for it. The clerk told her that as the druggist was not present he could not possibly comply with her wishes, whereupon she went out, much disappointed.

She returned 20 minutes later and asked for prussic acid. The article was again refused her, with the advice to return when the druggist would be back from dinner. Mr. Martel describes the caller as being about 26 years and weighing about 150 pounds. He said he could recognize her if he should see her.

A woman also called at Corneau & Latourneau's drug store on Pleasant street on the same date, but it was found out afterwards that it was the wife of Inspector McCaffrey who was then on a crusade against the drug stores. She is said to resemble Miss Borden.

At going to press it was stated by Marshal Hilliard that nothing would be done toward arresting any suspected party at the present, although a close surveillance is being held.

August 8, 1892

VISITED THE TOMB

Medical Examiner Dolan Examines Borden's Body.

AXE FAILS TO FIT SOME OF THE WOUNDS.

The Absence of Blood Continues a Puzzle.

Mrs. Borden's Letter as Yet Unaccounted For.

Minister Jubb Speaks About the Murder.

Four days have now past since the terrible Borden murder was perpetrated, and the murderer is still at large. For four days the police authorities have bent their best energies to the discovery of the perpetrator of the crime or his motive, and have reached one conclusion only. Still they hesitate, because their chain of evidence is purely circumstantial at best, and there are important missing links in it at that.

Andrew J. Jennings, who has followed the evidence carefully in behalf of the Borden estate, declares that he does not believe the police have evidence enough upon which to make an arrest. For the want of a better clue, public opinion has accepted the theory that the deed must have been done by somebody inside the Borden house. Accordingly a persistent clamour has been made for the arrests of the suspects. It may be reassuring to such people to know that from an hour after the murder every person who was in the Borden house has been practically under arrest. Night and day the police have stood guard there and have closely watched all the goings and comings, and there has been no chance for anybody to escape even if there was any desire to do so.

A SEARCH OF THE HOUSE.

Saturday and Sunday were devoid of startling revelations in the case, but during that time the best efforts of the police were made. While the bodies lay in the house no attempt was made to search the premises thoroughly. Faith was lodged in the officers to prevent the removal of any article from the house, and while the various clues were being run down by the detectives of the police force, the hunt for a concealed weapon inside of the house was deferred until after the funeral.

About 4 o'clock Marshal Hilliard, Assistant Marshal Fleet, Captain Desmond, Detective Seaver, Medical Examiner Dolan and Andrew J. Jennings, Esq., entered the house and proceeded to make a thorough hunt of the premises. Every facility was offered to them to carry on their search, and the members of the family volunteered any assistance in their power. This is in direct opposition to the story printed Saturday that Lizzie Borden had declined to admit the police into her room to make a search. The attic to which the visitors ascended was spacious. It contained four rooms and an open area, into which the stairway extends. The two rooms in the rear were found to be scantily furnished. One of them was occupied by the servant, Bridget Sullivan, whose personal effects were about all contained in a small trunk. The lid was quickly raised and the contents inspected. It contained only clothing and a few mementoes treasured by the owner, as might be judged by the careful manner in which they were preserved. The bed was carefully inspected, the mattress shaken up and pounded and the adjoining closet searched in vain. All that met the searchers' gaze were packages and boxes of heavy clothing stored for the summer, comforters for the beds and similar articles.

The search then extended to the second furnished room, which contained a painted set. The bed had the appearance of not having been used for some time. Every corner and every crevice in which an article might be secreted was examined, but nothing bearing on the murder was discovered. Nearly an hour was spent in the attic alone.

Then the party went downstairs. The ladies heard them coming and went further downstairs, leaving the searchers in full possession of their rooms. To illustrate the officer's movements, a description of the house is necessary. On the front, facing Second street, at the northern corner, is the guest chamber, which leads out of a spacious hall to the right. It was here the murder of Mrs. Borden took place, positively some time in advance of the husband's death, and there it was that Mr. Morse slept on the night preceding the tragedy. The room is large, with windows on two sides, and is handsomely papered. The windows are adorned with lace draperies. The furniture is a heavy set of black walnut. In one corner was the stain where the ill-fated victim fell, and where her life-blood colored the floor a deep crimson. While some of the men were inspecting the wall, carpet, floor and closet, the others were examining the bed, in which a hard spot was found. The mattress was quickly laid bare, and then a knife served to rip the ticking open. There was only stuffing within, the mysterious lump being nothing more than a portion of the contents which was matted together, a probable result of long use and insufficient shaking. The next room entered was Lizzie's, which is in the middle of the house, with windows on the south side. Every dress the occupant possessed, every skirt, wrapper and piece of clothing was rigorously scrutinized. On one of the skirts a blood stain was found. It was the only notable discovery in the room. Opening out of this chamber to the south is a small room, presumably used by the sisters as a study, and it next demanded the attention of the police. The contents of a desk were minutely examined, and then after nearly two hours work the remainder of the floor was gone over.

Then the visitors walked down to the ground floor, and as they did so the ladies went upstairs. A long time was consumed in a minute inspection of the parlor, library, sitting-room, dining-room and kitchen, which availed nothing. In the cellar the wood pile was overturned and every crevice and crack looked into. There was nothing that could shed any light upon the crime. About 6:30 o'clock Marshal Hilliard concluded that the search had been carried far enough.

THOSE AXES.

After the search of the house, Mayor Coughlin visited the police station to have a conference with Marshal Hilliard. Throughout this entire affair he has been a close adviser with the police. He was among the first at the house after the murder and was present at the autopsy. Since then, night and day, the mayor has devoted himself to the case, urging the police to do their utmost in their hunt for the murderer and assisting by his medical knowledge the workings of the clues which had their origin in the physical condition of the victim.

Two axes and a hatchet were picked up in the cellar on the day of the murder and carried to the police station. Mayor Coughlin closely examined these, and on one of them detected spots that looked like blood. It was a long handled axe, and there were three suspicious stains upon it. The microscope gave evidence of blood, and the axe will be saved for further examination. The mayor is determined to allow no clue to be left unworked, but he admits that he does not place great confidence in the importance of his find. These axes lay on the cellar floor just after the murder and were seen by a great many people who ranged through the cellar. Several persons picked them up and looked them over with curiosity. This was within ten minutes of the announcement of the murder. In order to remove the blood from the axe it would have been necessary to have dipped it into water, and the amateur detectives would have found the blade and handle wet when they made their inspection. It was reported that a spot of blood had been discovered on one of Lizzie Borden's garments, but little importance has been ascribed to that.

AN UNSATISFACTORY INTERVIEW.

After consulting for a long time, Mayor Coughlin and Marshal Hilliard got into the mayor's carriage and drove to the Borden house Saturday evening to have a conversation with the family. Mayor Coughlin assured the members that every means would be taken by the authorities to discover the murderer and to clear up the mystery. The police would be on hand to keep the crowd in the street from becoming annoying. An attempt was then made to elicit information from the Bordens or Morse, who were present during the conversation, which would be of advantage to the police. Mayor Coughlin first went into particulars concerning the whereabouts of the mother, Mrs. Borden, on the morning she met her death. To the astonishment of himself and the marshal, he learned that Mrs. Borden had not been seen after 9 o'clock, until she was found weltering in a sickening pool of blood.

"When did you last see your mother, Lizzie?" inquired the mayor.

"I don't think I saw mother after 9 o'clock. She went up stairs to put shams on the pillows."

The question was repeated several times, but Miss Borden seemed positive that she could not be mistaken as to the time.

51

She was then examined as to the door which leads from one of the lower rooms to the staircase in the front hall, which connects the first floor with the upper entry. As nearly as the young woman could recall, that door was closed. She had seen nobody open or close it, of course, but her impression was that it was closed and had remained closed during the morning, until Dr. Bowen ascended in search of her mother.

It would naturally be surmised that if the murderer passed through the house while Miss Lizzie was in the barn and before Mr. Borden returned from his trip down town, he would have left this door open. He found the coast clear when he descended the stairs, and a man as clever as he would have arranged to command as much of a view after the foul deed had been accomplished as possible. If, when he attempted to make his escape, he noticed that the rooms leading to the rear or side door were occupied, he could have sneaked back and waited for a more favorable opportunity. If he were concealed upstairs and had been in hiding for some time, he would have had to take his chances on doors of course, and as has been demonstrated, his chances from beginning to end were good fairies so far as his precious skin was concerned.

It appears then that nobody saw Mrs. Borden for two hours, unless the servant, who has not been questioned, can give some information of her whereabouts. It is plain, too, that nobody knows what she was doing. She could not have been busy in the spare chamber for that length of time, for there was absolutely nothing to do there. The bed was made, the shams were arranged on the pillows, the towels laid scrupulously clean on a rack, and the room was in perfect order when Dr. Bowen entered, all but that heavy form with the mangled head, which was stretched motionless on the floor. Mrs. Borden had not gone out during the morning, at least the gown indicated that she had not left the house, because she wore an old calico dress, much worn, and not her street gown.

RUMORS OF ALL SORTS.

Saturday night all sorts of strange rumors were rife upon the street, and crowds of people made their way into Second street to stare at the windows of the house and to speculate concerning the secret which it contained. Police officers guarded front and rear, and a squad kept the crowds from congregating in the roadway. Early in the night there was considerable commotion at police headquarters and rumors were thick to the effect that a fresh trail had been struck. The marshal hurried up to his office from the supper table and in company with a couple of officers drove off hastily. They refused to make known their errand, however, and the announcement was made to the press representatives that there would be no important developments before Sunday. That did not fit into a story which leaked out from another quarter, however, and the reporters concluded to sit up a while. Nothing of an alarming nature happened, however.

Sunday was a quiet day around the house. Emma Borden appeared at the door at 8 o'clock to take in the milk. The servant girl, Bridget Sullivan, could stand the strain no longer and left the house Saturday night to join her friends. She will be on hand when the police want her to testify in the case. None of the family ventured out to church, and there was nobody visible at the windows.

EVENT OF SUNDAY.

The event of the day was the arrival at the house of Supt. Hanscom of the Boston Pinkerton agency, who entered with Lawyer Jennings during the forenoon. Hanscom arrived at the Mellen house late Saturday night, and there was a big stir when it became known that he had been hired by the Bordens to look after their interests. This was intensified somewhat Sunday when it was learned that he chose to work on lines independent of the police, and had had little conversation with the local authorities.

Detective Hanscom talked at length to the reporters in the Mellen house, and his ideas do not correspond with the government theory. He reviewed the case at length, but admitted that he had been at work on it too short a time to form a definite opinion. He had questioned Lizzie, but found her too exhausted physically for a searching examination. The reaction had come and he did not want to weary her. He was favorably impressed with her appearance and stated that she, like her sister, Miss E., appeared to be sincere and truthful. He questioned particularly the time that she spent in the barn, and she was positive that she was there 20 minutes or possibly half an hour. The murder looked like the work of a lunatic, while Lizzie appeared to be a level-headed, self-possessed woman. If she was in the barn half an hour, a man might have entered the house, committed both murders, and escaped by the way of the basement through the door leading to the back yard. That door was found open after the murders, though it was usually closed. Detective Hanscom admitted that he had a varied experience, and usually began by looking for the cause of death and the motive. Here the cause was apparent, but he had as yet found no motive. He had attempted to discover if Mr. Borden had any enemy capable of the deed. The family and Mr. Jennings could recall but one person who had a serious difference with the murdered man, and that was not of a nature to arouse suspicion in the present instance. The detective did not question Miss Borden regarding the axe found in the cellar, but had learned from another source that a flock of pigeons belonging to the Bordens had been killed in June. That might account for the blood stains on one of the axes. This axe will be sent to Boston for examination.

53

At last account Lizzie Borden had given way under the great strain and excitement of the last four days and Dr. Bowen had been summoned twice last evening to attend her. It was expected that morbid curiosity would fill Oak Grove cemetery with crowds of pedestrians yesterday, but for some reason or other there were fewer visitors than usual. A friend of the Borden family called during the day and two of John Morse's acquaintances from South Dartmouth paid him a visit.

DR. DOLAN AT A LOSS.

There was no special excitement at police headquarters. Medical Examiner Dolan held a long interview with Marshal Hilliard in the latter's office, and Detective Hanscom had a talk with Andrew Jennings. The medical examiner states that the only discovery of importance made during the thorough search of the Borden house Saturday afternoon was in the spare bed room, where Mrs. Borden's body was found. Out near the window drops of blood were found, which indicated that the murdered woman had moved after the first blow was delivered. It is thought that that blow was the glancing one which has been described. The supposition is that the axe fell on the right side of the head, taking off the flesh and hair, and that the woman turned and reeled to the space between the dressing case and bureau where the mortal wound was delivered. After that, the blows fell thick and fast. It is believed that when she was approached, Mrs. Borden stood looking out of the window in this room, and her blood which stained it at this point bears out that view. Dr. Dolan says that the more he reflects on the small quantity of blood that was spilled, the more at a loss he is to account for it. To him it seems utterly inexplicable. Ordinarily, no matter how sharp the weapon used, the rooms would have been stained crimson had such a tragedy taken place in them. Even if no arterial blood made its appearance, and though the wounds were inflicted after death, the veins and brain would have discharged enough fluid and gray matter to have left their mark on the furniture. But with the exception of the stains near the window and the thick pool about the head of the unfortunate woman, the chamber was as clean as though it had been freshly washed and swept. Every time the axe fell it cut deeply, but there was no gush of blood from the frightful gashes. The same condition prevails in the sitting room below where Mr. Borden was butchered, and there was nothing to raise the suspicion that the murderer had cleaned anything, except the dripping axe.

That letter which it is alleged Mrs. Borden received on the morning of the tragedy continues to excite interest, and on this head Dr. Dolan likewise had a little information to give. He says, that both Lizzie Borden and the servant told him that Mrs. Borden had received such a letter, and when he asked Lizzie what had become of it, she told him that she had been unable to find it; she feared that it had been burned in the kitchen stove. Nobody in the household seems to be able to give anything more than a general idea of the contents of the letter or note. It was from a friend who was ill, but if Mrs. Borden made this much known, it is curious that she did not state who the friend was or that the person with whom she was conversing did not have the curiosity to inquire.

It is certain that, so far as the public is concerned, the time of all the occupants of the Borden homestead has not been satisfactorily accounted for. If Mrs. Borden disappeared at 9 o'clock to put shams on the pillows, and did not appear again, it is presumed that her step-daughter remained downstairs while she was occupied on the second floor. At some time before Mr. Borden was killed, Bridget Sullivan went upstairs, and she may have seen her mistress on the floor. If the latter were in the habit of attending to household duties on the second floor for two hours at a time, her absence would [not] have attracted attention, but if she visited all parts of the house like women do, it is a little singular that nobody missed her. At all events, no harm could come from ascertaining just what Miss Lizzie and the servant did with their time from the hour of rising until the murders were discovered.

EMPLOYED A MASON.

Another thorough research was made this morning. Among those present at the time outside of the regular inmates were Lawyer Jennings, Superintendent Hanscom of the Boston Pinkerton agency, City Marshal Hilliard, Capt. Desmond, State Detective Seaver, Sergt. Edson and Officer Quigley. Charles H. Bryant, the mason, was called in, and every fire place was opened and examined. Nothing could be found of the axe, and nothing looked as though it had been disturbed. The wood in the cellar was turned over, and every inch of the building was sounded in the endeavor to find some recent hiding place, but once more the police were baffled and the conclusion was arrived at that the weapon had been conveyed from the premises.

City Missionary Buck in an interview expressed himself as a firm believer in Lizzie Borden's innocence. He said "Aside from her christian character, her actions at the time of the murder count with me as indicating ignorance of the crime. I called on her in less than one hour after the discovery of her father's body. I asked her if there was anyone she suspected, and she replied in tears that she did not know of a person in the world who could have a motive for murdering her father. She highly endorsed the character of the Swede farm hand in Mr. Borden's employ, and said he was above suspicion. A guilty person takes every opportunity to throw suspicion on the innocent, Lizzie Borden did not do that."

As the case is involved at present it looks as if much would depend upon medical testimony. Dr. Dolan is taking care of that end of the case and will have the best experts obtainable to assist. In company with Assistant Marshal Fleet, Drs. Dolan and Leary visited the receiving vault Sunday and made a further examination of the bodies, taking measurements of the wounds and notes of other matters which will be of use when testimony is needed in these directions.

Late Sunday night it was learned that something of a sensational character is likely to occur. Just exactly what it will be could not be ascertained. It is believed that Medical Examiner Dolan will spring a surprise. He has been working harder than any man interested in the case, and he has had the least to say. It is believed that he will introduce some very important evidence at the inquest. It is probable that he will have the bloody clothes worn by the murdered people, which are buried in the yard of the Borden house, in the rear of the barn, dug up and produced in court. These clothes were buried at the request of Mr. Morse, who still remains at the house.

Dr. Bowen, the family physician of the Borden family, is likely to be a prominent witness before the inquest hearing. It is supposed that he knows considerably more about the status of the relations of the Borden family, in a professional way, than he has told, and that he may be brought out at the hearing. It is understood that he does not think Lizzie Borden is guilty of the crime, and that she is not insane or has ever showed any signs of insanity. Dr. Bowen was closeted with Mayor Coughlin in Marshal Hilliard's private office for over an hour last evening, but what the interview was all about could not be learned. It was thought that an effort was made to glean from him something further about the social relations of the members of the Borden family.

This morning Dr. Dolan heard from the package in which were sent the viscera to Dr. Wood, the Boston chemist. Dr. Wood is not in Europe, as had been stated, but was in Boston and has received the package, the examination of which will be begun today. Dr. Dolan was interviewed relative to the spots of blood and the weapon which it is said had been discovered. He declined to state what kind of weapon it was; neither did he care to affirm or deny a statement attributed to one of the officers in the case that hairs were found on it. From another source it is learned that the weapon in question is an axe.

AN IMPORTANT POINT.

The visit to the cemetery Sunday was an important one. The axe was taken along with Dr. Dolan and Assistant Marshal Fleet and was fitted into the wounds, with what conclusions cannot be stated at once. The blow which was delivered over the temple of both victims was with a dull edge, and it was impossible to tell whether the axe would fit the wound or not, so shattered was the bone. The cut which extended down the front of Mr. Borden's nose was in a soft part of the face, so that the entire edge of the weapon cut into the flesh. It was an easy matter to measure that, and it was found that while the exact length of the gash did not correspond with the width of the axe blade, yet it would readily have been made by such a weapon. None of the cuts on Mrs. Borden was so clean as that on the face of her husband. In every instance the axe had been brought up against the skull, and it was not imbedded the entire width.

At the house this morning, the condition of things had not materially changed. It appears that no orders had been issued to prevent anybody from entering or leaving the house. Several friends of the young ladies called and were received, and about 8 o'clock Inspector Hanscom entered. Later he was joined by Lawyer Jennings, and the pair remained in the house for several hours.

The story of Mrs. Chace about a man being seen sitting on the fence at the time of the tragedy has been thoroughly sifted by Detectives Seaver and McHenry. The man who was engaged taking the pears at the time was named Patrick McGowan, a mason's helper employed by John Crowe. He stood on a pile of lumber, and at the time there were two other men employed in the yard cutting wood and drilling a stone. Both these men are confident that no person left the yard by that exit.

SAW A MAN AT MIDNIGHT.

The residence of Dr. Chagnon on Third street is situated close to the Borden property, both being divided by a fence about seven feet high. Mrs. Chagnon and her daughter, Martha, say that Wednesday night about 12 o'clock they distinctly saw a man jump over the fence into the Borden yard, and subsequently they heard a slight noise in the barn. The women were much frightened and told the story to the doctor on the morning of the day when the murder took place. Owing to the darkness of the street, they could not see the man plainly enough to give any description of his appearance.

NOTES OF THE AFFAIR.

Seven out of the nine stories that were reported to the police have been investigated, and every one found to be a myth.

Dr. Bowen said this noon that the Bordens were suffering from nervous prostration. Lizzie is somewhat worse, as it was not until after returning from the funeral Saturday that she knew of the suspicion that was cast on her.

The statement of Mr. Morse that he had not been in the horse business since his return from the west was proven today by a visit to Westport by Officer Medley.

The Mrs. Borden who threw her three children into the cistern of the house south of Mr. Borden's residence is in no way related to any of the deceased. Thus no claim of insanity can be drawn from that quarter.

Marshal Hilliard ordered William Niles to be present at the house at 2:30 p. m. to dig up the clothes which were ordered to be buried behind the barn.

MINISTER JUBB

Appeals to the People to Refrain from Causeless Innuendos.

Mr. and Mrs. Borden were members of the Central Congregational church. Lizzie has been a teacher in the mission school connected with the parish, and has always been very active in the young people's societies and the work of the church. Sunday the central church worshippers met with the First Church congregation in the stone church on Main street. All of the pews were filled, many being in their seats some half hour before the service began. It was supposed that the Rev. W. Walker Jubb, who occupied the pulpit, would make some allusion to the awful experiences through which one family in his charge had been compelled to pass during the week, and the supposition was correct.

Mr. Jubb read for the morning lesson a portion of Matthew, containing the significant words which imply that what is concealed will be revealed. In his prayer, Mr. Jubb evoked the divine blessing on the community, rendering thanks for the blessings bestowed on many, and, pausing, referred to the murder of two innocent persons. He prayed fervently that right might prevail, and that in good time the terrible mystery might be cleared away; that the people of the city might do everything in their power to assist the authorities; and asked for divine guidance for the police, that they might prosecute unflinchingly and unceasingly the search for the murderer. Mr. Jubb prayed that their hands might be strengthened, that their movements might be characterized by discretion, and that wisdom and great power of discernment might be given to them in their work. "And while we hope," he continued, "for the triumph of justice, let our acts be tempered with mercy. Help us to refrain from giving voice to those insinuations and innuendoes which we have no right to utter. Save us from blasting a life, innocent and blameless; keep us from taking the sweetness from a future by our ill-advised words, and let us be charitable as we remember the poor, grief-stricken family and minister unto them."

The clergyman asked that those who were writing of the crime might be careful of the reputations of the living, which could so easily be undermined.

For his text Mr. Jubb took the first chapter of Ecclesiastes, ninth verse: "The thing that hath been is that which shall be; and that which is done is that which shall be done; and there is no new thing under the sun." The speaker considered the monotonies of life, and expatiated on the causes of indifference in persons who would be nothing if not geniuses, drawing lessons from successes in humble spheres. At the end of the sermon Mr. Jubb stepped to the side of the pulpit and said slowly and impressively: "I cannot close my sermon this morning without speaking of the horrible crime that has startled our beloved city this week, ruthlessly taking from our church household two respected and esteemed members. I cannot close without referring to my pain and surprise at the atrocity of the outrage. A more brutal, cunning, daring and fiendish murder I never heard of in all my life. What must have been the person who could have been guilty of such a revolting crime? One to commit such a murder must have been without heart, without soul, a fiend incarnate, the very vilest of degraded and depraved humanity, or he must have been a maniac. The circumstances, execution and all the surroundings cover it with mystery profound. Explanations and evidence as to both perpetrator and motive are shrouded in a mystery that is almost inexplicable. That such a crime could have been committed during the busy hours of the day, right in the heart of a populous city, is passing comprehension. As we ponder, we exclaim in our perplexity, Why was the deed done? What could have induced anybody to engage in such a butchery? Where is the motive? When men resort to crime it is for plunder, for gain, from enmity, in sudden anger or for revenge. Strangely, nothing of this nature enters into this case, and again I ask -- what was the motive? I believe, and am only voicing your feelings fully when I say that I hope the criminal will be speedily brought to justice. This city cannot afford to have in its midst such an inhuman brute as the murderer of Andrew J. Borden and his wife. Why, a man who could conceive and execute such a murder as that would not hesitate to burn the city.

"I trust that the police may do their duty and lose no opportunity which might lead to the capture of the criminal. I would impress upon them that they should not say too much and thus unconsciously assist in defeating the ends of justice. I also trust that the press (and I say this because I recognize its influence and power), I trust that it will use discretion in disseminating its theories and conclusions, and that pens may be guided by consideration and charity. I would wish the papers to remember that by casting a groundless or undeserved insinuation they may blacken and blast a life forever, like a tree smitten by a bolt of lightening; a life which has always commanded respect, whose acts and motives have always been pure and holy. Let us ourselves curb our tongues and preserve a blameless life from undeserved suspicions. I think I have a right to ask for the prayers of this church and of my own congregation. The murdered husband and wife were members of this church, and a daughter now stands in the same relation to each one of you, as you, as church members, do to each other. God help and comfort her. Poor, stricken girls, may they both be comforted, and may they both realize how fully God is their refuge."

DEAD BEFORE THE BUTCHERY.

A New Bedford Man's Theory of the Small Flow of Blood.

Josiah A. Hunt, keeper of the house of correction, who has had an extensive experience as an officer of the law in this city, in speaking of the tragedy advanced a theory which has thus far escaped the notice of the police, or, if it has not, they are putting the public on the wrong scent.

Said Mr. Hunt: "It is my opinion that both Mr. Borden and his wife were dead before the murderers struck a blow, probably poisoned by the use of prussic acid, which would cause instant death. The use of a hatchet was simply to mislead those finding the bodies. I believe this to be the real state of the case, for if they had been alive when the first blow was struck, the action of the heart would have been sufficient to have caused the blood to spatter more freely than is shown from the accounts furnished by the papers. There was altogether too much of a butchery for so little spattering of blood.

"In this connection it might be said that in the Johnson murder trial, in which Charles J. Tighe of Boston was found guilty, there was a great deal of evidence produced on this particular point. In that murder a lather's hatchet was used, and it will be remembered that the defence endeavored to break down the testimony touching upon spatters of blood which so completely covered his clothing. In both cases it is supposed that the weapons were in the hands of some one who stood just back of the victims. That so little blood was found in the Borden home is surprising."

III
Lizzie Goes to Trial

In the second week·after the murders, the case moved from the Borden home and the police station to the courts. The inquest, the preliminary hearing, the arrest, and the trial brought Lizzie Borden to the center of the stage. Given the society's deference for ladies of good family, the fact of police suspicion and the eventual arrest of Lizzie on a charge of murder indicate exceptionally strong evidence against her. Throughout, however, in hearings and trial, the tension between the demands of justice and society's preconceptions can be seen in court records and news accounts alike.

The Inquest

On August 9, 1892, Lizzie Borden was served with a subpoena summoning her to appear at the Second District Court in Fall River for an inquiry to determine the cause of death of her father and stepmother. This was the inquest, an investigative proceeding, less formal than a trial and required by Massachusetts law in homicide cases of unknown cause.

The law in force at the time of the Borden murders provided that the inquest may be private, and it left the matter to the court's discretion. Judge Josiah C. Blaisdell limited publicity regarding the inquest to brief news bulletins, and, in so doing, he carried out the implicit intent of the law: to maintain the secrecy of the inquest proceedings in order to protect the accused from any prejudicial pretrial publicity and to ensure a fair trial. Miss Borden's inquest testimony was not published until after the trial jury was selected and sequestered. The New Bedford *Evening Standard* printed the complete transcript on June 12, 1893.

Only at the inquest did Lizzie tell her own story under oath, and her testimony is therefore a significant feature of the Borden record. Here Lizzie described life in the Borden household, revealed her relationships with members of her family, and accounted for her own actions on the day of the murders.

There are inconsistencies in the account: Lizzie gave a variety of answers to the question of her whereabouts when her father returned from "downstreet" on the day of his death. Her story of her father's congress boots is contradicted by the photographs of the dead man taken soon after the crime. Lizzie's story sometimes strained the limits of credibility, particularly her account of the time she spent in the barn. Perhaps the precise recollection of ordinary activities is always difficult. Perhaps Lizzie was nervous and frightened by the District Attorney's questioning. And her memory might have been dulled by the sedative, morphine, prescribed by Dr. Bowen.

Lizzie's testimony is published here in full. It deserves careful assessment at first hand for it opens a rare window on Lizzie's character. One may, in the end, agree with District Attorney Hosea M. Knowlton that the inquest testimony was "Lizzie's confession." It should be remembered that this testimony was excluded from the trial and from the jurors' knowledge.

Transcript of Lizzie Borden's Testimony

A Note on the Text: The inquest testimony is reprinted here exactly as originally published. Irregular spelling and punctuation and the use of ungrammatical forms by speakers (e.g., "you was") appear here as in the original text.

Source: New Bedford *Evening Standard,* June 12, 1893

Q. (Mr. Knowlton) Give me your full name.
A. Lizzie Andrew Borden.
Q. Is it Lizzie or Elizabeth?
A. Lizzie.
Q. You were so christened?
A. I was so christened.
Q. What is your age, please?
A. Thirty-two.
Q. Your mother is not living?
A. No sir.
Q. When did she die?
A. She died when I was two and a half years old.
Q. You do not remember her, then?
A. No sir.
Q. What was your father's age?
A. He was seventy next month.
Q. What was his whole name?
A. Andrew Jackson Borden.
Q. And your stepmother, what is her whole name?
A. Abby Durfee Borden.
Q. How long had your father been married to your stepmother?
A. I think about twenty-seven years.
Q. How much of that time have they lived in that house on Second street?
A. I think, I am not sure, but I think about twenty years last May.
Q. Always occupied the whole house?
A. Yes sir.
Q. Somebody told me it was once fitted up for two tenements.
A. When we bought it it was for two tenements, and the man we bought it of stayed there a few months until he finished his own

62

house. After he finished his own house and moved into it there was no one else ever moved in; we always had the whole.

Q. Have you any idea how much your father was worth?

A. No sir.

Q. Have you ever heard him say?

A. No sir.

Q. Have you ever formed any opinion?

A. No sir.

Q. Do you know something about his real estate?

A. About what?

Q. His real estate?

A. I know what real estate he owned, part of it; I don't know whether I know it all or not.

Q. Tell me what you know of.

A. He owns two farms in Swanzey, the place on Second street and the A. J. Borden building and corner, and the land on South Main street where McMannus is, and then a short time ago he bought some real estate up further south that, formerly, he said belonged to a Mr. Birch.

Q. Did you ever deed him any property?

A. He gave us some years ago, Grandfather Borden's house on Ferry street, and he bought that back from us some weeks ago, I don't know just how many.

Q. As near as you can tell.

A. Well, I should say in June, but I am not sure.

Q. What do you mean by bought it back?

A. He bought it of us, and gave us the money for it.

Q. How much was it?

A. How much money? He gave us $5,000 for it.

Q. Did you pay him anything when you took a deed from him?

A. Pay him anything? No sir.

Q. How long ago was it you took a deed from him?

A. When he gave it to us?

Q. Yes.

A. I can't tell you; I should think five years.

Q. Did you have any other business transactions with him besides that?

A. No sir.

Q. In real estate?

A. No sir.

Q. Or in personal property?

A. No sir.

Q. Never?

A. Never.

Q. No transfer of property one way or the other?

A. No sir.
Q. At no time?
A. No sir.
Q. And I understand he paid you the cash for this property?
A. Yes sir.
Q. You and Emma equally?
A. Yes sir.
Q. How many children has your father?
A. Only two.
Q. Only you two?
A. Yes sir.
Q. Any others ever?
A. One that died.
Q. Did you ever know of your father making a will?
A. No sir, except I heard somebody say once that there was one several years ago; that is all I ever heard.
Q. Who did you hear say so?
A. I think it was Mr. Morse.
Q. What Morse?
A. Uncle John V. Morse.
Q. How long ago?
A. How long ago I heard him say it? I have not any idea.
Q. What did he say about it?
A. Nothing, except just that.
Q. What?
A. That Mr. Borden had a will.
Q. Did you ask your father?
A. I did not.
Q. Did he ever mention the subject of will to you?
A. He did not.
Q. He never told you that he had made a will, or had not?
A. No sir.
Q. Did he have a marriage settlement with your stepmother that you knew of?
A. I never knew of any.
Q. Had you heard anything of his proposing to make a will?
A. No sir.
Q. Do you know of anybody that your father was on bad terms with?
A. There was a man that came there that he had trouble with, I don't know who the man was.
Q. When?
A. I cannot locate the time exactly. It was within two weeks. That is I don't know the date or day of the month.
Q. Tell all you saw and heard.
A. I did not see anything. I heard the bell ring, and father went to the

door and let him in. I did not hear anything for some time, except just the voices; then I heard the man say, "I would like to have that place, I would like to have that store. Father says, "I am not willing to let your business go in there." And the man said, "I thought with your reputation for liking money, you would let your store for anything." Father said, "You are mistaken." Then they talked a while, and then their voices were louder, and I heard father order him out, and went to the front door with him.

Q. What did he say?
A. He said that he had stayed long enough, and he would thank him to go.
Q. Did he say anything about coming again?
A. No sir.
Q. Did your father say anything about coming again, or did he?
A. No sir.
Q. Have you any idea who that was?
A. No sir. I think it was a man from out of town, because he said he was going home to see his partner.
Q. Have you had any efforts made to find him?
A. We have had a detective; that is all I know.
Q. You have not found him?
A. Not that I know of.
Q. You can't give us any other idea about it?
A. Nothing but what I have told you.
Q. Beside that do you know of anybody that your father had bad feelings toward, or who had bad feelings toward your father?
A. I know of one man that has not been friendly with him; they have not been friendly for years.
Q. Who?
A. Mr. Hiram C. Harrington.
Q. What relation is he to him?
A. He is my father's brother-in-law.
Q. Your mother's brother?
A. My father's only sister married Mr. Harrington.
Q. Anybody else that was on bad terms with your father, or that your father was on bad terms with?
A. Not that I know of.
Q. You have no reason to suppose that man you speak of a week or two ago, had ever seen your father before, or has since?
A. No sir.
Q. Do you know of anybody that was on bad terms with your stepmother?
A. No sir.
Q. Or that your stepmother was on bad terms with?
A. No sir.

Q. Had your stepmother any property?

A. I don't know, only that she had half the house that belonged to her father.

Q. Where was that?

A. On Fourth Street.

Q. Who lives in it?

A. Her half-sister.

Q. Any other property beside that that you know of?

A. I don't know.

Q. Did you ever know of any?

A. No sir.

Q. Did you understand that she was worth anything more than that?

A. I never knew.

Q. Did you ever have any trouble with your stepmother?

A. No sir.

Q. Have you, within six months, had any words with her?

A. No sir.

Q. Within a year?

A. No sir.

Q. Within two years?

A. I think not.

Q. When last that you know of?

A. About five years ago.

Q. What about?

A. Her stepsister, half-sister.

Q. What name?

A. Her name now is Mrs. George W. Whitehead.

Q. Nothing more than hard words?

A. No sir, they were nòt hard words; it was simply a difference of opinion.

Q. You have been on pleasant terms with your stepmother since then?

A. Yes sir.

Q. Cordial?

A. It depends upon one's idea of cordiality, perhaps.

Q. According to your idea of cordiality?

A. Quite so.

Q. What do you mean by "quite so"?

A. Quite cordial. I do not mean the dearest of friends in the world, but very kindly feelings, and pleasant. I do not know how to answer you any better than that.

Q. You did not regard her as your mother?

A. Not exactly, no; although she came here when I was very young.

Q. Were your relations towards her that of daughter and mother?

A. In some ways it was, and in some it was not.

Q. In what ways was it?
A. I decline to answer.
Q. Why?
A. Because I don't know how to answer it.
Q. In what ways was it not?
A. I did not call her mother.
Q. What name did she go by?
A. Mrs. Borden.
Q. When did you begin to call her Mrs. Borden?
A. I should think five or six years ago.
Q. Before that time you had called her mother?
A. Yes sir.
Q. What led to the change?
A. The affair with her stepsister.
Q. So that the affair was serious enough to have you change from calling her mother, do you mean?
A. I did not choose to call her mother.
Q. Have you ever called her mother since?
A. Yes, occasionally.
Q. To her face, I mean?
A. Yes.
Q. Often?
A. No sir.
Q. Seldom?
A. Seldom.
Q. Your usual address was Mrs. Borden?
A. Yes sir.
Q. Did your sister Emma call her mother?
A. She always called her Abby from the time she came into the family.
Q. Is your sister Emma older than you?
A. Yes sir.
Q. What is her age?
A. She is ten years older than I am. She was somewhere about fourteen when she came there.
Q. What was your stepmother's age?
A. I don't know. I asked her sister Saturday, and she said sixty-four. I told them sixty-seven; I did not know. I told as nearly as I knew. I did not know there was so much difference between she and father.
Q. Why did you leave off calling her mother?
A. Because I wanted to.
Q. Is that all the reason you have to give me?
A. I have not any other answer.
Q. Can't you give me any better reason than that?

A.	I have not any reason to give, except that I did not want to.
Q.	In what other respect were the relations between you and her not that of mother and daughter, besides not calling her mother?
A.	I don't know that any of the relations were changed. I had never been to her as a mother in many things. I always went to my sister, because she was older and had the care of me after my mother died.
Q.	In what respects were the relations between you and her that of mother and daughter?
A.	That is the same question you asked before; I can't answer you any better now than I did before.
Q.	You did not say before you could not answer, but that you declined to answer.
A.	I decline to answer because I do not know what to say.
Q.	That is the only reason?
A.	Yes sir.
Q.	You called your father father?
A.	Always.
Q.	Were your father and mother happily united? (Witness pauses a little before answering.)
A.	Why, I don't know but that they were.
Q.	Why do you hesitate?
A.	Because I don't know but that they were, and I am telling the truth as nearly as I know it.
Q.	Do you mean me to understand that they were happy entirely, or not?
A.	So far as I know they were.
Q.	Why did you hesitate then?
A.	Because I did not know how to answer you any better than what came into my mind. I was trying to think if I was telling it as I should; that is all.
Q.	Do you have any difficulty in telling it as you should, any difficulty in answering my questions?
A.	Some of your questions I have difficulty in answering because I don't know just how you mean them.
Q.	Did you ever know of any difficulty between her and your father?
A.	No sir.
Q.	Did he seem to be affectionate?
A.	I think so.
Q.	As man and woman who are married ought to be?
A.	So far as I have ever had any chance of judging.
Q.	They were?
A.	Yes.
Q.	What dress did you wear the day they were killed?
A.	I had on a navy blue, sort of a bengaline; or India silk skirt, with a

navy blue blouse. In the afternoon they thought I had better change it. I put on a pink wrapper.

Q. Did you change your clothing before the afternoon?

A. No sir.

Q. You dressed in the morning, as you have described, and kept that clothing on until afternoon?

A. Yes, sir.

Q. When did Morse come there first, I don't mean this visit, I mean as a visitor, John V. Morse?

A. Do you mean this day that he came and stayed all night?

Q. No. Was this visit his first to your house?

A. He has been in the east a year or more.

Q. Since he has been in the east has he been in the habit of coming to your house?

A. Yes; came in any time he wanted to.

Q. Before that had he been at your house, before he came east?

A. Yes, he has been here, if you remember the winter that the river was frozen over and they went across, he was here that winter, some 14 years ago, was it not?

Q. I am not answering questions, but asking them.

A. I don't remember the date. He was here that winter.

Q. Has he been here since?

A. He has been here once since; I don't know whether he has or not since.

Q. How many times this last year has he been at your house?

A. None at all to speak of, nothing more than a night or two at a time.

Q. How often did he come to spend a night or two?

A. Really I don't know; I am away so much myself.

Q. Your last answer is that you don't know how much he had been here, because you had been away yourself so much?

A. Yes.

Q. That is true the last year, or since he has been east?

A. I have not been away the last year so much, but other times I have been away when he has been here.

Q. Do I understand you to say that his last visit before this one was 14 years ago?

A. No, he has been here once between the two.

Q. How long did he stay then?

A. I don't know.

Q. How long ago was that?

A. I don't know.

Q. Give me your best remembrance.

A. Five or six years, perhaps six.

Q. How long has he been east this time?

A. I think over a year; I am not sure.

Q. During the last year how much of the time has he been at your house?

A. Very little that I know of.

Q. Your answer to that question before was, I don't know because I have been away so much myself.

A. I did not mean I had been away very much myself the last year.

Q. How much have you been away the last year?

A. I have been away a great deal in the daytime, occasionally at night.

Q. Where in the daytime, any particular place?

A. No, around town.

Q. When you go off nights, where?

A. Never unless I have been off on a visit.

Q. When was the last time when you have been away for more than a night or two before this affair?

A. I don't think I have been away to stay more than a night or two since I came from abroad, except about three or four weeks ago I was in New Bedford for three or four days.

Q. Where at New Bedford?

A. At 20 Madison street.

Q. How long ago were you abroad?

A. I was abroad in 1890.

Q. When did he come to the house the last time before your father and mother were killed?

A. He stayed there all night Wednesday night.

Q. My question is when he came there.

A. I don't know; I was not at home when he came; I was out.

Q. When did you first see him there?

A. I did not see him at all.

Q. How did you know he was there?

A. I heard his voice.

Q. You did not see him Wednesday evening?

A. I did not; I was out Wednesday evening.

Q. You did not see him Thursday morning?

A. I did not; he was out when I came down stairs.

Q. When was the first time you saw him?

A. Thursday noon.

Q. You had never seen him before that?

A. No sir.

Q. Where were you Wednesday evening?

A. I spent the evening with Miss Russell.

Q. As near as you can remember, when did you return?

A. About nine o'clock at night.

Q. The family had then retired?

A. I don't know whether they had or not. I went right to my room; I don't remember.

Q. You did not look to see?
A. No sir.
Q. Which door did you come in at?
A. The front door.
Q. Did you lock it?
A. Yes sir.
Q. For the night?
A. Yes sir.
Q. And went right up stairs to your room?
A. Yes sir.
Q. When was it that you heard the voice of Mr. Morse?
A. I heard him down there about supper time -- no, it was earlier than that. I heard him down there somewhere about three o'clock, I think, I was in my room Wednesday, not feeling well, all day.
Q. Did you eat supper at home Wednesday night?
A. I was at home; I did not eat any supper, because I did not feel able to eat supper; I had been sick.
Q. You did not come down to supper?
A. No sir.
Q. Did you hear him eating supper?
A. No sir. I did not know whether he was there or not.
Q. You heard him in the afternoon?
A. Yes sir.
Q. Did you hear him go away?
A. I did not.
Q. You did not go down to see him?
A. No sir.
Q. Was you in bed?
A. No sir. I was on the lounge.
Q. Why did you not go down?
A. I did not care to go down, and I was not feeling well, and kept my room all day.
Q. You felt better in the evening?
A. Not very much better. I thought I would go out, and see if the air would make me feel any better.
Q. When you came back at nine o'clock, you did not look in to see if the family were up?
A. No sir.
Q. Why not?
A. I very rarely do when I come in.
Q. You go right to your room?
A. Yes sir.
Q. Did you have a night key?
A. Yes sir.

71

Q. How did you know it was right to lock the front door?
A. That was always my business.
Q. How many locks did you fasten?
A. The spring locks itself, and there is a key to turn, and you manipulate the bolt.
Q. You manipulated all those?
A. I used them all.
Q. Then you went to bed?
A. Yes, directly.
Q. When you got up the next morning, did you see Mr. Morse?
A. I did not.
Q. Had the family breakfasted when you came down?
A. Yes sir.
Q. What time did you come down stairs?
A. As near as I can remember, it was a few minutes before nine.
Q. Who did you find down stairs when you came down?
A. Maggie and Mrs. Borden. [Editors' note: The Bordens often referred to Bridget as "Maggie," presumably because this was the name of the former maid.]
Q. Did you inquire for Mr. Morse?
A. No sir.
Q. Did you suppose he had gone?
A. I did not know whether he had or not; he was not there.
Q. Your father was there?
A. Yes sir.
Q. Then you found him?
A. Yes sir.
Q. Did you speak to either your father or Mrs. Borden?
A. I spoke to them all.
Q. About Mr. Morse?
A. I did not mention him.
Q. Did not inquire anything about him?
A. No sir.
Q. How long before that time had he been at the house?
A. I don't know.
Q. As near as you can tell?
A. I don't know. He was there in June sometime, I don't know whether he was there after that or not.
Q. Why did you not go to Marion with the party that went?
A. Because they went sooner than I could, and I was going Monday.
Q. Why did they go sooner than you could; what was there to keep you?
A. I had taken the secretaryship and treasurer of our C. E. society, had the charge, and the roll call was the first Sunday in August, and I felt I must be there and attend to that part of the business.

Q. Where was your sister Emma that day?

A. What day?

Q. The day your father and Mrs. Borden were killed?

A. She had been in Fairhaven.

Q. Had you written to her?

A. Yes sir.

Q. When was the last time you wrote to her?

A. Thursday morning, and my father mailed the letter for me.

Q. Did she get it at Fairhaven?

A. No sir, it was sent back. She did not get it at Fairhaven, for we telegraphed for her, and she got home here Thursday afternoon, and the letter was sent back to this post office.

Q. How long had she been in Fairhaven?

A. Just two weeks to a day.

Q. You did not visit in Fairhaven?

A. No sir.

Q. Had there been anybody else around the house that week, or premises?

A. No one that I knew of, except the man that called to see him on this business about the store.

Q. Was that that week?

A. Yes sir.

Q. I misunderstood you probably, I thought you said a week or two before.

A. No, I said that week. There was a man came the week before and gave up some keys, and I took them.

Q. Do you remember of anybody else being then around the premises that week?

A. Nobody that I know of or saw.

Q. Nobody at work there?

A. No sir.

Q. Nobody doing any chores there?

A. No sir, not that I know of.

Q. Nobody had access to the house, so far as you know, during that time?

A. No sir.

Q. I ask you once more how it happened that, knowing Mr. Morse was at your house, you did not step in and greet him before you retired?

A. I have no reason, except that I was not feeling well Wednesday, and so did not come down.

Q. No, you were down. When you came in from out.

A. Do you mean Wednesday night?

Q. Yes.

A.   Because I hardly ever do go in. I generally went right up to my room, and I did that night.

Q.   Could you then get to your room from the back hall?

A.   No sir.

Q.   From the back stairs?

A.   No sir.

Q.   Why not? What would hinder?

A.   Father's bedroom door was kept locked, and his door into my room was locked and hooked, I think, and I had no keys.

Q.   That was the custom of the establishment?

A.   It had always been so.

Q.   It was so Wednesday, and so Thursday?

A.   It was so Wednesday, but Thursday they broke the door open.

Q.   That was after the crowd came; before the crowd came?

A.   It was so.

Q.   There was no access, except one had a key, and one would have to have two keys?

A.   They would have to have two keys if they went up the back way to get into my room. If they were in my room, they would have to have a key to get into his room, and another to get into the back stairs.

Q.   Where did Mr. Morse sleep?

A.   In the next room over the parlor in front of the stairs.

Q.   Right up the same stairs that your room was?

A.   Yes sir.

Q.   How far from your room?

A.   A door opened into it.

Q.   The two rooms connected directly?

A.   By one door, that is all.

Q.   Not through the hall?

A.   No sir.

Q.   Was the door locked?

A.   It has been locked and bolted, and a large writing desk in my room kept up against it.

Q.   Then it was not a practical opening?

A.   No sir.

Q.   How otherwise do you get from your room to the next room?

A.   I have to go into the front hall.

Q.   How far apart are the two doors?

A.   Very near, I don't think more than so far (measuring).

Q.   Was it your habit when you were in your room to keep your door shut?

A.   Yes sir.

Q.   That time, that Wednesday afternoon?

A.   My door was open part of the time, and part of the time I tried to

74

get a nap and their voices annoyed me, and I closed it. I kept it open in summer more or less, and closed in winter.

Q. Then, unless for some special reason, you kept your door open in the summer?

A. Yes sir, if it was a warm day. If it was a cool day, I should have closed it.

Q. Where was your father when you came down Thursday morning?

A. Sitting in the sitting room in his large chair, reading the Providence Journal.

Q. Where was your mother? Do you prefer me to call her Mrs. Borden?

A. I had as soon you called her mother. She was in the dining room with a feather duster dusting.

Q. When she dusted did she wear something over her head?

A. Sometimes when she swept, but not when dusting.

Q. Where was Maggie?

A. Just come in the back door with the long pole, brush, and put the brush on the handle, and getting her pail of water; she was going to wash the windows around the house. She said Mrs. Borden wanted her to.

Q. Did you get your breakfast that morning?

A. I did not eat any breakfast; I did not feel as though I wanted any.

Q. Did you get any breakfast that morning?

A. I don't know whether I ate half a banana; I don't think I did.

Q. You drank no tea or coffee that morning?

A. No sir.

Q. And ate no cookies?

A. I don't know whether I did or not. We had some molasses cookies; I don't know whether I ate any that morning or not.

Q. Were the breakfast things put away when you got down?

A. Everything except the coffee pot; I am not sure whether that was on the stove or not.

Q. You said nothing about Mr. Morse to your father or mother?

A. No sir.

Q. What was the next thing that happened after you got down?

A. Maggie went out of doors to wash the windows and father came out into the kitchen and said he did not know whether he would go down to the post office or not. And then I sprinkled some handkerchiefs to iron.

Q. Tell me again what time you came down stairs.

A. It was a little before nine, I should say about quarter; I don't know sure.

Q. Did your father go down town?

A. He went down later.

Q. What time did he start away?

A.   I don't know.

Q.   What were you doing when he started away?

A.   I was in the dining room I think; yes, I had just commenced, I think, to iron.

Q.   It may seem a foolish question. How much of an ironing did you have?

A.   I only had about eight or ten of my best handkerchiefs.

Q.   Did you let your father out?

A.   No sir; he went out himself.

Q.   Did you fasten the door after him?

A.   No sir.

Q.   Did Maggie?

A.   I don't know. When she went up stairs she always locked the door; she had charge of the back door.

Q.   Did she go out after a brush before your father went away?

A.   I think so.

Q.   Did you say anything to Maggie?

A.   I did not.

Q.   Did you say anything about washing the windows?

A.   No sir.

Q.   Did you speak to her?

A.   I think I told her I did not want any breakfast.

Q.   You do not remember of talking about washing the windows?

A.   I don't remember whether I did or not; I don't remember it. Yes, I remember; yes, I asked her to shut the parlor blinds when she got through, because the sun was so hot.

Q.   About what time do you think your father went down town?

A.   I don't know; it must have been after nine o'clock. I don't know what time it was.

Q.   You think at that time you had begun to iron your handkerchiefs?

A.   Yes sir.

Q.   How long a job was that?

A.   I did not finish them; my flats were not hot enough.

Q.   How long a job would it have been if the flats had been right?

A.   If they had been hot, not more than 20 minutes, perhaps.

Q.   How long did you work on the job?

A.   I don't know, sir.

Q.   How long was your father gone?

A.   I don't know that.

Q.   Where were you when he returned?

A.   I was down in the kitchen.

Q.   What doing?

A.   Reading an old magazine that had been left in the cupboard, an old Harper's Magazine.

Q.   Had you got through ironing?

A. No sir.

Q. Had you stopped ironing?

A. Stopped for the flats.

Q. Were you waiting for them to be hot?

A. Yes sir.

Q. Was there a fire in the stove?

A. Yes sir.

Q. When your father went away, you were ironing them?

A. I had not commenced, but I was getting the little ironing board and the flats.

Q. Are you sure you were in the kitchen when your father returned?

A. I am not sure whether I was there or in the dining room.

Q. Did you go back to your room before your father returned?

A. I think I did carry up some clean clothes.

Q. Did you stay there?

A. No sir.

Q. Did you spend any time up the front stairs before your father returned?

A. No, sir.

Q. Or after he returned?

A. No, sir. I did stay in my room long enough when I went up to sew a little piece of tape on a garment.

Q. What was the time when your father came home?

A. He came home after I came down stairs.

Q. You were not up stairs when he came home?

A. I was not up stairs when he came home; no, sir.

Q. What was Maggie doing when your father came home?

A. I don't know whether she was there or whether she had gone up stairs; I can't remember.

Q. Who let your father in?

A. I think he came to the front door and rang the bell, and I think Maggie let him in, and he said he had forgotten his key; so I think she must have been down stairs.

Q. His key would have done him no good if the locks were left as you left them?

A. But they were always unbolted in the morning.

Q. Who unbolted them that morning?

A. I don't think they had been unbolted; Maggie can tell you.

Q. If he had not forgotten his key it would have been no good?

A. No, he had his key and could not get in. I understood Maggie to say he said he had forgotten his key.

Q. You did not hear him say anything about it?

A. I heard his voice, but I don't know what he said.

Q. I understood you to say he said he had forgotten his key?

A. No, it was Maggie said he said he had forgotten the key.

Q. Where was Maggie when the bell rang?
A. I don't know, sir.
Q. Where were you when the bell rang?
A. I think in my room up stairs.
Q. Then you were up stairs when you father came home?
A. I don't know sure, but I think I was.
Q. What were you doing?
A. As I say, I took up these clean clothes, and stopped and basted a little piece of tape on a garment.
Q. Did you come down before your father was let in?
A. I was on the stairs coming down when she let him in.
Q. Then you were up stairs when your father came to the house on his return?
A. I think I was.
Q. How long had you been there?
A. I had only been upstairs just long enough to take the clothes up and baste the little loop on the sleeve. I don't think I had been up there over five minutes.
Q. Was Maggie still engaged in washing windows when your father got back?
A. I don't know.
Q. You remember, Miss Borden, I will call your attention to it so as to see if I have any misunderstanding, not for the purpose of confusing you; you remember, that you told me several times that you were down stairs, and not up stairs when your father came home? You have forgotten, perhaps?
A. I don't know what I have said. I have answered so many questions and I am so confused I don't know one thing from another. I am telling you just as nearly as I know.
Q. Calling your attention to what you said about that a few minutes ago, and now again to the circumstance you have said you were up stairs when the bell rang, and were on the stairs when Maggie let your father in; which now is your recollection of the true statement, of the matter, that you were down stairs when the bell rang and your father came?
A. I think I was down stairs in the kitchen.
Q. And then you were not up stairs?
A. I think I was not; because I went up almost immediately, as soon as I went down, and then came down again and stayed down.
Q. What had you in your mind when you said you were on the stairs as Maggie let your father in?
A. The other day somebody came there and she let them in and I was on the stairs; I don't know whether the morning before or when it was.

Q. You understood I was asking you exactly and explicitly about this fatal day?

A. Yes, sir.

Q. I now call your attention to the fact that you had specifically told me you had gone up stairs, and had been there about five minutes when the bell rang, and were on your way down, and were on the stairs when Maggie let your father in that day --

A. Yes, I said that, and then I said I did not know whether I was on the stairs or in the kitchen.

Q. Now how will you have it?

A. I think, as nearly as I know, I think I was in the kitchen.

Q. How long was your father gone?

A. I don't know, sir; not very long.

Q. An hour?

A. I should not think so.

Q. Will you give me the best story you can, so far as your recollection serves you, of your time while he was gone?

A. I sprinkled my handkerchiefs, and got my ironing board and took them in the dining room and left the handkerchiefs in the kitchen on the table and whether I ate any cookies or not I don't remember. Then I sat down looking at the magazine waiting for the flats to heat. Then I went in the sitting room and got the Providence Journal, and took that into the kitchen. I don't recollect of doing anything else.

Q. Which did you read first, the Journal or the magazine?

A. The magazine.

Q. You told me you were reading the magazine when your father came back?

A. I said in the kitchen, yes.

Q. Was that so?

A. Yes, I took the Journal out to read, and had not read it. I had it near me.

Q. You said a minute or two ago you read the magazine awhile, and then went and got the Journal and took it out to read?

A. I did, but I did not read it; I tried my flats then.

Q. And went back to reading the magazine?

A. I took the magazine up again, yes.

Q. When did you last see your mother?

A. I did not see her after when I went down in the morning and she was dusting the dining room.

Q. Where did you or she go then?

A. I don't know where she went. I know where I was.

Q. Did you or she leave the dining room first?

A. I think I did. I left her in the dining room.

Q. You never saw her or heard her afterwards?

A. No sir.

Q. Did she say anything about making the bed?

A. She said she had been up and made the bed up fresh, and had dusted the room and left it all in order. She was going to put some fresh pillow slips on the small pillows at the foot of the bed, and was going to close the room, because she was going to have company Monday and she wanted everything in order.

Q. How long would it take to put on the pillow slips?

A. About two minutes.

Q. How long to do the rest of the things?

A. She had done that when I came down.

Q. All that was left was what?

A. To put on the pillow slips.

Q. Can you give me any suggestions as to what occupied her when she was up there, when she was struck dead?

A. I don't know of anything except she had some cotton cloth pillow cases up there, and she said she was going to commence to work on them. That is all I know. And the sewing machine was up there.

Q. Whereabouts was the sewing machine?

A. In the corner between the north and west side.

Q. Did you hear the sewing machine going?

A. I did not.

Q. Did you see anything to indicate that the sewing machine had been used that morning?

A. I had not. I did not go in there until after everybody had been in there, and the room had been overhauled.

Q. If she had remained down stairs, you would undoubtedly have seen her?

A. If she had remained down stairs, I should have, if she had remained in her room, I should not have. If she had remained down stairs, I should have. If she had gone to her room, I should not have.

Q. Where was that?

A. Over the kitchen.

Q. To get to that room she would have to go through the kitchen?

A. To get up the back stairs.

Q. That is the way she was in the habit of going?

A. Yes, sir, because the other doors were locked.

Q. If she had remained down stairs, or had gone to her own room, you undoubtedly would have seen her?

A. I should have seen her if she had stayed downstairs; if she had gone to her room, I would not have seen her.

Q. She was found a little after 11 in the spare room, if she had gone to her own room she must have gone through the kitchen and up the

	back stairs, and subsequently have gone down and gone back again?
A.	Yes sir.
Q.	Have you any reason to suppose you would not have seen her if she had spent any portion of the time in her own room, or down stairs?
A.	There is no reason why I should not have seen her if she had been down there, except when I first came down stairs, for two or three minutes I went down cellar to the water closet.
Q.	After that you were where you practically commanded the view of the first story the rest of the time?
A.	I think so.
Q.	When you went up stairs for a short time, as you say you did, you then went in sight of the sewing machine?
A.	No, I did not see the sewing machine, because she had shut that room up.
Q.	What do you mean?
A.	I mean the door was closed. She said she wanted it kept closed to keep the dust and everything out.
Q.	Was it a room with a window?
A.	It has three windows.
Q.	A large room?
A.	The size of the parlor; a pretty fair sized room.
Q.	It is the guest room?
A.	Yes, the spare room.
Q.	Where the sewing machine was was the guest room?
A.	Yes, sir.
Q.	I ask again, perhaps you have answered all you care to, what explanation can you give, can you suggest, as to what she was doing from the time she said she had got the work all done in the spare room until 11 o'clock?
A.	I suppose she went up and made her own bed.
Q.	That would be in the back part?
A.	Yes sir.
Q.	She would have to go by you twice to do that?
A.	Unless she went when I was in my room that few minutes.
Q.	That would not be time enough for her to go and make her own bed and come back again?
A.	Sometimes she stayed up longer and sometimes shorter; I don't know.
Q.	Otherwise than that, she would have to go in your sight?
A.	I should have to have seen her once; I don't know that I need to have seen her more than once.
Q.	You did not see her at all?

A. No sir, not after the dining room.

Q. What explanation can you suggest as to the whereabouts of your mother from the time you saw her in the dining room, and she said her work in the spare room was all done, until 11 o'clock?

A. I don't know. I think she went back into the spare room, and whether she came back again or not, I don't know; that has always been a mystery.

Q. Can you think of anything she could be doing in the spare room?

A. Yes sir. I know what she used to do sometimes. She kept her best cape she wore on the street in there, and she used occasionally to go up there to get it and to take it into her room. She kept a great deal in the guest room drawers; she used to go up there and get things and put things; she used those drawers for her own use.

Q. That connects her with her own room again, to reach which she had to go down stairs and come up again?

A. Yes.

Q. Assuming that she did not go into her own room, I understand you to say she could not have gone to her own room without your seeing her?

A. She could while I was down cellar.

Q. You went down immediately you came down, within a few minutes, and you did not see her when you came back?

A. No sir.

Q. After that time she must have remained in the guest chamber?

A. I don't know.

Q. So far as you can judge?

A. So far as I can judge she might have been out of the house, or in the house.

Q. Had you any knowledge of her going out of the house?

A. No sir.

Q. Had you any knowledge of her going out of the house?

A. She told me she had had a note, somebody was sick, and said "I am going to get the dinner on the way," and asked me what I wanted for dinner.

Q. Did you tell her?

A. Yes, I told her I did not want anything.

Q. Then why did you not suppose she had gone?

A. I supposed she had gone.

Q. Did you hear her come back?

A. I did not hear her go or come back, but I supposed she went.

Q. When you found your father dead you supposed your mother had gone?

A. I did not know. I said to the people who came in "I don't know whether Mrs. Borden is out or in; I wish you would see if she is in her room."

Q. You supposed she was out at the time?
A. I understood so; I did not suppose anything about it.
Q. Did she tell you where she was going?
A. No sir.
Q. Did she tell you who the note was from?
A. No sir.
Q. Did you ever see the note?
A. No sir.
Q. Do you know where it is now?
A. No sir.
Q. She said she was going out that morning?
A. Yes sir.

(Hearing continued Aug. 10, 1892.)

Q. I shall have to ask you once more about that morning. Do you know what the family ate for breakfast?
A. No sir.
Q. Had the breakfast all been cleared away when you got down?
A. Yes sir.
Q. I want you to tell me just where you found the people when you got down that you did find there?
A. I found Mrs. Borden in the dining room. I found my father in the sitting room.
Q. And Maggie?
A. Maggie was coming in the back door with her pail and brush.
Q. Tell me what talk you had with your mother at that time?
A. She asked me how I felt. I said I felt better than I did Tuesday, but I did not want any breakfast. She asked me what I wanted for dinner, I told her nothing. I told her I did not want anything. She said she was going out, and would get the dinner. That is the last I saw her, or said anything to her.
Q. Where did you go then?
A. Into the kitchen.
Q. Where then?
A. Down cellar.
Q. Gone perhaps five minutes?
A. Perhaps. Not more than that; possibly a little bit more.
Q. When you came back did you see your mother?
A. I did not; I supposed she had gone out.
Q. She did not tell you where she was going?
A. No sir.
Q. When you came back was your father there?
A. Yes sir.
Q. What was he doing?
A. Reading the paper.
Q. Did you eat any breakfast?

83

A. No sir, I don't remember whether I ate a molasses cookie or not. I did not eat any regularly prepared breakfast.

Q. Was it usual for your mother to go out?

A. Yes sir, she went out every morning nearly, and did the marketing.

Q. Was it usual for her to be gone away from dinner?

A. Yes sir, sometimes, not very often.

Q. How often, say?

A. O, I should not think more than -- well I don't know, more than once in three months, perhaps.

Q. Now I call your attention to the fact that twice yesterday you told me, with some explicitness, that when your father came in you were just coming down stairs?

A. No, I did not, I beg your pardon.

Q. That you were on the stairs at the time your father was let in, you said with some explicitness. Do you now say you did not say so?

A. I said I thought first I was on the stairs; then I remembered I was in the kitchen when he came in.

Q. First you thought you were in the kitchen; afterwards you remembered you were on the stairs?

A. I said I thought I was on the stairs; then I said I knew I was in the kitchen. I still say that now. I was in the kitchen.

Q. Did you go into the front part of the house after your father came in?

A. After he came in from down street I was in the sitting room with him.

Q. Did you go into the front hall afterwards?

A. No sir.

Q. At no time?

A. No sir.

Q. Excepting the two or three minutes you were down cellar, were you away from the house until your father came in?

A. No sir.

Q. You were always in the kitchen or dining room, excepting when you went up stairs?

A. I went up stairs before he went out.

Q. You mean you went up there to sew a button on?

A. I basted a piece of tape on.

Q. Do you remember you did not say that yesterday?

A. I don't think you asked me. I told you yesterday I went up stairs directly after I came up from down cellar, with the clean clothes.

Q. You now say after your father went out, you did not go up stairs at all?

A. No sir, I did not.

Q. When Maggie came in there washing the windows, you did not appear from the front part of the house?

A.   No sir.

Q.   When your father was let in, you did not appear from up stairs?

A.   No sir. I was in the kitchen.

Q.   That is so?

A.   Yes sir, to the best of my knowledge.

Q.   After your father went out, you remained there either in the kitchen or dining room all the time?

A.   I went in the sitting room long enough to direct some paper wrappers.

Q.   One of the three rooms?

A.   Yes sir.

Q.   So it would have been extremely difficult for anybody to have gone through the kitchen and dining room and front hall, without your seeing them?

A.   They could have gone from the kitchen into the sitting room while I was in the dining room, if there was anybody to go.

Q.   Then into the front hall?

A.   Yes sir.

Q.   You were in the dining room ironing?

A.   Yes sir, part of the time.

Q.   You were in all of the three rooms?

A.   Yes sir.

Q.   A large portion of that time, the girl was out of doors?

A.   I don't know where she was, I did not see her. I supposed she was out of doors, as she had the pail and brush.

Q.   You know she was washing windows?

A.   She told me she was going to, did not see her do it.

Q.   For a large portion of the time, you did not see the girl?

A.   ˙ No sir.

Q.   So far as you know you were alone in the lower part of the house a large portion of the time, after your father went away, and before he came back?

A.   My father did not go away, I think until somewhere about 10, as near as I can remember, he was with me down stairs.

Q.   A large portion of the time after your father went away, and before he came back, so far as you know, you were alone in the house?

A.   Maggie had come in and gone up stairs.

Q.   After he went out, and before he came back; a large portion of the time after your father went out, and before he came back, so far as you know, you were the only person in the house?

A.   So far as I know, I was.

Q.   And during that time, so far as you know, the front door was locked?

A.   So far as I know.

Q.   And never was unlocked at all?

A.	I don't think it was.
Q.	Even after your father came home, it was locked up again?
A.	I don't know whether she locked it up again after that or not.
Q.	It locks itself?
A.	The spring lock opens.
Q.	It fastens it so it cannot be opened from the outside?
A.	Sometimes you can press it open.
Q.	Have you any reason to suppose the spring lock was left so it could be pressed open from the outside?
A.	I have no reason to suppose so.
Q.	Nothing about the lock was changed before the people came?
A.	Nothing that I know of.
Q.	What were you doing in the kitchen when your father came home?
A.	I think I was eating a pear when he came in.
Q.	What had you been doing before that?
A.	Been reading a magazine.
Q.	Were you making preparations to iron again?
A.	I had sprinkled my clothes, and was waiting for the flat. I sprinkled the clothes before he went out.
Q.	Had you built up the fire again?
A.	I put in a stick of wood. There was a few sparks. I put in a stick of wood to try to heat the flat.
Q.	You had then started the fire?
A.	Yes sir.
Q.	The fire was burning when he came in?
A.	No sir, but it was smoldering and smoking as though it would come up.
Q.	Did it come up after he came in?
A.	No sir.
Q.	Did you do any more ironing?
A.	I did not. I went in with him, and did not finish.
Q.	You did not iron any more after your father came in?
A.	No sir.
Q.	Was the ironing board put away?
A.	No sir, it was on the dining room table.
Q.	When was it put away?
A.	I don't know. Somebody put it away after the affair happened.
Q.	You did not put it away?
A.	No sir.
Q.	Was it on the dining room table when you found your father killed?
A.	I suppose so.
Q.	You had not put it away then?
A.	I had not touched it.

Q. How soon after your father came in, before Maggie went up stairs?

A. I don't know. I did not see her.

Q. Did you see her after your father came in?

A. Not after she let him in.

Q. How long was your father in the house before you found him killed?

A. I don't know exactly, because I went out to the barn. I don't know what time he came home. I don't think he had been home more than fifteen or twenty minutes; I am not sure.

Q. When you went out to the barn, where did you leave your father?

A. He had laid down on the sitting room lounge, taken off his shoes, and put on his slippers, and taken off his coat and put on the reefer. I asked him if he wanted the window left that way.

Q. Where did you leave him?

A. On the sofa.

Q. Was he asleep?

A. No sir.

Q. Was he reading?

A. No sir.

Q. What was the last thing you said to him?

A. I asked him if he wanted the window left that way. Then I went into the kitchen, and from there to the barn.

Q. Whereabouts in the barn did you go?

A. Up stairs.

Q. To the second story of the barn?

A. Yes sir.

Q. How long did you remain there?

A. I don't know, fifteen or twenty minutes.

Q. What doing?

A. Trying to find lead for a sinker.

Q. What made you think there would be lead for a sinker up there?

A. Because there was some there.

Q. Was there not some by the door?

A. Some pieces of lead by the open door, but there was a box full of old things up stairs.

Q. Did you bring any sinker back from the barn?

A. I found no sinker.

Q. Did you bring any sinker back from the barn?

A. Nothing but a piece of a chip I picked up on the floor.

Q. Where was that box you say was up stairs, containing lead?

A. There was a kind of a workbench.

Q. Is it there now?

A. I don't know, sir.

Q. How long since have you seen it there?

A. I have not been out there since that day.

Q. Had you been in the barn before?

A. That day, no sir.

Q. How long since you had been in the barn before?

A. I don't think I had been into it. I don't know as I had in three months.

Q. When you went out did you unfasten the screen door?

A. I unhooked it to get out.

Q. It was hooked until you went out?

A. Yes sir.

Q. It had been left hooked by Bridget if she was the last one in?

A. I suppose so; I don't know.

Q. Do you know when she did get through washing the outside?

A. I don't know.

Q. Did you know she washed the windows inside?

A. I don't know.

Q. Did you see her washing the windows inside?

A. I don't know.

Q. You don't know whether she washed the dining room and sitting room windows inside?

A. I did not see her.

Q. If she did, would you not have seen her?

A. I don't know. She might be in one room and I in another.

Q. Do you think she might have gone to work and washed all the windows in the dining room and sitting room and you not know it?

A. I don't know. I am sure, whether I should or not, I might have seen her, and not know it.

Q. Miss Borden, I am trying in good faith to get all the doings that morning of yourself and Miss Sullivan, and I have not succeeded in doing it. Do you desire to give me any information or not?

A. I don't know it -- I don't know what your name is.

Q. It is certain beyond reasonable doubt she was engaged in washing the windows in the dining room or sitting room when your father came home. Do you mean to say you know nothing of either of those operations?

A. I knew she washed the windows outside; that is, she told me so. She did not wash the windows in the kitchen, because I was in the kitchen most of the time.

Q. The dining room and sitting room; I said.

A. I don't know.

Q. It is reasonably certain she washed the windows in the dining room and sitting room, inside while your father was out, and was engaged in this operation when your father came home; do you mean to say you know nothing of it?

88

A.   I don't know whether she washed the windows in the sitting room and dining room or not.

Q.   Can you give me any information how it happened at that particular time you should go into the chamber of the barn to find a sinker to go to Marion with to fish the next Monday?

A.   I was going to finish my ironing; my flats were not hot; I said to myself "I will go and try and find that sinker; perhaps by the time I get back the flats will be hot." That is the only reason.

Q.   How long had you been reading an old magazine before you went to the barn at all?

A.   Perhaps half an hour.

Q.   Had you got a fish line?

A.   Not here; we had some at the barn.

Q.   Had you got a fish hook?

A.   No sir.

Q.   Had you got any apparatus for fishing at all?

A.   Yes, over there.

Q.   Had you any sinkers over there?

A.   I think there were some. It is so long since I have been there; I think there were some.

Q.   You had no reason to suppose you were lacking sinkers?

A.   I don't think there were any on my lines.

Q.   Where were your lines?

A.   My fish lines were at the farm here.

Q.   What made you think there were no sinkers at the farm on your lines?

A.   Because some time ago when I was there I had none.

Q.   How long since you used the fish lines?

A.   Five years, perhaps.

Q.   You left them at the farm then?

A.   Yes, sir.

Q.   And you have not seen them since?

A.   Yes, sir.

Q.   It occurred to you after your father came in it would be a good time to go to the barn after sinkers, and you had no reason to suppose there was not abundance of sinkers at the farm and abundance of lines?

A.   The last time I was there there were some lines.

Q.   Did you not say before you presumed there were sinkers at the farm?

A.   I don't think I said so.

Q.   You did say so exactly. Do you now say you presume there were not sinkers at the farm?

A.   I don't think there were any fish lines suitable to use at the farm; I don't think there were any sinkers on any line that had been mine.

Q. Do you remember telling me you presumed there were lines, and sinkers and hooks at the farm?

A. I said there were lines I thought, and perhaps hooks. I did not say I thought there were sinkers on my lines. There was another box of lines over there beside mine.

Q. You thought there were not sinkers?

A. Not on my lines.

Q. Not sinkers at the farm?

A. I don't think there were any sinkers at the farm. I don't know whether there were or not.

Q. Did you then think there were no sinkers at the farm?

A. I thought there were no sinkers anywhere, or I should not have been trying to find some.

Q. You thought there were no sinkers at the farm to be had?

A. I thought there were no sinkers at the farm to be had.

Q. That is the reason you went into the second story of the barn to look for a sinker?

A. Yes, sir.

Q. What made you think you would find sinkers there?

A. I went to see, because there was lead there.

Q. You thought there might be lead there made into sinkers?

A. I thought there might be lead with a hole in it.

Q. Did you examine the lead that was down stairs near the door?

A. No sir.

Q. Why not?

A. I don't know.

Q. You went straight to the upper story of the barn?

A. No, I went under the pear tree and got some pears first.

Q. Then went to the second story of the barn to look for sinkers for lines you had at the farm, as you supposed, as you had seen them there five years before that time?

A. I went up to get some sinkers, if I could find them. I did not intend to go to the farm for lines; I was going to buy some lines here.

Q. You then had no intention of using your own line and hooks at the farm?

A. No sir.

Q. What was the use of telling me a little while ago you had no sinkers on your line at the farm?

A. I thought I made you understand that those lines at the farm were no good to use.

Q. Did you not mean for me to understand one of the reasons you were searching for sinkers was that the lines you had at the farm, as you remembered them, had no sinkers on them?

A. I said the lines at the farm had no sinkers.

90

Q. I did not ask you what you said. Did you not mean for me to understand that?

A. I meant for you to understand I wanted the sinkers, and was going to have new lines.

Q. You had not then bought your lines?

A. No sir, I was going out Thursday noon.

Q. You had not bought any apparatus for fishing?

A. No hooks.

Q. Had bought nothing connected with your fishing trip?

A. No sir.

Q. Was going to go fishing the next Monday, were you?

A. I don't know that we should go fishing Monday.

Q. Going to the place to go fishing Monday?

A. Yes sir.

Q. This was Thursday and you had no idea of using any fishing apparatus before the next Monday?

A. No sir.

Q. You had no fishing apparatus you were preparing to use the next Monday until then?

A. No sir, not until I bought it.

Q. You had not bought anything?

A. No sir.

Q. Had not started to buy anything?

A. No sir.

Q. The first thing in preparation for your fishing trip the next Monday was to go to the loft of that barn to find some old sinkers to put on some hooks and lines that you had not then bought?

A. I thought if I found no sinkers I would have to buy the sinkers when I bought the lines.

Q. You thought you would be saving some time by hunting in the loft of the barn before you went to see whether you should need lines or not?

A. I thought I would find out whether there were any sinkers before I bought the lines; and if there was, I should not have to buy any sinkers. If there were some, I should only have to buy the lines and the hooks.

Q. You began the collection of your fishing apparatus by searching for the sinkers in the barn?

A. Yes sir.

Q. You were searching in a box of old stuff in the loft of the barn?

A. Yes sir, up stairs.

Q. That you had never looked at before?

A. I had seen them.

Q. Never examined them before?

A. No sir.

Q.	All the reason you supposed there was sinkers there was your father had told you there was lead in the barn?
A.	Yes, lead; and one day I wanted some old nails; he said there was some in the barn.
Q.	All the reason that gave you to think there was sinkers was your father said there was old lead in the barn?
A.	Yes sir.
Q.	Did he mention the place in the barn?
A.	I think he said up stairs; I am not sure.
Q.	Where did you look up stairs?
A.	On that work bench, like.
Q.	In anything?
A.	Yes, it was a box, sort of a box, and then some things lying right on the side that was not in the box.
Q.	How large a box was it?
A.	I could not tell you. It was probably covered up with lumber, I think.
Q.	Give me the best idea of the size of the box you can.
A.	Well, I should say, I don't know, I have not any idea.
Q.	Give me the best idea you have.
A.	I have given you the best idea I have.
Q.	What is the best idea you have?
A.	About that large, (measuring with hands).
Q.	That long?
A.	Yes.
Q.	How wide?
A.	I don't know.
Q.	Give me the best idea you have.
A.	Perhaps about as wide as it was long.
Q.	How high?
A.	It was not very high.
Q.	About how high?
	(Witness measures with her hands.)
Q.	About twice the length of your forefinger?
A.	I should think so. Not quite.
Q.	What was in the box?
A.	Nails, and some old locks, and I don't know but there was a door knob.
Q.	Anything else?
A.	I don't remember anything else.
Q.	Any lead?
A.	Yes, some pieces of tea lead, like.
Q.	Foil, what we call tin foil, the same as you use on tea chests?
A.	I don't remember seeing any tin foil; not as thin as that.
Q.	Tea chest lead?

A. No, sir.

Q. What did you see in shape of lead?

A. Flat pieces of lead, a little bigger than that; some of them were doubled together.

Q. How many?

A. I could not tell you.

Q. Where else did you look beside in the box?

A. I did not look anywhere for lead except on the work bench.

Q. How full was the box?

A. It was not nearly as full as it could have been.

Q. You looked on the bench, beside that where else?

A. Nowhere except on the bench.

Q. Did you look for anything else beside lead?

A. No, sir.

Q. When you got through looking for lead did you come down?

A. No, sir. I went to the west window over the hay, to the west window, and the curtain was slanted a little. I pulled it down.

Q. What else?

A. Nothing.

Q. That is all you did?

A. Yes, sir.

Q. That is the second story of the barn?

A. Yes, sir.

Q. Was the window open?

A. I think not.

Q. Hot?

A. Very hot.

Q. How long do you think you were up there?

A. Not more than fifteen or twenty minutes, I should not think.

Q. Should you think what you have told me would occupy four minutes?

A. Yes, because I ate some pears up there.

Q. Do you think all you have told me would take you four minutes?

A. I ate some pears up there.

Q. I asked you to tell me all you did.

A. I told you all I did.

Q. Do you mean to say you stopped your work, and then, additional to that, sat still and ate some pears?

A. While I was looking out of the window, yes sir.

Q. Will you tell me all you did in the second story of the barn?

A. I think I told you all I did that I can remember.

Q. Is there anything else?

A. I told you I took some pears up from the ground when I went up; I stopped under the pear tree and took some pears up when I went up.

93

Q. Have you now told me everything you did up in the second story of the barn?

A. Yes sir.

Q. I now call your attention, and ask you to say whether all you have told me -- I don't suppose you stayed there any longer than necessary?

A. No sir, because it was close.

Q. I suppose that was the hottest place there was on the premises?

A. I should think so.

Q. Can you give me any explanation why all you have told me would occupy more than three minutes?

A. Yes, it would take me more than three minutes.

Q. To look in that box that you have described the size of on the bench and put down the curtain and then get out as soon as you conveniently could; would you say you were occupied in that business twenty minutes?

A. I think so, because I did not look at the box when I first went up.

Q. What did you do?

A. I ate my pears.

Q. Stood there eating the pears, doing nothing?

A. I was looking out of the window.

Q. Stood there, looking out of the window eating the pears?

A. I should think so.

Q. How many did you eat?

A. Three, I think.

Q. You were feeling better than you did in the morning?

A. Better than I did the night before.

Q. You were feeling better than you were in the morning?

A. I felt better in the morning than I did the night before.

Q. That is not what I asked you. You were then, when you were in that hot loft, looking out of the window and eating three pears, feeling better, were you not, than you were in the morning when you could not eat any breakfast?

A. I never eat any breakfast.

Q. You did not answer my question, and you will, if I have to put it all day. Were you, then when you were eating those three pears in that hot loft, looking out of that closed window, feeling better than you were in the morning when you ate no breakfast?

A. I was feeling well enough to eat the pears.

Q. Were you feeling better than you were in the morning?

A. I don't think I felt very sick in the morning, only -- Yes, I don't know but I did feel better. As I say, I don't know whether I ate any breakfast or not, or whether I ate a cookie.

Q. Were you then feeling better than you did in the morning?

94

A. I don't know how to answer you, because I told you I felt better in the morning anyway.

Q. Do you understand my question? My question is whether, when you were in the loft of that barn, you were feeling better than you were in the morning when you got up?

A. No, I felt about the same.

Q. Were you feeling better than you were when you told your mother you did not care for any dinner?

A. No sir, I felt about the same.

Q. Well enough to eat pears, but not well enough to eat anything for dinner?

A. She asked me if I wanted any meat.

Q. I ask you why you should select that place, which was the only place which would put you out of sight of the house, to eat those three pears in?

A. I cannot tell you any reason.

Q. You observe that fact, do you not? You have put yourself in the only place perhaps, where it would be impossible, for you to see a person going into the house?

A. Yes sir, I should have seen them from the front window.

Q. From anywhere in the yard?

A. No sir, not unless from the end of the barn.

Q. Ordinarily in the yard you could see them, and in the kitchen where you had been, you could have seen them?

A. I don't think I understand.

Q. When you were in the kitchen, you could see persons who came in at the back door?

A. Yes sir.

Q. When you were in the yard, unless you were around the corner of the house, you could see them come in at the back door?

A. No sir, not unless I was at the corner of the barn; the minute I turned I could not.

Q. What was there?

A. A little jog like, the walk turns.

Q. I ask you again to explain to me why you took those pears from the pear tree?

A. I did not take them from the pear tree.

Q. From the ground, wherever you took them from. I thank you for correcting me; going into the barn, going up stairs into the hottest place in the barn, in the rear of the barn, the hottest place, and there standing and eating those pears that morning?

A. I beg your pardon, I was not in the rear of the barn. I was in the other end of the barn that faced the street.

Q. Where you could see anybody coming into the house?

A. Yes sir.

Q. Did you not tell me you could not?

A. Before I went into the barn, at the jog on the outside.

Q. You now say when you were eating the pears, you could see the back door?

A. Yes sir.

Q. So nobody could come in at that time without your seeing them?

A. I don't see how they could.

Q. After you got through eating your pears you began your search?

A. Yes sir.

Q. Then you did not see into the house?

A. No sir, because the bench is at the other end.

Q. Now I have asked you over and over again, and will continue the inquiry, whether anything you did at the bench would occupy more than three minutes?

A. Yes, I think it would, because I pulled over quite a lot of boards in looking.

Q. To get at the box?

A. Yes sir.

Q. Taking all that, what is the amount of time you think you occupied in looking for that piece of lead which you did not find?

A. Well, I should think perhaps I was ten minutes.

Q. Looking over those old things?

A. Yes sir, on the bench.

Q. Now can you explain why you were ten minutes doing it?

A. No, only that I can't do anything in a minute.

Q. When you came down from the barn, what did you do then?

A. Came into the kitchen.

Q. What did you do then?

A. I went into the dining room and laid down my hat.

Q. What did you do then?

A. Opened the sitting room door, and went into the sitting room, or pushed it open; it was not latched.

Q. What did you do then?

A. I found my father, and rushed to the foot of the stairs.

Q. What were you going into the sitting room for?

A. To go up stairs.

Q. What for?

A. To sit down.

Q. What had become of the ironing?

A. The fire had gone out.

Q. I thought you went out because the fire was not hot enough to heat the flats.

A. I thought it would burn, but the fire had not caught from the few sparks.

Q. So you gave up the ironing and was going up stairs?

A. Yes, sir, I thought I would wait till Maggie got dinner and heat the flats again.

Q. When you saw your father where was he?

A. On the sofa.

Q. What was his position?

A. Lying down.

Q. Describe anything else you noticed at that time.

A. I did not notice anything else, I was so frightened and horrified. I ran to the foot of the stairs and called Maggie.

Q. Did you notice that he had been cut?

A. Yes; that is what made me afraid.

Q. Did you notice that he was dead?

A. I did not know whether he was or not.

Q. Did you make any search for your mother?

A. No, sir.

Q. Why not?

A. I thought she was out of the house; I thought she had gone out. I called Maggie to go to Dr. Bowen's. When they came I said, "I don't know where Mrs. Borden is." I thought she had gone out.

Q. Did you tell Maggie you thought your mother had come in?

A. No, sir.

Q. That you thought you heard her come in?

A. No, sir.

Q. Did you say to anybody that you thought she was killed up stairs?

A. No, sir.

Q. To anybody?

A. No, sir.

Q. You made no effort to find your mother at all?

A. No, sir.

Q. Who did you send Maggie for?

A. Dr. Bowen. She came back and said Dr. Bowen was not there.

Q. What did you tell Maggie?

A. I told her he was hurt.

Q. When you first told her?

A. I says "Go for Dr. Bowen as soon as you can. I think father is hurt."

Q. Did you then know that he was dead?

A. No, sir.

Q. You saw him?

A. Yes, sir.

Q. You went into the room?

A. No, sir.

Q. Looked in at the door?

A. I opened the door and rushed back.

Q. Saw his face?

A. No, I did not see his face, because he was all covered with blood.
Q. You saw where the face was bleeding?
A. Yes, sir.
Q. Did you see the blood on the floor?
A. No, sir.
Q. You saw his face covered with blood?
A. Yes, sir.
Q. Did you see his eye ball hanging out?
A. No, sir.
Q. See the gashes where his face was laid open?
A. No, sir.
Q. Nothing of that kind?
A. No sir. (Witness covers her face with her hand for a minute or two; then examination is resumed.)
Q. Do you know of any employment that would occupy your mother for the two hours between nine and eleven in the front room?
A. Not unless she was sewing.
Q. If she had been sewing you would have heard the machine?
A. She did not always use the machine.
Q. Did you see, or were there found, anything to indicate that she was sewing up there?
A. I don't know. She had given me a few weeks before some pillow cases to make.
Q. My question is not that. Did you see, or were there found, anything to indicate that she had done any sewing in that room that morning?
A. I don't know. I was not allowed in that room; I did not see it.
Q. Was that the room where she usually sewed?
A. No sir.
Q. Did you ever know her to use that room for sewing?
A. Yes sir.
Q. When?
A. Whenever she wanted to use the machine.
Q. When she did not want to use the machine, did you know she used that room for sewing?
A. Not unless she went up to sew a button on; or something.
Q. She did not use it as a sitting room?
A. No sir.
Q. Leaving out the sewing, do you know of anything else that would occupy her for two hours in that room?
A. No, not if she had made the bed up, and she said she had when I went down.
Q. Assuming the bed was made?
A. I don't know anything.
Q. Did she say she had done the work?

A. She said she had made the bed, and was going to put on the pillow cases, about 9 o'clock.

Q. I ask you now again, remembering that.

A. I told you that yesterday.

Q. Never mind about yesterday. Tell me all the talk you had with your mother when you came down in the morning?

A. She asked me how I felt. I said I felt better, but did not want any breakfast. She said what kind of meat did I want for dinner. I said I did not want any. She said she was going out, somebody was sick, and she would get the dinner, get the meat, order the meat. And, I think she said something about the weather being hotter, or something; and I don't remember that she said anything else. I said to her, "Won't you change your dress before you go out." She had on an old one. She said, "No, this is good enough." That is all I can remember.

Q. In this narrative you have not again said anything about her having said that she had made the bed?

A. I told you that she said she made the bed.

Q. In this time saying, you did not put that in. I want that conversation that you had with her that morning. I beg your pardon again, in this time of telling me, you did not say anything about her having received a note.

A. I told you that before.

Q. Miss Borden, I want you now to tell me all the talk you had with your mother, when you came down, and all the talk she had with you. Please begin again.

A. She asked me how I felt. I told her. She asked me what I wanted for dinner. I told her not anything, what kind of meat I wanted for dinner. I told her not any. She said she had been up and made the spare bed, and was going to take up some linen pillow cases for the small pillows at the foot, and then the room was done. She says: "I have had a note from somebody that is sick, and I am going out, and I will get the dinner at the same time." I think she said something about the weather. I don't know. She also asked me if I would direct some paper wrappers for her, which I did.

Q. She said she had had a note?

A. Yes sir.

Q. You told me yesterday you never saw the note?

A. No sir, I never did.

Q. You looked for it?

A. No sir, but the rest have.

Q. She did not say where she was going?

A. No sir.

Q. Does she usually tell you where she is going?

A. She does not generally tell me.

Q. Did she say when she was coming back?
A. No sir.
Q. Did you know that Mr. Morse was coming to dinner?
A. No sir, I knew nothing about him.
Q. Was he at dinner the day before?
A. Wednesday noon? I don't know. I had not seen him; I don't think he was.
Q. Were you at dinner?
A. I was in the house. I don't know whether I went down to dinner or not. I was not feeling well.
Q. Whether you ate dinner or not?
A. I don't remember.
Q. Do you remember who was at dinner the day before?
A. No sir. I don't remember, because I don't know whether I was down myself or not.
Q. Were you at tea Wednesday night?
A. I went down, but I think, I don't know, whether I had any tea or not.
Q. Did you sit down with the family?
A. I think I did, but I am not sure.
Q. Was Mr. Morse there?
A. No sir, I did not see him.
Q. Who were there to tea?
A. Nobody.
Q. The family were there, I suppose?
A. Yes, sir; I mean nobody but the family.
Q. Did you have an apron on Thursday?
A. Did I what?
Q. Have an apron on Thursday?
A. No sir, I don't think I did.
Q. Do you remember whether you did or not?
A. I don't remember sure, but I don't think I did.
Q. You had aprons, of course?
A. I had aprons, yes sir.
Q. Will you try and think whether you did or not?
A. I don't think I did.
Q. Will you try and remember?
A. I had no occasion for an apron on that morning.
Q. If you can remember, I wish you would.
A. I don't remember.
Q. That is all the answer you can give me about that?
A. Yes sir.
Q. Did you have any occasion to use the axe or hatchet?
A. No sir.
Q. Did you know where they were?

A. I knew there was an old axe down cellar; that is all I knew.
Q. Did you know anything about a hatchet down cellar?
A. No sir.
Q. Where was the old axe down cellar?
A. The last time I saw it it was stuck in the old chopping block.
Q. Was that the only axe or hatchet down cellar?
A. It was all I knew about.
Q. When was the last you knew of it?
A. When our farmer came to chop wood.
Q. When was that?
A. I think a year ago last winter; I think there was so much wood on hand he did not come last winter.
Q. Do you know of anything that would occasion the use of an axe or hatchet?
A. No sir.
Q. Do you know of anything that would occasion the getting of blood on an axe or hatchet down cellar?
A. No sir.
Q. I do not say there was, but assuming an axe or hatchet was found down cellar with blood on it?
A. No sir.
Q. Do you know whether there was a hatchet down there before the murder?
A. I don't know.
Q. You are not able to say your father did not own a hatchet?
A. I don't know whether he did or not.
Q. Did you know there was found at the foot of the stairs a hatchet and axe?
A. No sir, I did not.
Q. Assume that is so, can you give me any explanation of how they came there?
A. No sir.
Q. Assume they had blood on them, can you give any occasion for there being blood on them?
A. No sir.
Q. Can you tell of any killing of an animal? or any other operation that would lead to their being cast there, with blood on them?
A. No sir, he killed some pigeons in the barn last May or June.
Q. What with?
A. I don't know, but I thought he wrung their necks.
Q. What made you think so?
A. I think he said so.
Q. Did anything else make you think so?
A. All but three or four had their heads on, that is what made me think so.

Q. Did all of them come into the house?
A. I think so.
Q. Those that came into the house were all headless?
A. Two or three had them on.
Q. Were any with their heads off?
A. Yes sir.
Q. Cut off or twisted off?
A. I don't know which.
Q. How did they look?
A. I don't know, their heads were gone, that is all.
Q. Did you tell anybody they looked as though they were twisted off?
A. I don't remember whether I did or not. The skin I think was very tender, I said why are these heads off? I think I remember of telling somebody that he said they twisted off.
Q. Did they look as if they were cut off?
A. I don't know, I did not look at that particularly.
Q. Is there anything else besides that that would lead, in your opinion so far as you can remember, to the finding of instruments in the cellar with blood on them?
A. I know of nothing else that was done.

(Judge Blaisdell) -- Was there any effort made by the witness to notify Mrs. Borden of the fact that Mr. Borden was found?

Q. Did you make any effort to notify Mrs. Borden of your father being killed?
A. No sir, when I found him I rushed right to the foot of the stairs for Maggie. I supposed Mrs. Borden was out. I did not think anything about her at the time, I was so --
Q. At any time did you say anything about her to anybody?
A. No sir.
Q. To the effect that she was out?
A. I told father when he came in.
Q. After your father was killed?
A. No sir.
Q. Did you say you thought she was up stairs?
A. No sir.
Q. Did you ask them to look up stairs?
A. No sir.
Q. Did you suggest to anybody to search up stairs?
A. I said, "I don't know where Mrs. Borden is;" that is all I said.
Q. You did not suggest that any search be made for her?
A. No sir.
Q. You did not make any yourself?
A. No sir.

102

Q. I want you to give me all that you did, by way of word or deed, to see whether your mother was dead or not, when you found your father was dead.

A. I did not do anything, except what I said to Mrs. Churchill. I said to her: "I don't know where Mrs. Borden is. I think she is out, but I wish you would look."

Q. You did ask her to look?

A. I said that to Mrs. Churchill.

Q. Where did you intend for her to look?

A. In Mrs. Borden's room.

Q. When you went out to the barn did you leave the door shut, the screen door?

A. I left it shut.

Q. When you came back did you find it shut or open?

A. No, sir; I found it open.

Q. Can you tell me anything else that you did, that you have not told me, during your absence from the house?

A. No, sir.

Q. Can you tell me when it was that you came back from the barn, what time it was?

A. I don't know what time it was.

Q. Have you any idea when it was that your father came home?

A. I am not sure, but I think it must have been after 10, because I think he told me he did not think he should go out until about 10. When he went out I did not look at the clock to see what time it was. I think he did not go out until 10, or a little after. He was not gone so very long.

Q. Will you give me the best judgment you can as to the time your father got back? If you have not any, it is sufficient to say so.

A. No, sir, I have not any.

Q. Can you give me any judgment as to the length of time that elapsed after he came back, and before you went to the barn?

A. I went right out to the barn.

Q. How soon after he came back?

A. I should think not less than five minutes; I saw him taking off his shoes and lying down; it only took him two or three minutes to do it. I went right out.

Q. When he came into the house did he not go into the dining room first?

A. I don't know.

Q. And there sit down?

A. I don't know.

Q. Why don't you know?

A. Because I was in the kitchen.

Q. It might have happened, and you not have known it?

103

A.	Yes sir.
Q.	You heard the bell ring?
A.	Yes sir.
Q.	And you knew when he came in?
A.	Yes sir.
Q.	You did not see him?
A.	No sir.
Q.	When did you first see him?
A.	I went into the sitting room, and he was there; I don't know whether he had been in the dining room before or not.
Q.	What made you go into the sitting room?
A.	Because I wanted to ask him a question.
Q.	What question?
A.	Whether there was any mail for me.
Q.	Did you not ask him that question in the dining room?
A.	No sir, I think not.
Q.	Was he not in the dining room sitting down?
A.	I don't remember his being in the dining room sitting down.
Q.	At that time was not Maggie washing the windows in the sitting room?
A.	I thought I asked him for the mail in the sitting room; I am not sure.
Q.	Was not the reason he went in the dining room because she was in the sitting room washing windows?
A.	I don't know.
Q.	Did he not go upstairs to his own room before he sat down in the sitting room?
A.	I did not see him go.
Q.	He had the key to his room down there?
A.	I don't know whether he had it; it was kept on the shelf.
Q.	Don't you remember he took the key and went into his own room and then came back?
A.	No, sir; he took some medicine; it was not doctor's medicine; it was what we gave him.
Q.	What was it?
A.	We gave him castor oil first and then Garfield tea.
Q.	When was that?
A.	He took the castor oil some time Wednesday. I think some time Wednesday noon, and I think the tea Wednesday night; Mrs. Borden gave it to him. She went over to see the doctor.
Q.	When did you first consult Mr. Jennings?
A.	I can't tell you that; I think my sister sent for him; I don't know.
Q.	Was it you or your sister?
A.	My sister.
Q.	You did not send for him?

A. I did not send for him. She said did we think we ought to have him. I said do as she thought best. I don't know when he came first.

Q. Now, tell me once more, if you please, the particulars of that trouble that you had with your mother four or five years ago.

A. Her father's house on Fourth street was for sale --

Q. Whose father's house?

A. Mrs. Borden's father's house. She had a stepmother and a half sister, Mrs. Borden did, and this house was left to the stepmother and a half sister, if I understood it right, and the house was for sale. The stepmother, Mrs. Oliver Gray, wanted to sell it, and my father brought out the Widow Gray's share. She did not tell me and he did not tell me, but some outsiders said that he gave it to her. Put it in her name. I said if he gave that to her, he ought to give us something. Told Mrs. Borden so. She did not care anything about the house herself. She wanted it so this half sister could have a home, because she had married a man that was not doing the best he could, and she thought her sister was having a very hard time and wanted her to have a home. And we always thought she persuaded father to buy it. At any rate he did buy it, and I am quite sure she did persuade him. I said what he did for her people, he ought to do for his own children. So he gave us grandfather's house. That was all the trouble we ever had.

Q. You have not stated any trouble yet between you and her?

A. I said there was feeling four or five years ago when I stopped calling her mother. I told you that yesterday.

Q. That is all there is to it then?

A. Yes, sir.

Q. You had no words with your stepmother then?

A. I talked with her about it and said what he did for her he ought to do for us; that is all the words we had.

Q. That is the occasion of his giving you the house that you sold back to him?

A. Yes, sir.

Q. Did your mother leave any property?

A. I don't know.

Q. Your own mother?

A. No, sir; not that I ever knew of.

Q. Did you ever see that thing? (Wooden club.)

A. Yes, sir, I think I have.

Q. What is it?

A. My father used to keep something similar to this, that looked very much like it under his bed. He whittled it out himself at the farm one time.

Q. How long since you have seen it?

105

A. I have not seen it in years.

Q. How many years?

A. I could not tell you. I should think 10 or 15 years; not since I was quite a little girl, it must be as much as that.

Q. When was the last time the windows were washed before that day?

A. I don't know.

Q. Why don't you know?

A. Because I had nothing to do with the work down stairs.

Q. When was the last time that you ate with the family, that you can swear to, before your mother was killed?

A. Well, I ate with them all day Tuesday, that is, what little we ate, we sat down to the table; and I think I sat down to the table with them Wednesday night, but I am not sure.

Q. All day Tuesday?

A. I was down at the table.

Q. I understand you to say you did not come down to breakfast?

A. That was Wednesday morning.

Q. I understood you to say that you did not come down to breakfast?

A. I came down, but I did not eat breakfast with them. I did not eat any breakfast. Frequently I would go into the dining room and sit down to the table with them and not eat any breakfast.

Q. Did you give to the officer the same skirt you had on the day of the tragedy?

A. Yes, sir.

Q. Do you know whether there was any blood on the skirt?

A. No, sir.

Q. Assume that there was, do you know how it came there?

A. No, sir.

Q. Have you any explanation of how it might come there?

A. No, sir.

Q. Did you know there was any blood on the skirt you gave them?

A. No, sir.

Q. Assume that there was, can you give any explanation of how it came there, on the dress skirt?

A. No, sir.

Q. Assume that there was, can you suggest any reason how it came there?

A. No, sir.

Q. Have you offered any?

A. No, sir.

Q. Have you ever offered any?

A. No, sir.

Q. Have you said it came from flea bites?

A. On the petticoats I said there was a flea bite. I said it might have been. You said you meant the dress skirt.

Q. I did. Have you offered any explanation how that came there?
A. I told those men that were at the house that I had had fleas; that is all. ["Having fleas" was a Victorian euphemism for menstruating. -- Eds.]
Q. Did you offer that as an explanation?
A. I said that was the only explanation that I knew of.
Q. Assuming that the blood came from the outside, can you give any explanation of how it came there?
A. No, sir.
Q. You cannot now?
A. No, sir.
Q. What shoes did you have on that day?
A. A pair of ties.
Q. What color?
A. Black.
Q. Will you give them to the officer?
A. Yes.
Q. Where are they?
A. At home.
Q. What stockings did you have on that day?
A. Black.
Q. Where are they?
A. At home.
Q. Have they been washed?
A. I don't know.
Q. Will you give them to the officer?
A. Yes, sir.
Q. The window you was at is the window that is nearest the street in the barn?
A. Yes, sir; the west window.
Q. The pears you ate, you got from under the tree in the yard?
A. Yes, sir.
Q. How long were you under the pear tree?
A. I think I was under there very nearly four or five minutes. I stood looking around. I looked up at the pigeon house that they have closed up. It was no more than five minutes, perhaps not as long. I can't say sure.

(Judge Blaisdell) Was this witness on Thursday morning in the front hall or front stairs or front chamber, any part of the front part of the house at all?

Q. What do you say to that?
A. I had to come down the front stairs to get into the kitchen.
Q. When you came down first?
A. Yes, sir.

Q. Were you afterwards?
A. No, sir.
Q. Not at all?
A. Except the few minutes I went up with the clean clothes, and I had to come back again.
Q. That you now say was before Mr. Borden went away?
A. Yes, sir.

(Miss Borden recalled Aug. 11, 1892.)

Q. (Mr. Knowlton) Is there anything you would like to correct in your previous testimony?
A. No, sir.
Q. Did you buy a dress pattern in New Bedford?
A. A dress pattern?
Q. Yes, a dress pattern.
A. I think I did.
Q. Where is it?
A. It is at home.
Q. Where?
A. Where at home?
Q. Please.
A. It is in a trunk.
Q. In your room?
A. No, sir; in the attic.
Q. Not made up?
A. O, no, sir.
Q. Where did you buy it?
A. I don't know the name of the store.
Q. On the principal street there?
A. I think it was on the street that Hutchinson's book store is on. I am not positive.
Q. What kind of a one was it, please?
A. It was a pink stripe and a white stripe, and a blue stripe corded gingham.
Q. Your attention has already been called to the circumstance of going into the drug store of Smith's, on the corner of Columbia and Main streets, by some officer, has it not, on the day before the tragedy?
A. I don't know whether some officer has asked me, somebody has spoken of it to me; I don't know who it was.
Q. Did that take place?
A. It did not.
Q. Do you know where the drug store is?
A. I don't.
Q. Did you go into any drug store and inquire for prussic acid?

A.   I did not.

Q.   Where were you on Wednesday morning that you remember?

A.   At home.

Q.   All the time?

A.   All day, until Wednesday night.

Q.   Nobody there but your parents and yourself and the servant?

A.   Why, Mr. Morse came sometime in the afternoon, or at noon time, I suppose, I did not see him.

Q.   He did not come so to see you?

A.   No, sir, I did not see him.

Q.   He did not come until afternoon anyway, did he?

A.   I don't think he did; I am not sure.

Q.   Did you dine with the family that day?

A.   I was down stairs, yes, sir. I did not eat any breakfast with them.

Q.   Did you go into the drug store for any purpose whatever?

A.   I did not.

Q.   I think you said yesterday that you did not go into the room where your father lay, after he was killed, on the sofa, but only looked in at the door?

A.   I looked in; I did not go in.

Q.   You did not step into the room at all?

A.   I did not.

Q.   Did you ever, after your mother was found killed, go into that room?

A.   No, sir.

Q.   Did you afterwards go into the room where your father was found killed, any more than to go through it to go up stairs?

A.   When they took me up stairs they took me through that room.

Q.   Otherwise than that did you go into it?

A.   No, sir.

Q.   Let me refresh your memory. You came down in the night to get some water with Miss Russell, along towards night, or in the evening, to get some water with Miss Russell?

A.   Thursday night? I don't remember it.

Q.   Don't you remember coming down sometime to get some toilet water?

A.   No, sir, there was no toilet water down stairs.

Q.   Or to empty the slops?

A.   I don't know whether I did Thursday evening or not. I am not sure.

Q.   You think it may have been some other evening?

A.   I don't remember coming down with her to do such a thing, I may have, I can't tell whether it was Thursday evening or any other evening.

Sarah Borden. (Courtesy of the Fall River Historical Society)

Andrew Borden. (Courtesy of the Fall River Historical Society)

Abby Borden. (Courtesy of the Fall River Historical Society)

Lizzie. (Courtesy of the Fall River Historical Society)

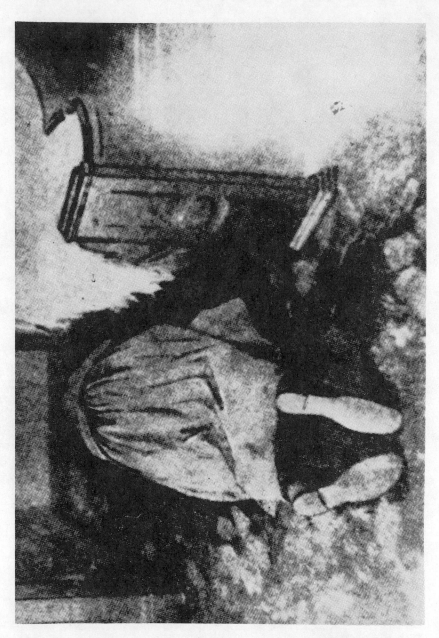

Abby Borden's body in the guest room. (Courtesy of the Fall River Historical Society)

Body of Andrew Borden on the sofa. (Courtesy of the Fall River Historical Society)

Q. Other than that, if that did take place, you don't recollect going into that room for any purpose at any time?

A. No, sir.

Q. Was the dress that was given to the officers the same dress that you wore that morning?

A. Yes, sir.

Q. The India silk?

A. No, it is not an India silk. It is silk and linen; some call it bengaline silk.

Q. Something like that dress there? (Pongee.)

A. No, it was not like that.

Q. Did you give to the officer the same shoes and stockings that you wore?

A. I did, sir.

Q. Do you remember where you took them off?

A. I wore the shoes ever after that, all around the house Friday, and Saturday until I put on my shoes for the street.

Q. That is to say you wore them all that day, Thursday, until you took them off for the night?

A. Yes, sir.

Q. Did you tell us yesterday all the errand that you had at the barn?

A. Yes, sir.

Q. You have nothing to add to what you said?

A. No, sir.

Q. You had no other errand than what you have spoken of?

A. No, sir.

Q. Miss Borden, of course you appreciate the anxiety that everybody has to find the author of this tragedy, and the questions that I put to you have been in that direction; I now ask you if you can furnish any other fact, or give any other, even suspicion, that will assist the officers in any way in this matter?

A. About two weeks ago --

Q. Was you going to tell the occurrence about the man that called at the house?

A. No, sir. It was after my sister went away. I came home from Miss Russell's one night, and as I came up, I always glanced towards the side door as I came along by the carriage way, I saw a shadow on the side steps. I did not stop walking, but I walked slower. Somebody ran down the steps, around the east end of the house. I thought it was a man, because I saw no skirts, and I was frightened, and of course I did not go around to see. I hurried to the front door as fast as I could and locked it.

Q. What time of night was that?

A. I think about quarter of 9; it was not after 9 o'clock, anyway.

Q. Do you remember what night that was?

116

A.   No, sir; I don't. I saw somebody run around the house once before last winter.

Q.   One thing at a time. Do you recollect about how long ago that last occurrence was?

A.   It was after my sister went away. She has been away two weeks today, so it must have been within two weeks.

Q.   Two weeks today? Or two weeks at the time of the murder?

A.   Is not today Thursday?

Q.   Yes, but I thought you said she was gone two weeks the day of the murder?

A.   Is not today Thursday?

Q.   Yes, but that would be three weeks; I thought you said the day your father was murdered she had been away just two weeks?

A.   Yes, she had.

Q.   Then it would be three weeks today -- your sister went away, a week has elapsed?

A.   Yes, I had forgotten that a whole week had passed since the affair.

Q.   Different from that you cannot state?

A.   No, sir; I don't know what the date was.

Q.   This form when you first saw it was on the steps of the backdoor?

A.   Yes, sir.

Q.   Went down the rear steps?

A.   Went down towards the barn.

Q.   Around the back side of the house?

A.   Disappeared in the dark; I don't know where they went.

Q.   Have you ever mentioned that before?

A.   Yes, sir; I told Mr. Jennings.

Q.   To any officer?

A.   I don't think I have, unless I told Mr. Hanscomb.

Q.   What was you going to say about last winter?

A.   Last winter when I was coming home from church one Thursday evening, I saw somebody run around the house again. I told my father of that.

Q.   Did you tell your father of this last one?

A.   No, sir.

Q.   Of course you could not identify who it was either time?

A.   No, I could not identify who it was, but it was not a very tall person.

Q.   Have you sealskin sacks?

A.   Yes, sir.

Q.   Where are they?

A.   Hanging in a large white bag in the attic, each one separate.

Q.   Put away for the summer?

A.   Yes, sir.

Q.   Do you ever use prussic acid on your sacks?

A. Acid? No, sir; I don't use anything on them.

Q. Is there anything else that you can suggest that even amounts to anything whatever?

A. I know of nothing else, except the man who came, and father ordered him out, that is all I know.

Q. That you told about the other day?

A. I think I did; yes, sir.

Q. You have not been able to find that man?

A. I have not; I don't know whether anybody else has or not.

Q. Have you caused search to be made for him?

A. Yes, sir.

Q. When was the offer of reward made for the detection of the criminals?

A. I think it was made Friday.

Q. Who suggested that?

A. We suggested it ourselves, and asked Mr. Buck if he did not think it was a good idea.

Q. Whose suggestion was it, yours or Emma's?

A. I don't remember. I think it was mine.

New York Times Reports

A Note on the Text: Typographical errors have been removed from the text for this edition, but errors of grammar, errors of fact, and irregular punctuation have been retained.

August 10, 1892

THE BORDEN MURDER MYSTERY.

The Inquest Begun But Nothing Of Importance Developed.

FALL RIVER, Mass., Aug. 9. -- This morning Bridget Sullivan, the servant girl in the Borden family, was summoned to the Central Police Station. She walked down in company with an officer, and talked freely on the way. She looked worried, and was pale. She told the officer that it was annoying to be watched so closely, but said she was willing to have the police or any one else examine her every action since the time she arose Thursday until she was asked to go to the police station with the officer. She said that she wanted to leave two or three times, but was urged to remain by Mrs. Borden. She was taken into the City Marshal's presence and also into the presence of District Attorney Knowlton and Medical Examiner Dolan and underwent an examination as to the facts before and after the murders as far as she knew them.

While the servant was in the court-room locked up with the authorities, J. V. Morse was walking through Main Street and down to the banks, closely followed by an officer. When shown the statement of

G. E. Fish of Hartford, to the effect that he believed that Lizzie Borden and Morse concocted the murder of the old couple, and hired some one to do it, Morse said: "You know as well as I do what grounds there are for such an absurd charge as that. It is entirely unreasonable. That is all I will say."

Attorney General Pillsbury has arrived in town, presumably on business in connection with the Borden cases.

Lizzie Borden was brought to the Central Police Station this afternoon in a hack containing Marshal Hilliard, Officer Harrington, and Mrs. James W. Bingham. Miss Borden was served with a subpeona summoning her to attend at an inquiry at the Second District Court to determine the cause of the death of her father and mother. Mrs. Bingham, who is a lady about her own age, was visiting Miss Borden at the time, and she consented to accompany her at the request and consent of Marshal Hilliard.

The stopping of the carriage at the Borden homestead was followed by the gathering of a great crowd. The drive to the station was through a crowd. At the police station the crowd was augmented and the police court alley was filled with curious business men and loiterers. This morning at the house she was visited by her counsel, Mr. Jennings, and her private detective, Mr. Hanscom.

The private inquiry was in reality an inquest, ordered by Judge Blaisdell at the suggestion of District Attorney Knowlton as a result of the midnight conference of the authorities.

Search is being made for the prescription which Dr. Bowen gave to the family when the members were ill a week ago.

The following bulletin was to-night given out by State Detective Seaver: "The inquest into the Borden murder began before Judge Blaisdell at 10 A.M. District Attorney Knowlton conducting the investigation. Bridget Sullivan and Lizzie Borden were questioned separately. The examination of neither was concluded. The inquest adjourned until 10 A.M. Wednesday. Nothing was developed for publication."

After adjournment Bridget Sullivan was taken from the Central Station. She was accompanied by Officer Doherty and went to 80 Division Street, where she has relatives. She has hardly eaten or slept at the Borden house since the tragedy. District Attorney Knowlton told her that he regarded her as the most important witness in the case and promised to allow her to go on her own recognizance until the trial, if one takes place, provided she would not go away without first acquainting the City Marshal. While the principal parties at the inquest were at dinner, Bridget was placed in charge of Matron Russell and told her the whole story, saying that she could not tell all before, as there were so many men about. At 2 o'clock, while Bridget was walking up stairs to the courtroom, she was crying bitterly.

Miss Borden was not examined very closely, owing to the advent of Attorney General Pillsbury, who went up stairs at the Mellen House without registering. He sent for Mr. Knowlton, who, with Marshal Hilliard, Medical Examiner Dolan, and others, went to the Mellen House, where they remained in consultation with Mr. Pillsbury for about half an hour. About 4:30 P.M. Prof. Wood, the Harvard analyst, Mr. MacKenzie of this city, and Dr. Dolan joined the other officials at the Mellen House. Attorney General Pillsbury started for Boston on the 4:50 train. Before going he declined to say anything about the murder cases. After his departure there was more secrecy than ever among the authorities.

The analysis of the stomachs has not been completed yet, and probably will not be for some days longer. It is said that Dr. Wood was called here to assist, if possible, in giving some information which would justify the officials in serving warrants. At the present time the officers are in great doubt about how to proceed. An officer who is very close to the head of the department said to-night that he had no doubt of the ultimate arrest of some one in the family, but which one he would not or could not say. After the adjournment of the inquest Miss Borden was taken to her home on Second Street, accompanied by Mrs. Bingham and City Marshal Hilliard.

Last night's *News* says: Dr. Handy furnishes a very suggestive hint as to the probable murderer of Mr. and Mrs. Borden. He says that about 10 A.M. on Thursday he saw a man standing on Second Street, a little south of the Borden residence, the man having such a terribly unusual appearance to attract his attention. The stranger was ghastly white, and seemed very much agitated. His eyes were particularly wild. He wore a small black mustache. The doctor could certainly identify the man he observed, as he was so struck by his desperate look that he turned around his carriage and gazed at him for a time.

Late last evening the police began to put some credence in this rumor, as it was said that a man answering this description was seen by Officer Hyde about the same time.

August 11, 1892

THE BORDEN MURDER MYSTERY.

The Inquest Adjourned -- No Clues To The Murderers.

FALL RIVER, Mass., Aug. 10. -- To-night it cannot be said that the police have any substantial clue to the murderers of Mr. and Mrs. Andrew J. Borden. Theories are plentiful, but reliable evidence is wanting. At 5 o'clock this afternoon State Detective Seaver handed the following bulletin to the reporters:

"The inquest was continued at 10 o'clock to-day. The witnesses examined were Miss Lizzie Borden, John V. Morse, Emma L. Borden, Dr. S. W. Bowen, Adelaide B. Churchill, and Hiram C. Harrington. Adjourned until 10 A.M. Thursday; nothing developed for publication."

This was all that was given out after examination lasting more than four and a half hours. The principal witness was Lizzie Borden. The change in Miss Borden's appearance after her examination was the chief topic of conversation in the police station to-night. Whatever the police may think of the strength of their clues, it is certain that the opinions of Miss Borden's many friends are entirely in favor of her innocence. This feeling is gaining more adherents every hour. Dr. Bowen told a straightforward story, covering the time since he was called to the Borden house a few days before the murder. He incidentally gave some evidence which startled the authorities.

The nature of this will not be given for publication, but it was learned that to-morrow an examination of the dead bodies will be made at Oak Grove Cemetery. Hiram Harrington could give little testimony regarding the circumstances surrounding the murders, as he said that he was not in the vicinity when they occurred. Taken all altogether, in connection with an authoritative statement volunteered to-night, the police have presented very insufficient and meagre evidence against any member of the family.

Prof. Wood, the analyst, appeared at the station early to-day in company with Medical Examiner Dolan. Shortly after the inquest was resumed the two men were admitted and were behind closed doors twenty minutes. When they reappeared they were followed by a couple of policemen carrying a trunk containing bloody clothing and other evidences of the crime.

Prof. Wood took the 11:03 train for Boston, and the trunk was checked for the same place.

A carpenter was at work in the Borden house this afternoon. Shortly before 2 o'clock Marshal Hilliard, Detective Seaver, and Officer Harrington arrived at the police station carrying three boxes. Two were wrapped up and one was open. The open one contained sheet lead and was taken from the barn where Miss Lizzie Borden said she had gone to look for lead for sinkers.

The inquest was resumed at 2:30 o'clock.

The Arrest

Lizzie Borden was arrested on August 11, 1892, for the murder of her father, Andrew Borden, with no mention made in the warrant of her stepmother's death. Not until December 2 was Lizzie formally charged with the murder of her stepmother, Abby Borden. At her arraignment on August 12, Lizzie, represented by attorney Andrew

Jennings, entered a plea of not guilty to the charge. Since murder was a non-bailable offense, Lizzie was taken to nearby Taunton Jail to await her preliminary hearing.

New York Times Report

August 12, 1892

MISS BORDEN ARRESTED

Charged With Murdering Her Father And His Wife.

She Appeared Calm When The Warrant Was Read To Her -- Another Autopsy Upon The Bodies Of Mr. And Mrs. Borden -- What Was Done At The Inquest.

FALL RIVER, Mass., Aug. 11. -- Lizzie Borden is under arrest charged with murdering her father and step-mother last Thursday morning at their home on Second Street.

She was brought into the Second District Court room about 3 o'clock this afternoon, presumably to give further evidence at the inquest. Miss Borden was accompanied by her sister and Mrs. Brigham. As was the case yesterday, all the proceedings were carried on behind locked doors.

When Miss Lizzie returned from the third inquiry she was a physical and mental wreck and was conducted to the matron's room. The inquest was adjourned about 4 o'clock.

District Attorney Knowlton and other officials went to the Marshal's private office, where they remained closeted for two hours.

Shortly after 6 o'clock City Marshal Hilliard and District Attorney Knowlton drove to the home of Andrew Jennings, who had been the family's attorney for some years. They returned at about 7 o'clock, and went into the matron's room, where Miss Borden was lying on a sofa.

The reading of the warrant was waived. The lady took the announcement of her arrest with surprising calmness. Two women who were with her were much more visibly affected.

The excitement on the street was very great when the news of the arrest became known, although some hours previous it was generally understood that Miss Borden was soon to be made a prisoner.

Miss Borden was searched by Mrs. Russell shortly after she was formally placed in custody.

All the afternoon a machinist has been at work on the safe at the Borden homestead, but up to this hour he has not been able to open it.

Other witnesses examined at the inquest this afternoon were Eli Bence, who is supposed to have refused to sell poison to the prisoner; his assistant, Fred Hart, and Frank Kilroy, who was in the store when it is alleged Miss Borden made the request. Their testimony is said to have clinched the suspicions of the police, but is believed in no way to have affected the previous statements made by them.

The City Marshal's guard will be kept around the house for some time longer. The police will still keep watch on the actions of Miss Sullivan and John V. Morse. Miss Sullivan is still with her relatives.

A second autopsy was made to-day on the bodies of Mr. and Mrs. Borden. Mrs. Borden's body was exhumed first. The new fact discovered was a bruise on the back, near the left shoulder, about the width of an axe, and shaped like the head of an axe. It gives another idea of the exact position held by Mrs. Borden when the murder was committed. The physicians next examined Mr. Borden's body. The physicians were Dr. Draper of Boston and Medical Examiner Dolan and Drs. Leary and Cone of this city.

At the inquest continued to-day Charles Sawyer, who had guarded the door of the Borden home while Officer Allen ran to the Central Station, was the first witness. He testified that he ran to the house when he saw Mrs. [Miss - Eds.] Russell, and that he was with Officer Doherty and a reporter when Dr. Bowen discovered that Mrs. Borden did not die of heart disease.

Officer George Allen was called, and he testified to having seen Mr. Borden lying on the sofa, stabbed, as he supposed.

Mrs. George Whitehead, a stepsister of Mrs. Borden; Mrs. Tripp, a neighbor, and Mrs. Russell, who was placed in charge of the household, were examined as to the relations of the members of the family. The deposition of Mrs. Hiram C. Harrington was also taken.

The evidence thus far points to a member of the household being guilty of the double murder.

Last night Officer Harrington went to Boston to identify a person answering the description of a "wild looking man," seen last Thursday morning by a doctor as he was driving by the Borden house. He was not the man. The police have also run down a man who, it was said, boarded the New-Bedford train at Pleasant and rode into the city. He proved an alibi.

Marshal Hilliard said to-day, in answer to questions as to whether or not the police had given up all hopes of locating a murderer outside of the Borden family, that three clues were already being run down and none of them would in any way implicate a member of the household. He said he had not been stinted in money nor men by the City Government because of political complications.

It has been proved that the milk drank by the Borden family was not poisoned when it was taken from the Borden farm and brought to the city. Members of the family in charge of the farm drank it, and they were affected in no noticeable way.

Arrest Records of the Fall River Police Department

The records of the police department provide a thorough -- and socially telling -- profile of those arrested for crimes in Fall River. The "booking" involved not only a prisoner's name and the charges but also his or her age and sex, height, skin color, and other physical features, and the alleged criminal's place of birth and occupation. The following abbreviated version of the Fall River police records for the week of Lizzie's arrest reveals the social composition of the people who fell afoul of the law in early August, 1892.

Source: Fall River Historical Society.

1892				Descriptive Record of Prisoners Arrested		
	Name	Age	Sex	Born In	Occupation	Arrested on Charge of
Aug 7	John or Jeremiah Sullivan	28	Male	Ireland	Painter	Drunkenness
	Michael O'Neil	32	Male	Ireland	Steamboat-hand	Drunkenness
	William Young	28	Male	Sweden	Fisherman	Drunkenness
	Margaret McMahon	20	Female	England	Weaver	Drunkenness
Aug 8	Harry England	30	Male	New York	Machinist	Drunkenness
	Patrick Hagle	33	Male	England	Hostler	Drunkenness
	Michael Hogan	30	Male	Ireland	Laborer	Drunkenness
	Louie A. Bowcock	25	Male	Fall River	Paper hanger	Drunkenness
	Delia Gray	33	Female	Ireland	Servant	Drunkenness
	Ellen Prescott	41	Female	Ireland	Servant	Drunkenness
	Maria Thompson	33	Female	England	[?] Speeder tender	Drunkenness
	James O'Connell	29	Male	Ireland	Stone Mason	Assault & Battery on James Hogan
	Michael McCormick	28	Male	England	Weaver	Assault & Battery on Wife Ellen
	James Holahan	59	Male	Ireland	Canvasser	Dist. the Peace
	William H. Fanning	28	Male	Rhode Island	Spinner	Dist. the Peace
	Edward Cooney	24	Male	England	Weaver	Dist. the Peace
	Mary J. Rockett	36	Female	Ireland	Weaver	Dist. the Peace
Aug 10	William McKing	23	Male	Fall River	[ms. illeg.]	Drunkenness
	Thomas McAloon	50	Male	Ireland	Blacksmith	Drunkenness

124

	Dennis Sullivan	52	Male	Ireland	Laborer	Dist. the Peace
	Joseph Gendron	45	Male	Canada	Weaver	Dist. the Peace
	Jane Dennis	37	Female	Fall River	Weaver	Dist. the Peace
Aug 11	James Lewis	42	Male	England	Weaver	Neglect to Support Family
	Adam Ridge	27	Male	England	Weaver	Larceny of coat & vest from Nathaniel Stockley
	Edward Dwelly	24	Male		Laborer	Larceny from the person $5.00 from Fred K.E. Manchester
	Born June 9, 1860 Lizzie A. Borden	32	Female	Fall River	at home with parents	Murder of Father & Step Mother
	Adeline St. Pierre	37	Female	Canada	Housekeeper	Safe Keeping
	William Hunter	35	Male	England	Laborer	Drunkenness
Aug 12	Edward R. Howard	26	Male	Bay Head Mass.	Hostler	Drunkenness
	Edward Rogers	35	Male	Fall River	Laborer	Drunkenness
	Julia Murphy	36	Female	Fall River	[?] Speeder tender and Housekeeper	Dist. the Peace
	Sarah Powers	37	Female	England	[?] Speeder tender	Dist. the Peace
	Mary Elisabeth Campbell	32	Female	Worcester- Mass.	Servant	Dist. the Peace
	Edward Rogers	35	Male	Fall River	Laborer	Assault on Wife Bridget
Aug 13	Sarah Powers	37	Female	England	[?] Speeder tender	Loud & lascivious behavior
	Mary E. Campbell	32	Female	Worcester Mass.	Servant	Loud & lascivious behavior
	Thomas Ratcliff	45	Male	England	Store Keeper	Assault & Battery on Mary Ratcliff
	John Irving	23	Male	England		Assault & Battery on Catherine Baker
	Solomon H. Baxter	50	Male	Falmouth Mass.	Mason	Assault & Battery

Preliminary Hearing

Judge Blaisdell had heard the evidence presented at the closed inquest held before Lizzie's arrest. On that ground, Andrew Jennings and Melvin O. Adams, Lizzie's lawyers, raised objections to his presiding over the preliminary hearing that began on August 25, 1892. Blaisdell overruled their objections and conducted the hearing to determine whether there was probable cause to believe that Lizzie had murdered her father. In so doing he ignored the old adage in the law that "the appearance of fairness is as important as fairness itself," for Blaisdell allowed himself to sit in judgment on the evidence at two separate stages of these proceedings.

The prosecution called more than twenty witnesses to the stand during the week of August 25 to 30. In addition, the prosecution was permitted to read into the record portions of Lizzie Borden's testimony from the inquest. After her statements were read aloud, Judge Blaisdell, who had known Lizzie and her family since her childhood, sadly announced that it was more probable than not that she had committed the murder of her father. She was ordered back to Taunton Jail and her case bound over for consideration by the Bristol County Grand Jury.

The questioning at this hearing suggests some of the issues and matters of evidence that were of particular interest to the prosecution in their conduct of the case. The testimony of witnesses gives us an opportunity to consider what others observed about Lizzie's relations with her family and her conduct before and after the murders. Their accounts reveal some of the contradictory evidence that made the investigation and prosecution of the Borden case so difficult.

A Note on the Text: Errors of grammar, punctuation, and spelling appear in the original transcript and are retained here.

Source: The following testimony is selected from the transcript of the preliminary hearing, a copy of which (containing Jennings' handwritten notes) was provided to the editors by the Fall River Historical Society.

Testimony of Assistant Marshal John Fleet

Q: (District Attorney): Did you have any talk with her?
A: I did, yes sir.
Q: Tell me what that was, please.
A: I asked her if she knew anything about who had killed her father and mother. . . . She said it was not her mother, that her mother was dead. She said it was not her mother, it was her step mother.
    . . . .
A: Dr. Bowen was in there, and he held the door. I told him what I wanted to do, I wanted to get in there, and search the room and search the house pretty thoroughly. He said he would see Miss Lizzie. He said she had been bothered considerable, and he would see Miss Lizzie. "Just wait a moment." I waited.
Q: He was in the room?
A: Yes; so he turned and said something to her. Of course I do not know what it was. He came back and says "is it absolutely necessary that you should search this room, Lizzie wants to

know?" I says "yes, I have got to do my duty as an officer, and I cannot leave the premises until I have searched the whole of this house." So he said something to her, and then opened the door, and I went in. I spoke to her and told her that I had got to search the house. She says "how long will it take you?" I says "it won't take me long. I have got to search it though." "I do hope you will get through soon," she says, "it will make me sick."

. . . .

Q: Have you told all you can remember that Miss Lizzie told you?
A: All I think of.
Q: Do you remember of her saying anything about the possibility of getting into her room?
A: O yes, when I went in there she said ----
Q: Which time was that?
A: The second time, when the two officers were with me.
Q: Those two, Minnehan and Wilson?
A: Yes sir. That time when I went in, she said "it is no use in searching this room" she says, "Nobody can get in here, or put anything in." She says "I always lock my door when I leave it. There is no possibly way for anybody to get anything in there."

. . . .

Q: What was Lizzie's appearance when you saw her in her room?
A: Cool and collected. (Objected to.)
Q: Was she in tears?
A: No sir.
Q: At any of the time was she in tears?
A: Not any of the time.

. . . .

Testimony of Bridget Sullivan

Q: Up to the time you let Mr. Borden in, had you seen Miss Lizzie?
A: She was up stairs at the time I let him in.
Q: Where up stairs?
A: She might be in the hall, for I heard her laugh.
Q: Up the back or front stairs?
A: The front stairs.
Q: At the time you let Mr. Borden in?
A: Yes sir.

. . . .

Q: How soon did you see her?
A: It might be five or ten minutes after, she came down stairs;
Q: When she came down, what room did she come into from the front hall?
A: In the sitting room where I was; then she went into the dining room.

127

Q: That is where Mr. Borden was?

A: Yes.

Q: Did you hear her say anything to Mr. Borden?

A: I heard her ask him if he had any mail for her. I heard her telling her father *very slowly* [underlined by Jennings in transcript] that her mother got a note, that Mrs. Borden had a note that morning, and had gone out.

Q: You heard her telling that very slowly?

A: Yes Sir, to her father.

Q: Had got a note?

A: From some sick person. Of course the conversation was very low, I did not pay any attention to it; but I heard her telling her father that.

. . . .

Testimony of Alice Russell

. . . .

Q: Do you remember of asking her where she was when her father was killed?

A: I do not remember of asking her; I might have.

Q: Do you remember of her telling you where she was when her father was killed?

A: I remember of hearing her tell it, I do not remember who asked it or whether she told it to me.

Q: What did she say?

A: She said she had come in from the barn, and saw him lying on the sofa with his face all ---

Q: Did she say anything more than that?

A: I do not know. Someone was asking her questions all the time, that I heard.

Q: Did she say what she went to the barn for?

A: I asked her that. She said she went out to get a piece of tin or iron to fix her screen or window.

Q: When was it you asked her that?

A: I do not remember that.

Q: What was it you said to her?

A: I said "what were you out in the barn for, Lizzie?"

Q: Did she say anything more in answer to it than what you have already said?

A: I do not remember; I do not think she did.

Q: Did she say what window she wanted to fix?

A: I do not remember that she did; I do not think she did.

. . . .

Q: Do you remember what kind of shoes she usually wore in the morning?

A: No Sir. I noticed nothing unusual that would attract my attention.

Q: You noticed nothing at all about her dress or appearance unusual?

A: No Sir.

Q: Did you notice whether she seemed to be panting from exertion, or anything of that kind?

A: She was not panting.

. . . .

Q: After Miss Lizzie went up stairs to her room did the officers come in there afterwards?

A: In her room, yes, I think they were coming all day; it seemed to me they were.

Q: Asking her questions?

A: Yes Sir.

Q: Did she answer them freely?

A: Yes Sir.

. . . .

Testimony of Mrs. Adelaide Churchill

. . . .

Q: Now when was this talk that you have spoken of with Lizzie where she said she thought that her father had an enemy, or must have had an enemy?

A: She sat on the stairs.

Q: That was before Miss Russell came?

A: Yes Sir.

Q: Just what was it that she said?

A: She said "father must have an enemy, for we have all been sick, and we think the milk must have been poisoned."

Q: Was there any time when something was said about some Portuguese having done it, some farm hand?

A: The policeman inquired of Miss Lizzie about a man who worked on the farm. I heard them talking about it.

. . . .

Lizzie In Jail

Lizzie was in jail for ten months, from the day of her arrest until the end of the trial. Little evidence exists of her thoughts during this period. Our only insight may come from an article that appeared in the New York *Recorder* on September 20, 1892, reporting on an interview between Lizzie Borden and the author, a Mrs. M'Guirk. Edwin Porter, in *The Fall River Tragedy,* maintains that this news story was a "magnificent fake." Others have taken the report at face value. If the account is true, it does indeed present Lizzie "in a new light." We may see in this report the portrait of a suffering woman -- or a consummate actress.

New York Recorder Interview

September 20, 1892

IN A NEW LIGHT

Lizzie Borden in Jail Awaiting Trial

How She Appeared to a Recent Visitor in Her Cell

Feels Badly Over the Talk that She Shows no Grief

"I know I am innocent, and I have made up my mind that, no matter what happens, I will try to bear it bravely and make the best of it."

The speaker was a woman. The words came slowly, and her eyes filled with tears that did not fall before they were wiped away. The woman was Lizzie Borden, who had been accused of the murder of her father, and personally has been made to appear in the eyes of the public as a monster, lacking in respect for the law, and stolid in her demeanor to such an extent that she never showed emotion at any stage of the tragedy, inquest or trial, and, as far as the Government would allow they knew, had never shown any womanly or human emotion of any sort since the public first crossed the threshold of the Borden house.

I was anxious to see if this girl, with whom I was associated several years ago in the work of the Fall River Fruit and Flower Mission, had changed her character and become a monster since the days when she used to load up the plates of vigorous young newsboys and poor children at the annual turkey dinner provided during the holidays for them and take delight in their healthy appetites.

I sought her in the Taunton Jail and found her unchanged, except that she showed traces of the great trial she has just been through. Her face was thinner, her mouth had a patient look, as if she had been schooling herself to expect and to bear any treatment, however unpleasant, and her eyes were red from the long nights of weeping. A dark shade now protects them from the glaring white light reflected from the walls of her cell.

*   *   *   *   *

"How do you get along here, Miss Borden?" I asked her as soon as extra chairs had been secured for the two visitors.

"To tell the truth, I am afraid it is beginning to tell on my health. This lack of fresh air and exercise is hard for me. I have always been out of doors a great deal, and that makes it harder. I cannot sleep nights now, and nothing they give me will produce sleep. If it were not for my friends I should break down, but as long as they stand by me I can bear it. They have been, with few exceptions, true to me all through it, and I appreciate it. If they had not, I don't know how I could have gone through with it. I certainly should have broken down. Some things

130

have been unpleasant, but while every one had been so kind to me I ought not to think of those. Marshall Hilliard has been very gentlemanly and kind to me in every way possible.

"The hardest thing for me to stand here is the night, when there is no light. They will not allow me to have even a candle to read by, and to sit in the dark all the evening is very hard; but I do not want any favors that are against the rules. Mr. Wright and his wife are very kind to me, and try to make it easier to bear, but of course, they must do their duty.

"There is one thing that hurts me very much. They say I don't show any grief. Certainly I don't in public. I never did reveal my feelings, and I cannot change my nature now. They say I don't cry. They should see me when I am alone, or sometimes with my friends. It hurts me to think people say so about me. I have tried hard" -- and Miss Borden raised her eyes to mine -- "to be brave and womanly through it all. I know I am innocent, and I have made up my mind that no matter what comes to me I will try to bear it bravely and make the best of it.

"I read and sew and write. Letters are my greatest comfort and I am allowed to correspond with my friends. I find that I have a great many friends -- more than I ever knew I had. I receive a great many letters of sympathy from people whom I don't even know. I try to answer them, but I cannot reply to all. Some of them are anonymous, and are so comforting that I wish the writers would sign them.

"Mrs. Ward -- Elizabeth Stuart Phelps -- wrote me a very sympathetic letter. Mrs. S. S. Fessenden has been a great comfort to me. She came and has told me that the Boston women were trying to get a petition signed to secure my release on bail. They tell me that is against the laws of the State, and, while I am very, very grateful to all the people who are working for me, I think perhaps it is better to stay here, but their sympathy helps to keep me up.

"I have received a great many letters from members of the W.C.T.U. and Christian Endeavor Society all over the country, and that is another help.

"It is a little thing, I suppose, but it hurt me when they said I was not willing to have my room searched. Why, I had seen so many different men that first day, and had been questioned about everything till my head was confused and in such a whirl that I could not think. I was lying down and Dr. Bowen was just preparing some medicine for me when a man came to my room and began to question me. I knew he was a policeman because he had brass buttons on his clothes. I asked the doctor:

" 'Must I see all these people now? It seems as if I cannot think a moment longer, my head pains me so.'

"He went out. When he returned he said I must see them, and then the policeman came back with another man. They spoke about my mother, and that was the time I said, 'She is not my mother, but my

131

stepmother.' I suppose, if it was necessary that I must talk to them just then, I must tell as near as I could what was right.

"As to our not putting on mourning, of which people spoke unfavorably, there was not a moment when I could think of such a thing as a hat or dress. Somebody was talking to me, it seemed, all the time about the murder and asking me questions, and I could not think of anything else. I don't suppose we would have put it on anyway, because my father was very much opposed to the practice, and had always expressed himself to us so.

"If people would only do me justice that is all I ask, but it seems as if every word I have uttered has been distorted and such a false construction placed on it that I am bewildered. I can't understand it."

There was not a trace of anger in her tones -- simply a pitiful expression. She recovered herself with an effort, and we said "good-by."

Miss Borden stood in the door of her cell looking after us until we turned the corner of the corridor.

*   *   *   *   *

The undertaker came to one of the women in the house and said: "You cannot imagine how natural Mr. Borden looks. I think it would be a comfort to the girls to see him once more."

The lady went in, and, seeing how careful all traces of the wounds had been concealed by the undertaker's art, went to Miss Emma Borden and, explaining the condition, asked her if she cared to go down to see her father and Mrs. Borden. Miss Borden had said good-by to her father when she started on her visit to Fairhaven a week before, and it seemed to her that she preferred to always carry with her the picture of him as she saw him then. Any other would be an added grief to her.

But Miss Lizzie's case was different. Before her would always be the sight of that bloody corpse that appeared to her as she discovered her father lying dead on the sofa. If it could be replaced by some other recollection her friends thought it would be better.

When the house had become a little quiet, Lizzie, accompanied by another lady and the undertaker's assistant, went down stairs to the parlor. In the dark lay the victims of the awful murder. One woman carried a light, whose rays fell on the face of the father. The daughter looked at it earnestly.

"How old father looks," she said.

How many times have other daughters said just the same thing. New England women always think of such things.

The undertaker had washed away the blood, had smoothed out the little curl that always wound about Mr. Borden's ear, and he did look older.

"How much he looks like grandfather."

And then, releasing herself from the supporting arm of the friend, she bent over and kissed her father's cold lips. Then the tears came in a great flood, and the daughter, who had tried to bear up all day and be calm because of her sister, who was not strong and who she feared would be prostrated by the blow, broke down and almost frightened the two women with her grief.

Was that "insensibility?" Was that young woman a "sphinx of coldness?"

* * * * *

The reason the house was without such conveniences was that the girls desired Mr. Borden not to make improvements, because he was talking of moving up "on the hill." Fall River's aristocracy live "on the hill," and Mr. Borden had declared to real estate agents that he was looking for a house in that section and that, although he would just as soon live in the old house, the girls desired to move and he wanted to gratify them.

He said that over a year ago to a well-known real estate agent, who had it in mind and was looking for a bargain for him.

More than that, he had offered $15,000 for a handsome house on Main street, that had just been sold, and found that his namesake, a prominent mill Treasurer, was also trying to buy it for the same sum. He told him if the younger man would get certain land at a bargain he would take half of it, and the two Andrew Bordens would build houses alike and live side by side. This was a few months ago. Naturally any one who contemplated buying a new house and removing to it would not fix up his old house, which was in a district of tenements, as he would if he intended to remain in it.

When Mr. Borden wanted to put in modern improvements, the wife and daughters said they preferred to stand it rather than have the house torn up for piping.

This does not indicate that Lizzie Borden's father was niggardly in his dealings with his family, thereby arousing the girl's indignation and supplying her with a motive for a brutal murder.

They have also tried to urge as a motive that she was kept on a mere pittance, had no spending money nor even enough for necessities, and that she was hard pressed to pay her pew rent sometimes. The fact is that both Emma and Lizzie Borden had more money than they knew how to spend. Their bank books show that they not only had $2500 in cash each, the proceeds of the sale of the old Borden homestead to their father, but Lizzie had mill and other stocks in her own name. The average dividends on mill stocks in Fall River for the past five years was over 8 per cent. Lizzie did not dress poorly. She had handsome cloth gowns and silk dresses and a fine seal sacque. She had just such an outfit as any young woman in her position had who did

133

not try to keep ahead of the fashions. Everything she wore was of fine material. She took trips whenever she pleased. Her father, a few years ago, on the return of his namesake's family from Europe, expressed his regret that he hadn't known of it in time, as the girls wanted to go to Europe and he would have been glad to send them with the Bordens. When Miss Borden did go two years ago she did not have to sell property to secure funds.

In arranging entertainments in the church or for charitable purposes, if there was any especial expense to be borne, it was always assumed by Lizzie Borden. If there was any discrepancy in footing up the results, it was she who made it up. When she bought anything the order was always for the best material and accompanied by the injunction not to spare any cost. She was not extravagant, however.

That she had plenty of money and to spare is shown by the addition she had been making regularly every month to her bank account. It is evident that lack of money could never have supplied a motive in this case.

The Grand Jury

The grand jury is a secret pre-trial proceeding where evidence presented by the prosecutor is considered by a jury to determine whether an accused person should be formally charged with a crime (by an indictment) and stand trial.

The Bristol County Grand Jury began consideration of the Borden case on November 18, 1892, adjourned on November 21, and re-convened on December 1. After hearing new testimony from Alice Russell that Lizzie had burned a dress on August 7, 1892, Lizzie was formally charged on December 2 with three crimes -- the murder of her father, the murder of her stepmother, and the murder of both. Lizzie was taken back to Taunton Jail until her arraignment in New Bedford Superior Court on May 8, 1893. She pleaded not guilty to all charges and trial was set by Judge Hammond for June 5, 1893, in New Bedford.

Public support for Lizzie grew. Many had wept in the courtroom when Jennings plead for her at the preliminary hearing. Prosecuting attorney Knowlton received letters supporting Lizzie, and one newspaper portrayed her as "the poor girl who discovered the terrible deed."

On the eve of her trial, Lizzie, on advice of counsel, dressed in mourning clothes for the first time since the murders. When she entered the courtroom on the morning of June 5, she was wearing a black dress and a black hat.

The Trial

By the time of the trial, Lizzie Borden's name had become a household word in many parts of the country, in large part because of news media fascination with the case. Covering the investigation and legal proceedings must have been a reporter's dream: some of New England's finest and best-known lawyers (one a former three-time governor of the Commonwealth) confronted each other as adversaries in the trial of a socially prominent woman charged with the brutal axe murders of both her parents!

Accounts of the trial from the New York *Times* are published here because of the *Times*'s preeminent position among the nation's newspapers. Because it was somewhat removed from the carnival-like atmosphere of southeastern Massachusetts, it might have been less influenced by regional biases and prejudices associated with the Borden case.

The *Times* reports provide a concise day-by-day account of the conduct of the trial. They show how both prosecution and defense built their cases and, in the process, reveal their attempts to exploit social, ethnic, and sexual stereotypes and values in order to influence the jurors. The *Times* reports also provide a sustained look at late nineteenth-century styles of reporting. The reporters' accounts themselves reflect American attitudes and values at this period.

New York Times Reports

A Note on the Text: Following is the full text of the *Times* coverage of the Borden case from jury selection to verdict. Typographical errors in the original have been corrected here, but errors of grammar and fact and irregular punctuation have been retained.

June 6, 1893

BORDEN MURDER TRIAL BEGUN

Jurors Impaneled to Try the Celebrated Case.

They Are to Decide the Fate of a Young Woman Accused of Murdering Her Father and Stepmother -- Crowds Surround the Court House -- No Spectators Admitted to the Trial Chamber -- The Jury to View the Premises at Fall River Where the Crime Was Committed.

NEW BEDFORD-MASS., June 5 -- The trial of Lizzie Andrew Borden for the murder of her father and stepmother began here to-day. At an early hour crowds gathered about the Court House on County Street, and many remained there all day in the hope of securing a sight of the accused young woman. Hundreds attempted to gain entrance to the building, but the rule that there should be no spectators in the courtroom was rigidly enforced.

The selection of the jury was all that was done to-day. This work was completed before 5 o'clock. The ease with which the jury was secured was a surprise to everybody, particularly as almost every man examined had formed an opinion about the case, and many of the candidates were opposed to capital punishment. The majority of the jury are farmers. All are advanced at least to middle age, both sides having objected to the presence of young men in the box.

The prosecution is represented by District Attorneys H. M. Knowlton and H. W. Moody. The attorneys for the defense are Andrew J. Jennings of Fall River, Col. Melvin O. Adams of Boston, and ex-Gov. George D. Robinson.

Each side had twenty-two challenges. When the jury was finally selected the prosecution has exhausted fourteen and the defense twenty-two. The jury is made up as follows:

Augustus Swift, New-Bedford.
John C. Finn, Taunton.
Louis D. Hedges, Taunton.
William F. Dean, Taunton.
George Potter, Westport.
Fredrick C. Wilber, Raynham.
John Wilber, Somerset.
Frank G. Cole, Attleborough.
Charles L. Richards, North Attleborough.
Lemnelk Wilber, Easton.
William Westcott, Seekonk.
Allen H. Wordell, Dartmouth.

The prisoner reached the courtroom at 11 o'clock. She entered the chamber from the jury room. She paused for a moment in the doorway and glanced over the room, apparently as self-possessed as ever. She looked unusually well. She wore a black brocade dress and black lace hat.

Presently, as she stood there, the pink flush, which those who have watched her have learned to know denotes excitement, came to her cheeks.

She stepped forward as her attorneys, Mr. Jennings and Col. Adams, advanced to meet her. She gave her hand to each and smiled as she greeted them.

The three Judges who are to preside at the trial came in soon after. Those in the chamber rose as the Judges entered. Proceedings began with prayer by the Rev. M. C. Jullen of the New-Bedford Congregational Church. He prayed that the innocent might be protected and the guilty exposed.

Then District Attorney Knowlton opened the trial. After announcing that, on account of the illness of the Attorney General,

William H. Moody of Haverhill, State's Attorney of the Eastern District, had been assigned to assist him, he moved that the jury be selected.

After a few words relating to qualifications of jurors from Chief Justice Mason, the clerk, Simeon Borden, who by the way is not a relative of the accused, called the prisoner and informed her of her right of challenge, adding that all challenges must be made before the jury was sworn. Edward G. Baker was called. Mr. Baker is an elderly man with a gray beard and pleasant features. He stood before the court and the following interrogations were propounded by the Chief Justice, this being the form in each instance:

"Are you related to the prisoner, or to Andrew J. or Abby D. Borden?"

"Have you formed or expressed an opinion in relation to this case?"

"Are you sensible of any bias or prejudice in it?"

"Have you formed any opinion that would preclude you from finding the defendant guilty of an offense punishable by death?"

Mr. Baker had an opinion, he said, that could not be changed, and he was interrogated no further.

George Winslow was the next name called, and against him the first peremptory challenge of the defense was made. He is a man with a fierce black mustache. He had expressed no opinion, and appeared perfectly willing to serve.

"Juror, look on the prisoner," commanded the Chief Justice.

Winslow rolled his eyes toward the desk.

"Prisoner, look upon the juror."

As this sentence was spoken, Attorney Jennings hurried from his seat to that of his client and whispered to her.

She arose and addressing the court, uttered the word, "Challenge."

Mr. Winslow retired.

The next man called, George Potter, was accepted as a juror. William F. Dean was accepted as the second juror. After this the proceedings took on a routine nature and the afternoon was a dull one.

The day was warm, the atmosphere inside the courtroom was oppressive, and it was an absolute relief to all concerned when the last man took his position in the jury box. To-morrow morning the indictment will be read and the prisoner will be arraigned. Then the jury will probably go to Fall River to view the scene of the tragedy.

LIZZIE BORDEN IN A FAINT

Overcome by the Prosecution's Story of the Murder

Second Day of the Great Trial at New-Bedford -- The State Opens Its Case and Examines One Witness -- Great Crowds About the Court House -- Jury Goes to Fall River and Takes a Careful View of the Borden House and Its Surroundings.

NEW-BEDFORD, MASS., June 6 -- The trial of Lizzie Borden for the murder of her father and stepmother was continued to-day. A few spectators were admitted into the court chamber, but hundreds sought admission in vain. Today, as yesterday, when the trial opened, great crowds surrounded the Court House and gazed at the brick wall of the building, as though by so doing they might gain some slight information of the celebrated trial in progress within. There were no empty seats in the courtroom, though there was by no means a crowd.

The majority of the spectators were men, but a score or more of women were in attendance.

After the reading of the indictment the outline of the Government's case was given by District Attorney William H. Moody, a young man with an earnest and impressive air.

The prisoner sat behind the Deputy Sheriff and listened to Mr. Moody's careful address with the closest attention, as calm and unmoved as ever. Her eyes looked straight toward the speaker. Indeed, the spectators seemed as much interested in the prosecutor's words as did Miss Borden, and but for the uniformed Sheriff sitting beside her she might have been taken by a stranger for one of those who had come to the courtroom with no greater interest than that of curiosity.

It was a great surprise, therefore, to everybody when just as Mr. Moody finished speaking, Miss Borden fell back in her chair in a faint.

Mr. Moody's exposition of the circumstances attending the murder of the Bordens was clear and succinct, and he evidently left a favorable impression on the minds of the jury.

He first gave a description of the house and the location of the rooms. The happenings in the Borden residence on the day of the murder were carefully gone into and dwelt upon at length. The hypothesis that none but the prisoner could have committed the murder was prominent at every point.

The two most important subjects touched related to the burning of the dress and the estrangement between Lizzie and her stepmother. The dress story was made public for the first time, and in referring to it Mr. Moody said:

"It will appear that soon after the alarm an officer was attracted by Dr. Bowen doing something at the stove, and he looked in and saw

138

what appeared to be a large roll of burned paper. The prisoner had a light-blue dress, with a small figure, which she was in the habit of wearing. Dr. Bowen will say that she had on a cheap drab-colored dress that morning."

"Mrs. Churchill will say that she had on, early, a light-blue ground dress with a diamond figure of navy blue, and the dress with light spots was not the one she had on when Mrs. Churchill arrived at the house."

"Miss Russell and the prisoner went to her bedroom soon after the former came, and the prisoner said she wanted Winwood for an undertaker. When Miss Russell came back from her errand to the undertaker's she found Lizzie coming from Emma's room with the pink wrapper. On Sunday morning Miss Russell went to the house and there saw the prisoner with a skirt in her arm, one which the prisoner had purchased that Spring, a light-blue dress, as described by Mrs. Churchill. The dress ordinarily worn in the morning was also bought in the Spring."

"She saw the prisoner standing at the stove and she was asked by Emma what she was going to do."

"I am going to burn the dress; it's all covered with paint," she answered.

"Then she commenced to tear the dress up, and was requested to be careful not to let anyone see her, and she stepped aside."

"The next day Emma said to Lizzie: 'I'm afraid the burning of the dress was the worst thing you could have done,' and Lizzie said: " 'Oh! Why did you let me do it!' "

In reference to the cause for the murder, Mr. Moody said:

"There was or come to be between prisoner and stepmother an unkindly feeling. From the nature of the case it will be impossible for us to get anything more than suggestive glimpses of this feeling from outsiders. The daughters thought that something should be done for them by way of dividing the property after thay had learned that the stepmother had been amply provided for. Then came a division and ill-feeling, and the title of 'mother' was dropped."

The prosecution would show, Mr. Moody said, that when a dress-maker of the family had spoken of the stepmother as "mother," Lizzie had chided her and said:

"Don't call her mother; we hate her; she's a mean, spiteful thing."

"When," said Mr. Moody, "an officer was seeking information from the prisoner, right in sight of the woman who had sunken under the assassin's blows, and asked: "When did you last see your mother; my mother died when I was an infant."

It would be shown, continued Mr. Moody, that there was an impossible barrier built up between the daughters and the stepmother, socially and by locks and bars.

For two hours the attorney spoke, calling attention to the constant presence of the prisoner in the house on that morning, of her careless, indifferent demeanor after the crime, and of the various incriminating incidents which marked her conduct.

Then calmly and deliberately he delivered his peroration:

"The time for hasty and inexact reasoning is past. We are to be guided from this time forth by the law and the evidence only. I adjure you gentlemen to keep your minds in the same open attitude which you have maintained to-day to the end. When that end comes, after you have heard the evidence on both sides, the arguments of the counsel and the instruction of the court, God forbid that you should step one step against the law or beyond the evidence.

"But if your minds, considering all these circumstances, are irresistibly brought to the conclusion of the guilt of the prisoner, we ask you in your verdict to declare her guilt. By so doing, and only by so doing, shall you make true deliverance of the great issues which has been submitted to you."

As the District Attorney ceased speaking the prisoner, who, with her face covered by the fan, had sat motionless for the last hour, suddenly succumbed to the strain that had been put upon her nervous system and lost consciousness. The Rev. Mr. Jubb, sitting directly in front of her and separated only by the dock rail, turned to her assistance, and Mr. Jennings, the attorney, hurried to the place from his position. Smelling salts and water were brought into immediate requisition, and soon entire consciousness returned.

In the meantime, the jury had retired to enjoy a short recess, and when they returned, Miss Borden again resumed her old position of interest, though marks of agitation were still plainly visible.

The first witness was then called. Thomas Kiernan, a civil engineer. His testimony related to plans of the house and vicinity, and before the examination was concluded a recess until to-morrow morning was ordered to allow the jury to visit the scene of the murder at Fall River.

FALL RIVER, MASS., June 6 -- The Borden jury arrived in the city from New-Bedford this afternoon at 1:20 o'clock. The jury examined carefully the inner part of the Borden house, made a survey of the outside adjoining yard, marked the distance from the house to the fence, and the situation of the lumber pile and barn loft. The jury then filed out from the yard and walked up Second Street to Dr. Bowen's house, and other points figuring in the trial were shown and looked over.

Passing to Third Street, considerable time was spent in Crowe's stoneyard, where masons were at work at the time the murder is alleged to have been committed, and the position and distance of the porch in

Dr. Chagnon's house, where the doctor's daughter was seated at the time of the murder, was also noted.

The tour was finished at 4 P.M.

June 8, 1893

BRIDGET SULLIVAN A WITNESS

The Borden's Servant Tells Her Story of the Murders.

Her Testimony Establishes the Presence of Lizzie in the House at the Time the Crime Was Committed. She Weakens the State's Case, However, by Declaring that Lizzie and Her Stepmother Lived Together Peaceably. The Prisoner's Uncle Also Testifies.

NEW BEDFORD, MASS., June 7 -- Properly speaking, this was the first day of the Borden trial, for, while the two previous days had been occupied in the preparation of preliminaries, this day was marked by the rapid presentation of testimony. The progress made was marked, and was entirely in keeping with the course presaged by the prompt selection of the jury.

Judges and attorneys are alike, interested in securing celerity, and the trial will now proceed as rapidly as possible to its conclusion.

The witnesses of the day comprised a number of persons who testified in relation to Andrew Borden's presence in the business portion of the city half an hour before his murder. John V. Morse, uncle of the prisoner, and Bridget Sullivan also testified.

Bridget Sullivan was the strongest witness of the day, but while her testimony placed Lizzie Borden, the accused, in the home at the hour of the murders, the effect of it was weakened by the statement, reiterated with emphasis, that between the accused and her stepmother there had never been, to witness's knowledge, an unkind word.

The Government needs a motive and must have one in its presentation of its side of the case. Bridget Sullivan helped the District Attorney out a bit on that point.

When she told of the food served at the Borden household, she laughed, and there was a smile on the lips of the prisoner. Others have been amused at the parsimony of the man whose possessions were more than a quarter of a million, and who fed his family on a diet of mutton and cold mutton and mutton broth.

Again the prisoner laughed when John V. Morse, her uncle, went through some mathematical calculations, the deduction of which was that the prisoner was thirty-three years of age. The latter shook her head vigorously at the assertion, and there spoke the woman.

The weakness of yesterday had vanished, and today her strong will was again in evidence. She appeared highly interested in the proceedings and watched the developments closely. Tomorrow it was expected that Medical Examiner Bowen will be a witness and the skulls will be produced.

Proceedings opened with the recall of Mr. Kiernan, the civil engineer, whose examination stopped yesterday when the jury started for Fall River to view the scene of the murder. Mr. Kiernan's testimony was devoted to locating various points upon the Borden place, describing the fences, barns, and outbuildings, explaining the arrangement of the rooms, stairs, and closets. He also gave the results of certain experiments that he had made to determine from what points of view the bodies of Mr. and Mrs. Borden could have been seen.

After Mr. Kiernan came a photographer, who exhibited pictures which he had made of the premises and of the bodies of the murdered man and his wife.

John V. Morse, uncle of the prisoner and brother of Mr. Borden's first wife, was the next witness. Mr. Morse is sixty years old. He lives at South Dartmouth. He said Mr. Borden was first married about forty-seven years ago and had three children by his first wife, one of whom was dead. He said Lizzie was thirty-three years old and Emma was forty-one.

On Wednesday, August 3, last, he went to the Borden house. He had been a visitor there several weeks before. The last time he saw Lizzie Borden before that visit he could not place. He arrived at the Borden house at 1:30 o'clock. He did not see anybody that day except Mr. and Mrs. Borden and Bridget. He ate dinner that day, but ate it alone. He left the house between three and four p.m. and got back about 8:30. He entered the front door, having been let in by Mrs. Borden. The door was shut after he went in.

He saw nobody there but the family. He went into the sitting room and went to bed about 10:30. Mrs. Borden went to bed first, going out of the rear door to the back stairs.

"While we were sitting there," said Mr. Morse, "somebody entered the front door and went upstairs to Lizzie's room. Mr. Borden and I went to bed at the same time, I going into the guest room. The prisoner's room door was closed when I went into my room, but I don't know whether it was locked or not."

The next morning witness was up at 6 o'clock and breakfasted at 7 o'clock with Mr. and Mrs. Borden on mutton, bread, coffee, sugar cakes, and bananas. He didn't recall that there was fried johnny cake on the table. At 8:40 he left the house and did not return until after the murder. Reaching the back yard he ate part of a pear before going into the house. It was not until after he had seen the bodies of Mr. and Mrs. Borden that he caught site of Lizzie Borden. On cross examination witness said that on reaching the Borden house after the murder he saw no officers in the yard, that the barn door was closed, and he heard no one inside. This contradicted the Government's allegation that officers, by immediate examination of the barn, ascertained that the prisoner could not have been there at the time of the murder.

Witness said that at the last meal Mrs. Borden brought in the food, and he saw nothing of Bridget Sullivan. On the evening previous to the murder both Mr. and Mrs. Borden were sick. Of his own knowledge he did not know whether Bridget was in the house or not. He first saw her at breakfast the day of the murder.

Abraham G. Hart, Treasurer of the Union Savings Bank of Fall River, of which Mr. Borden was President, and others were called to show at what time Mr. Borden was about town the morning of the murders. Their testimony established that he went toward his home soon after 10:30 o'clock.

Counsel Robinson stated that it was agreed, to save time, that Mr. Borden died intestate and that his property was estimated at between $200,000 and $300,000.

A buzz of excitement went around the room at 10:30 when Mr. Moody called "Bridget Sullivan." She was dressed in a maroon colored, fashionably made dress, and wore a large hat, with a large feather and black kid gloves. She leaned on the left side against the rail, looked straight at Mr. Moody and spoke so low that he had to tell her to speak louder. The prisoner remained leaning back in the seat, but changed posture so as to see witness plainly, and watched her steadily with her large eyes wide open.

Bridget said that she had worked for the Bordens for two years and ten months doing general housework, but having no care of any sleeping room except her own. She remembered Mr. Morse's visit the night before the murder. She remembered, too, that Mr. and Mrs. Borden were ill Wednesday night. She herself felt well until Thursday morning, when she waked up with a headache. She was out Wednesday night until 10:30 o'clock. She entered the house by the back door, and locked and bolted it.

Thursday, the day of the murder, she was up at 6:15 o'clock. She found all doors downstairs just as she had left them the night before. Witness then went on to detail minutely what happened at the house from the time of her getting up until the discovery of the murders.

At 1:00 o'clock the Court took a recess until 2:15.

In the afternoon Miss Borden took her seat for the first time within the bar inclosure and near her counselor. She appeared to be in good spirits and fondled a small cluster of pansies, which seem to be her favorite flowers.

While Bridget Sullivan was taking a rest, Mrs. Caroline Kelley, who lives next door to the Borden house, was put on the stand to fix the time when Mr. Borden entered his house. According to her clock it was 10:32 o'clock when she saw him at the front door.

Resuming her testimony, Bridget Sullivan said that after Mr. and Mrs. Borden and Mr. Morse had finished their breakfast Lizzie Borden came to the kitchen and said that she would have coffee and cookies for her breakfast. Bridget left Lizzie in the kitchen and went outdoors feeling ill. When she came back there was nobody in the kitchen. She fastened the screen door on the inside as she came in.

About 9 o'clock Mrs. Borden told her to wash the windows, and she went to work at once obeying the order. Her work took her first to the front of the house, where she spent some time washing the outside of the parlor windows. She passed from the front of the house to the barn several times, and also entered the kitchen. At no time did she see any strangers about the premises.

She opened the door for Mr. Borden when he came in from down town. There were several locks on the door.

"I was so bothered by those locks," said Bridget, "that I said: 'Oh, pshaw!' and Lizzie, who was either at the head of the stairs or in her room, laughed at me."

"When I let Mr. Borden in," continued the witness, "I did speak to him. He had a parcel in his hand. When he went into the dining room he sat in a chair at the head of the lounge and I went on washing my windows. Miss Lizzie came downstairs about five minutes after, and went into the dining room. I heard her ask her father if he had any mail, and she told him Mrs. Borden had received a note and had gone out. Then Mr. Borden took the key of his bedroom door and went up the back stairs. When he came down some time after he took a rocking chair in the sitting room, and I went on washing my windows. This time in the dining room."

"While I was doing this Lizzie came into the room, took the ironing board from the kitchen, and placed it in position. She asked me if I was going out that afternoon and I said I did not think I was. She said, 'Well, if you do, be sure and lock the doors, for Mrs. Borden has gone out on a sick call, and I may go out myself.' "

"Then I went up to my room and lay down, the first notice I took of any time was when I heard the City Hall clock strike 11. I think I had been there three or four minutes. Don't think I went to sleep. Heard no noise. Am able to hear the opening and closing of the screen door if its done by a careless person."

"The next thing I heard was when Lizzie called me to come down, as her father was dead; that was at least fifteen minutes after."

Counsel asked witness to describe the dress Lizzie had on that morning but objections stopped an answer. She remembered a light blue dress with a sprig on it of darker blue, bought the previous Spring.

Continuing her narrative, witness said:

"When I heard the outcry from Lizzie I went downstairs and first saw Lizzie. I cannot tell what dress she had on that morning. When I

144

came down the back way the wooden door was open, and she was leaning against the door. The screen door was shut, but I could not tell whether it was hooked or not. I went to go into the sitting room, and she said: 'Maggie' -- I was sometimes called by that name -- 'I've got to have a doctor right away. I was out in the backyard, and when I came in the screen door was open and I found father dead. Do you know where Miss Russell lives?'

"I did not, and she told me. I didn't see Dr. Bowen. Then I went to the corner of Second and Borden Streets for Miss Russell and she was not there. Then I found where she did live and told her what Lizzie wanted. I guess I ran to Dr. Bowen's but I don't know. When I came back I found Mrs. Churchill. I said when I came back, that if I knew where Mrs. Whitehead lived I would go and tell Mrs. Borden, if she was there, that Mr. Borden was very sick, and Lizzie said: 'Oh, Maggie! I'm almost sure I heard her come in; go upstairs and see if she is there.'

"I said, 'I will not go upstairs alone,' and Mrs. Churchill went up with me.

"When I got far enough on the stairs to see into the room I saw the body on the floor and ran in and stood by the foot of the bed. The door was wide open.

"When I came downstairs Lizzie was on the lounge with Miss Russell. Then I went for the second time to Dr. Bowen's house. The first I heard of the note was when Lizzie spoke to me of it. No one, to my knowledge, came to the house on that day with a message for Mrs. Borden."

On cross-examination Bridget said: "I never saw or heard anything out of the way in the family relations, and during my nearly three years of service everything was pleasant. There were times when the girls did not eat at the same table with their parents -- most of the time. They rarely arose when the old people got up. There were times when they ate alone, or separately. Lizzie and her mother always spoke to each other.

"I heard them all talking in the sitting room that morning, and Mrs. Borden asked Lizzie some questions and she answered them civilly and properly. So far as I could see, they lived congenially and pleasantly. I waited on the table when all were there, and they conversed usually in a pleasant manner.

"I don't remember anything about my conversation about Christmas time."

Here Ex-Gov. Robinson asked Bridget if she had not stated at the preliminary hearing that there was talk about Christmas time, and she replied that she did not remember saying "if Mrs. Borden was sick Lizzie did all she could for her."

Cross-examined about the screen door, Bridget admitted that she was not absolutely sure that on coming into the house after washing the windows she fastened it with the hand. All the time she was washing windows that door was unhooked. She had told Lizzie that she needn't hook it, because she would look after it, but as a matter of fact she never went near it again until she went in. Any person could walk through that door at any time, she said, without her seeing him.

There was also a chance, she said, while she was at the back of the house talking to another servant girl over the fence for anybody to enter the front of the house without her knowledge.

Speaking of the intercourse between Mr. Borden and his daughter just before the murder witness said that they got along pleasantly and that she noticed nothing unusual in Lizzie's behavior.

She said that when Lizzie called for her to come downstairs she called in such a voice that witness asked her what was the matter, and Lizzie said, "Come down quickly, Maggie, father is killed."

Asked if she had stated this the same way as before, if she had not used the word "dead," the witness replied she could not remember; it was all the same, anyhow; he was dead.

"When I got back," witness said, "from going after the people, I found Mrs. Churchill there and Dr. Bowen. Lizzie was on the lounge. Her dress was free from spots of blood and her hair was not disarranged."

At the close of Bridget Sullivan's examination, at 4:55, the court adjourned.

June 9, 1893

TWO IMPORTANT WITNESSES

Testimony That Bears Hard Against Lizzie Borden.

Miss Russell Tells How Prisoner Burned up a Dress, a Policeman Describes the Hatchet With Which It Is Alleged Mr. and Mrs. Borden Were Killed -- Counsel For Defense Say This Evidence is of Small Account -- They Expect Acquittal or Disagreement.

NEW BEDFORD, MASS., June 9 -- This has been an anxious day for Lizzie Borden, on trial here for murdering her father and stepmother. Two of the state's most important witnesses have testified and have furnished the evidence upon which reliance for a conviction is largely based by the prosecutors.

Miss Russell, a friend of the accused, told how she saw Lizzie Borden burn up a dress in the kitchen stove three days after the murders were committed, and in the story incorporated a conversation between herself and Lizzie that evidently interested the jury.

146

The impression gained from her story was that Miss Borden had some other motive for destroying the dress than to get rid of it because it was soiled and spotted with paint. This dress, the State alleges, is the one which Lizzie Borden wore when, according to its theory, she struck the blows which killed Mr. and Mrs. Borden.

Their allegations were that this dress was hidden somewhere about the house while the officers were making their search and was brought out to be destroyed at a time when no member of the police force or a detective was about.

The other important witness was the Assistant Marshal of Fall River. The striking part of his testimony was his account of the finding of the hatchet with which the State alleges the murders were committed.

Besides these two, Dr. Bowen and Mrs. Churchill were interesting witnesses. Mrs. Churchill was the first person from outside to reach the house after the murders. She came in at Lizzie Borden's request, having been called from the window of her own house which is next to the Borden place. Her account of Lizzie Borden's behavior and of the discovery of Mr. Borden's body, though not knowingly having already been told at the inquest, was followed closely by court and jury.

Dr. Bowen was the first man upon the premises after the commission of the crime. He related what he saw and repeated his conversation with Lizzie Borden. The proceedings were enlivened somewhat while the doctor was under examination by the answers he gave when counsel tried to get from him a description of the dress Lizzie Borden wore the morning of the murder. The doctor's account of his treatment of Miss Borden when she was prostrated the day of the murder and subsequently brought out the fact that he prescribed morphine quite freely. Counsel for the defense seemed to consider this statement extremely important.

It developed today that the lawyers who are fighting for Miss Borden propose to make a vigorous defense. Ex-Gov. Robinson gave the first hints today of the part he intended playing in the drama now on the boards at the New-Bedford Court House. He is going to make a more bitter fight against the Commonwealth than he ever engaged in, and every movement of the enemy will be met as far as possible with counter efforts of the most brilliant nature.

His plan was illustrated when Miss Sullivan was on the stand. He cross-examined her at length, and in his easy, subtle manner brought out a few facts of interest to him and of confusion to the other side, and while Bridget made an excellent witness, and while it was plain she was doing her best to tell the truth and nothing but the truth, there was a slight discrepancy between her statements of today and of last fall in the preliminary hearing, slight to be sure, but sufficient to make those listeners who could not understand the trend of her evidence believe that the Government was losing ground.

The defense scored one point today by getting before the jury the fact that a year before the murders the Borden house was robbed in the daytime and that five months before the barn had been robbed. The court ruled the objection out, taking the ground that the evidence described was so remote in this matter of time that they had nothing to do with the case. But ruled out or not, the jurors had heard the testimony.

Dr. Bowen, the physician who was summoned to the Borden house by Bridget Sullivan immediately after the murders, was the first witness of the day.

The Doctor said that on reaching the house he found Lizzie Borden, the accused, and Mrs. Churchill in the hall. Mrs. Churchill was a neighbor of the Bordens. He asked Lizzie what was the matter, and she replied:

"Father has been killed or stabbed."

"Where is your father?" asked the doctor.

When told that he was in the sitting room the doctor went in and there saw Mr. Borden's body lying on the sofa. He examined it and found that it was covered with blood and that the head had been cut with a sharp instrument.

Finding that Mr. Borden was dead, the doctor asked Lizzie, "Have you seen anyone?"

"No," she answered.

"Where have you been?"

"Out in the barn looking for a piece of iron."

"She told me," continued the doctor, "that she was afraid her father had had trouble with some of his tenants."

Having covered the body with a sheet, the doctor went out to telegraph for Emma Borden, Lizzie having him to do it. Just before he started for the telegraph office he asked: "Where is Mrs. Borden?"

One of the two women -- Lizzie Borden he believed -- answered the question by saying that Mrs. Borden had gone out in response to a note that had been brought to the house.

Having sent the telegram the doctor returned to the house. The first person he met was Mrs. Churchill. She told him that Mrs. Borden's body had been found upstairs. He went up to the room where it was and examined it.

"I went through the dining room and sitting room," said the doctor, "and up the front stairs, stopping a moment in the door of the guest chamber. At that point I looked over the bed and saw the prostrate form of Mrs. Borden; then I was standing in the doorway. I went around at the foot of the bed, placed my hand on her head and found a wound in the head; then I felt her pulse and found she was dead.

"I never said to anyone that she had died of fright or in a faint; but I will say this: my first thought was that she had fainted. I went downstairs and told the people Mrs. Borden was dead, that I thought she was killed by the same instrument with which Mr. Borden was killed, and that I considered it fortunate that Lizzie was out of the way."

Questioned as to Lizzie Borden's dress, the doctor said: "When I was in the house in the morning I saw that Lizzie had exchanged her dress for a pink wrapper, but didn't notice the first dress worn as to color or material."

The doctor was reminded that at the inquest he had said he had noticed the color of this dress -- it was drab. The doctor explained the variance between the two statements by saying:

"I don't pretend to describe a woman's dress, and I never did so. I only gave my impression as to its color."

District Attorney Moody showed the blue dress that is one of the exhibits in the case and got all the women in the courtroom laughing while he walked around it as it lay upon the floor and gazed at it earnestly, vainly endeavoring to locate the waist line. Lawyer Knowlton, who is a married man, came to Mr. Moody's relief and the two managed to spread the dress in such a way to display its general style. Then the doctor was asked if that was the dress that Miss Borden had on and what its color was.

"I don't know," he answered, "whether this is the dress she had on that morning or not, I call this dress a dark blue."

"When I went downstairs first," said the doctor to Mr. Adams, who cross-examined him, "Lizzie was in the kitchen, Mrs. Churchill, Miss Russell, and my wife and Bridget were in the kitchen too; they were fanning her and working over her. She afterward went to the dining room, and I told her then that she had better go to her room, where I saw her that day between 1:00 and 2:00.

"Miss Russell came to me about some medicine for her and I gave her bromo caffeine to relieve nervous excitement. I left instructions and a second dose, and carried a bottle there for her.

"I ordered morphine for her on Friday and on Saturday and Sunday. On Friday I gave her one-eighth of a grain, on Saturday I doubled it, and continued the treatment all the time up to her arrest and while she was in the station."

"Doctor, is it true that for several days before that secret inquest at Fall River she had been taking double doses of morphine?" asked Mr. Adams.

"Yes, sir."

"I suppose all physicians agree that the continued use of morphine to allay nervous irritation affects the mind, produces hallucination, does it not?"

"Yes, it does."

"That's all," said Mr. Adams triumphantly.

Bridget Sullivan was then recalled for cross-examination. After telling about the finding of the hatchets by the officers she was questioned as to the dress she wore the morning of the murder.

"I had on a blue calico dress," said she, "with a clover leaf figure in white on a dark blue background. The waist was of the same material as the skirt. I kept it on until I got a chance to change it in the afternoon for a blue gingham, plain, with a white border, which was part of the cloth. This was a lighter blue than I had on in the morning."

In answer to another question Bridget said: "While I was living in the family there was a robbery there, it occurred in the day, about 12 months before."

The court asked how this was material, occurring so far back, and Mr. Robinson explained that the robbery occurred in the middle of the day, when all the family was there.

"There was a burglary in the barn also," said Bridget, "but it was in the night-time."

The testimony concerning the robberies was excluded, an exception being noted in each case.

Bridget was asked if she had found Lizzie crying when she came downstairs in response to her cries the morning of the murder.

"I did not," she answered.

Mr. Robinson read from the stenographic report of the inquest the statement by Bridget that she had seen Miss Lizzie crying.

"That must be wrong," said Bridget; "I never said that!"

"Well," remarked Mr. Robinson, "your memory is better now than it was then, isn't it."

"I don't care what my memory is," answered Bridget, "I knew that I didn't say that, because I never saw her crying."

"Will you swear to that?"

"Yes, I'll swear to it."

Mrs. Adelaide B. Churchill, a neighbor of the Bordens, came next to the witness stand. She said that looking out of her window just after Bridget Sullivan had been sent for a doctor, "I saw Lizzie Borden inside the screen door leaning against the side of the casing." Going on with the testimony, she said:

"I opened the window and asked Lizzie: 'What is the matter?' "

"She said: 'Oh, Mrs. Churchill, come over, someone has killed father.'

"I went right out the front door over to their house. When I stepped inside the screen door she was sitting on the second step; I put my hand on her right arm and said:

"Oh, Lizzie, how did it happen?"

"She said: 'I don't know.' "

"Where were you?"

" 'I was in the barn to get a piece of iron, and when I came back I found the screen door open.' "

"She said they must have some enemies, and thought they had all been poisoned, as they were all sick in the night."

Passing on to the finding of Mrs. Borden's body, witness said:

"Then Miss Russell came, and Lizzie said she wished somebody would try to find Mrs. Borden, as she thought she heard her come in. I volunteered to go up with Bridget, and as we went up the stairs and when my head was on a level with the floor, I saw the body. Then I turned about and went back. Miss Russell said:

" 'Is there another?' and I said, 'Yes she is up there.' "

"On the day of the tragedy the agitation of Lizzie was not manifested by tears. I don't remember whether Lizzie said to me that the reason she came in from the barn was because she heard a distressed noise.

"The dress she had on while I was there was a light-blue calico or cambric, with dark, navy-blue diamond, printed. The whole dress was alike."

"I did not see any blood on her dress that morning, although I was right over her fanning and bathing her. I think I might have seen it if there was any there."

"Did she have on more than one dress?"

"I don't know."

"Anything to indicate that there was more than one dress?"

"Not a thing."

"She was afterward lying on the lounge, wasn't she, as any person would?"

"Yes."

"Bridget said to me after I got there," continued witness: " 'Mrs. Borden had a note. She hurried off. She was dusting the sitting room. She did not tell me where she was going. She generally does.' "

"Now, you've got that right?" asked counsel.

"Yes," and witness repeated the statement.

"While there," she went on, "some policemen came and asked about a 'Portuguese' who worked for Mr. Borden, and Lizzie corrected them by saying he wasn't a Portuguese, he was a Swede, and that he wasn't in Fall River, and further, that she did not suspect him. She spoke out promptly and with perfect sincerity."

When Miss Alice M. Russell, the next witness, was called, Miss Borden straightened up in her chair and began to watch the door. When Miss Russell came in she looked everywhere but where Lizzie was seated.

After a few preliminary statements, witness said: "On Wednesday night, August 3, Lizzie came to see me. We conversed, and during the evening we spoke about going to Marion. I think when she came in she

151

said: " 'I have taken your advice and am going to Marion.' " I said: 'I'm glad you're going.' I spoke about her having a good time, but she said: " 'I don't know; I feel distressed. When I was at Marion the other day the girls were laughing, and they asked me what was the matter with me.' "

"Then she spoke of her father and mother, and her being sick the night before, but Maggie was not sick. She spoke of the bread and the milk, and we talked about that, and I said it couldn't possibly be the bread, because others would have been sick.

"Lizzie said her father had enemies, and spoke of a man who came there and wanted to hire a place and of a quarrel. Then she spoke of seeing a man about the place at night, about the barn being broken into, and about the burglary in the house.

"I said," witness continued, "that I never heard of the burglary before, and Lizzie said her father had forbidden them to speak of it. She described the robbery to me, and said it was down in Mrs. Borden's room.

"Lizzie said she was afraid somebody would burn the house down, and that she was afraid to go to sleep at night. Lizzie also spoke about the manner in which her father treated his friends, and particularly of how he used Dr. Bowen at one time."

Witness went to the house the morning of the murder and staid there for several days. She is the person who saw Lizzie burn a dress. The story of the burning she told as follows:

"On Sunday I saw Lizzie standing by the stove, Emma by the sink. Lizzie had a dress skirt, and I asked her what she was going to do with it, and she said she was going to burn it, as it was all covered with paint. I said nothing and went out. When I came into the room Lizzie was tearing the dress. I said:

" 'I wouldn't let anybody see me doing that,' and she stepped one step back.

"It was the waist she was tearing: I don't remember about the skirt.

"I said: 'I'm afraid the worst thing you could have done was to burn that dress. I have been asked about your dresses,' and she said: 'Why did you let me do it?' "

The next witness, John Cunningham, raised a laugh by saying that he saw Mrs. Churchill running "triangularly" across toward the Borden house.

"Not triangularly; diagonally, you mean," suggested Mr. Adams, while Lizzie bowed her head in laughter and the court and counsel joined.

The important part of Cunningham's testimony was his statement that immediately after the murders he found the cellar door locked. This was considered a strong point for the prosecution.

152

The testimony the first part of the afternoon was tame. After the cross-examination of Cunningham, Officer Allen and Deputy Sheriff Wixon testified to their search of the Borden premises after the murder.

Then Officer Fleet was put on the stand. After corroborating the testimony of the two preceding witnesses, he described his finding the hatchets without a handle, produced by Mr. Moody in opening. This hatchet, he said, was found on the day of the murders in a box next to the chimney in the cellar. A fragment of the handle showed a free break, and the iron was covered with ashes.

Said witness examined the dresses in the house closely, but found no paint or blood on any dress.

Officer Fleet said that after viewing the body of Mrs. Borden the morning of the murders, he had a talk with Lizzie Borden.

"I asked her," said witness, "if she knew anything about the murder. She said all she knew was that her father came home at 10:30 or 10:45, went into the sitting room, sat down, took out some papers and looked over them. She was ironing at the time in the dining room, and seeing that her father was feeble she went in and assisted him.

"After she had seen him on the sofa, she went out into the barn. Went up in the loft, and remained there half an hour. When she came in she said she found the body as it then was.

"I asked her if she had any idea who had killed her father and mother. Then she said:

"'She is not my mother, Sir, but my stepmother; my mother died when I was a child.'

"Miss Russell said: 'Tell him all; tell him what you told me.' "

Witness told of his searching the house, and particularly described his examination of the dresses he found.

"Were you looking for paint?" asked counsel.

"No."

"Were you looking for blood?"

"Yes."

"If there had been any blood there do you think you could have seen it?"

"I think I could. If there had been any paint there I don't think I could have seen it, unless I looked closely."

At this point the court adjourned until 9:00 o'clock tomorrow.

FALL RIVER, Mass., June 8 -- There is much talk in this city tonight about Assistant Marshall Fleet's story in New-Bedford regarding the axe found in the Borden house, supposed to have been used in the Borden murder.

For many weeks stories about the hatchet and axes have been published, but in the ten months that have passed the Assistant Marshall has kept the secret that the probable weapon was found the day the murder took place.

Mr. Fleet's description of the weapon was so minute, and his reputation for veracity and honorable dealing in police and private matters is so well known here that belief is general that he has really found the weapon with which the deed was committed.

Many of Lizzie Borden's friends feel much exercised over the testimony.

June 10, 1893

BREAK IN THE STATE'S CASE

Police Witnesses in the Borden Case Disagree

One of Them Swears That He Saw the Piece of Hatchet Handle Alleged to be Missing in the Very Box Where the Hatchet Was Found -- If He Did the Prosecution's Theory of the Murders Falls in an Important Respect -- A Momentous Question to be Decided.

NEW BEDFORD, MASS., June 9 -- The police of Fall River told their story of the Borden tragedy today. All the details of the affair were rehearsed with a painful exactness; all the scenes in and about that ill-fated house were placed in clear, and almost startling colors.

But while these witnesses told stories damaging to the defense, in the same breath they nearly destroyed the Government's hope of producing the instrument with which the deed was done and nearly, although not completely, disposed of the last hatchet which has been brought forward as the instrument which took the lives of Andrew Borden and his wife.

Each witness by his evidence assisted to place the prisoner in the house at the hour and almost the moment when the homicides were committed. So far all went well for the prosecution, but then came an open discrepancy in the Government's testimony.

Assistant Marshal Fleet told his story of the finding of a hatchet without a handle. It was discovered in the cellar of the Borden house on the very day of the tragedy. Its blade was covered with ashes as if someone might have been trying to remove blood stains from it, and the fact that the handle was broken close to the steel looked suspicious.

Marshal Fleet said that the break was a fresh one, and that the broken handle was not to be found.

Then came Officer Mullaly to tell the story of the finding of the hatchet. He said that there was a broken piece of wood beside the hatchet when it was found which seemed to belong to the hatchet. He further testified that Fleet took this supposed handle and examined it.

Assistant Marshal Fleet, when he was recalled, flatly denied the statement of Mullaly.

Here was a break in the prosecution's case, and the attorneys for the defense were greatly elated.

One of the witnesses today testified that the blood from Mr. Borden's body when first examined was clear, while Mrs. Borden's was dark and thick. The purpose of this testimony was to show that Mrs. Borden was killed some time before her husband.

An interesting question is to be discussed tomorrow by counsel. It is whether or not the evidence given by Lizzie Borden at the inquest shall be read to the jury.

The attorneys for the defense will take the negative on this question. They will set up, in the first place, that Miss Borden was practically forced to testify at that inquest, and will urge that anything she may have said at that time should not be brought out in this trial, inasmuch as her statements were not freely made.

Further than this, they will assert that, even if Miss Borden had testified at the inquest without coercion, she was in such a condition that she hardly knew what she was about. In support of this proposition the testimony of Dr. Bowen given yesterday will be cited.

The doctor said that from the day of the murders up to the time of the inquest he was giving Miss Borden doses of morphine, doses of one-eighth of a grain at first and double that much later.

Yesterday, Mr. Adams while examining the doctor, asked him if the continual use of opium to allay nervous irritation would not affect the patient's mind and produce hallucinations. The doctor answered this question in the affirmative and Mr. Adams seemed well pleased.

Since court opened, Assistant Marshal Fleet was recalled for cross-examination. Ex-Gov. Robinson questioned him. He said that he arrived at the Borden house before 12 o'clock and at once visited all the rooms downstairs and upstairs.

"Then", said he, "I went to the cellar and found Officers Mullaly and Devine in the cellar. The former had some axes on the floor of the washroom -- two of them and two hatchets. I was told by Mullaly that the hatchets were taken from the middle cellar on the southside. The hatchets were found near the chimney, in the same box where the broken-handled hatchet was found.

"I put the claw-handled hatchet in the cellar room over the stairs. Officer Harrington saw me put it there."

"Oh, he was there, was he? You haven't told me about that," said Mr. Robinson.

"There's a good many things I haven't told you about," answered the officer.

"I afterward searched the clothes closets. Then I went to the attic. I searched all the rooms, but did not open a trunk; we just looked in, but did not disturb anything. We looked into everything we could look into, but not very closely. We were not there long. There was some clothing in one of the rooms, but we did not take it down. I didn't discover any blood on Bridget's dresses; I did not look closely, and I didn't say today there was or there was not blood on them."

"What did you really look at these dresses for?"

"For blood or anything else."

"And yet you didn't see anything at all or make a very thorough examination?"

"Not very."

"The doors in all parts of the house," continued the witness, "were generously supplied with locks. There was nothing extraordinary that Lizzie's room should have a lock or that the door leading to the father's room should be locked, or that the guest chamber should be provided with a lock. Wherever we went the doors were all provided with locks. Even in the attic the same conditions existed."

"When did you find the hatchet with the broken handle?"

"On the second visit."

"Why didn't you tell me so?"

"You didn't ask me."

"Don't you know I am asking for all the information I can get about this case?"

"Yes, but you didn't ask me about this. I found it in the box where other tools were. It was in the box by the chimney."

"There was ash dust," said witness, "however, all over everything, just like any other cellar where ashes are kept. It was natural ashes should be on these things. The claw-head, apparently had been cleaned. There was a spot on the handle, but I don't see it now. It was a small spot, but I couldn't say what it was. It was red, and might be red paint or blood.

"Miss Lizzie had no chance to clean that hatchet. I am sure of that.

"When I first saw that clawhead there was one red spot on the blade."

Counsel showed the clawhead hatchet to the jury, calling attention to the location of a mark on the blade.

"There was dust on the broken-handled hatchet," continued witness, "as though it might have got into the ashpile. There were ashes on the end, on the handle, but none on the broken end, I think."

It was shown to witness that yesterday he had said there was ash dust on the broken part. He said that he must have misunderstood the question, and he could explain in no other way why he had made different statements. He was asked to take his pick of the two statements, and said he would say he did not discover any ashes there, although there might have been some there. He would leave the matter by saying that he did not know whether there were any ashes on the broken part or not.

On his redirect examination witness said that the reason why he kept the claw-head hatchet was because it looked as though it had been washed and had a spot on it which looked like blood.

Officer Harrington of the Fall River police was the next witness. He said that soon after he reached the Borden house he had a talk with Lizzie Borden.

"I asked her," said the officer, "to tell me all she knew, but she said:

" 'I can tell you nothing at all. Father came home from the Post Office with a small package in his hand. I asked him if he had any mail for me, then I went away in the yard and into the barn. I heard nobody in the meantime.'

"She said she was up in the loft. I asked her if the motive was robbery and she said no -- everything was all right, even to the watch in her father's pocket and the ring on his finger. I asked her if she had any reason to suspect anybody and she said 'No,' hesitantly.

"I asked her why she hesitated, and then she told me about the man with whom her father had quarrelled before that date."

Witness said in answer to a question as to Lizzie's condition at the time she was being questioned by him that she was cool, and at no time was she in tears. At no time was there any breaking of the voice.

"I asked her," continued witness, "how she fixed the time of her stay in the barn so accurately, and she said she was sure she was there 20 minutes and not a half an hour."

Witness gave such a detailed description of Lizzie Borden's dress that she smiled and others laughed.

"When I was in the kitchen," said witness, "I saw Dr. Bowen with some scraps of paper in his hand. I asked him what they were, and he answered that he guessed they were nothing, and he started to arrange them so as to show me what they were. I saw the word "Ellen" written in lead pencil. The doctor then lifted the lid from the stove, and I noticed the fire was nearly extinguished. There had been some paper burned which still held a cylindrical form about a foot long and perhaps two inches in diameter. I can't tell what sort of paper it was.

"About that time," witness went on, "Dr. Dolan came in with three hatchets, I think, in his hand, and two or three cans. I stood guard over them until I was sent away by the City Marshal."

On cross-examination, Officer Harrington contradicted Assistant Marshal Fleet as to the place where the clawhead hatchet was found. He said the hatchet was found on the chopping block.

Capt. Patrick Doherty of the Fall River police, who was the next to testify, said that he reached the Borden house just before noon the day of the murders. He described his going into the house and his wanderings about. He was asked to state what Dr. Bowen had said

157

about the body, but the court ruled the question out as being incompetent.

"Mrs. Borden," said witness, "when I saw her was lying face down, with her hands up over her head; the head was close to the wall, six or seven inches away. I lifted the head and looked at it. The furniture in the room was not disturbed that I remember. On the floor was a bunch of hair as big as my fist, which appeared to have been cut off. The first time I went there I did not see Miss Borden, Miss Russell, or Mrs. Churchill.

"During the afternoon I saw Miss Borden in the kitchen. I asked her where she was when this was done. She said it must have been while she was in the barn. She heard no outcries or screams, but she did hear some noise like scraping. Then I had some talk with Bridget and Mr. Mullaly and I went about the house and looked it over pretty thoroughly.

"I saw Miss Borden in her room that day before I went away. I went to her room and she came to the door and said, 'One minute,' and went in and about the door. It was a minute before she opened it. She looked about the room. When she was downstairs I thought she had on a light blue dress, with a small spot, and there was a bosom to the dress."

Dress shown with light sprigs on a dark blue ground. Witness said he did not think this was the one.

Cross-examined, witness said:

"I don't know if I ever saw that broken-handled hatchet before today. Lieut. Edson brought away the two axes and two hatchets. This was on Friday morning about 6:30."

Officer Michael Mullaly of the Fall River police, who followed Hogarty on the witness stand, said he was sent to the Borden house and arrived there at 11:37 o'clock. He looked at his watch when he got there.

"I saw Miss Borden for a moment," said witness, "and she told me she was in the yard, and when she came in her father was dead on the sofa. She told me what property her father had on his person and she told me what it was.

"I asked her if there were any hatchets or axes on the premises, and she said Bridget Sullivan would show me where they were.

"Officer Doherty searched the body and found things as Lizzie had said they were. Then I went to where Mrs. Borden was lying and found much blood of a thicker nature. Then I went to the attic. Bridget was with us, opened all the doors for us, and we searched them.

"Then we looked into the cellar, looking for the hatchets. Bridget accompanied us. She took from a box two hatchets. This was in the wood cellar, near the chimney. The box was on a shelf, which she reached up for, taking them out and handing them to me."

Witness described his going to the barn, and told how he went about the house again and to the cellar the second time, searched about there again.

"In the afternoon," he said, "I was down there with Fleet when he took from a box a hatchet like this, (pointing to the broken-handled one), and then he put it back again. The break in the wood was a fresh one."

Resuming his testimony after recess, Mullaly spoke of the little hatchet and described its appearance about as did the other witnesses. He examined the cellar thoroughly, but found nothing. Went through the attic again and outside on the premises, but found nothing of a suspicious nature, nor did he find any appearance of blood anywhere. Miss Borden told him about seeing a man about the house a short time before who was dressed in dark clothes and was about the size of Officer Hyde.

On cross-examination Mullaly said he had made, so far as he knew, a thorough search of the premises, but had found nothing of moment. He went into Bridget's room and looked about, but did not remove the clothing on the bed. He was not sure there was a trunk in her room, and did not think there was a closet there. He did not examine any dresses there. He had no recollection of visiting Mr. Borden's room. Officer Doherty was with him most of the time. At the time he went into the cellar Officers Allen and Doherty and Bridget Sullivan were with him.

Mullaly and Bridget showed him where the hatchets were because Miss Borden told him she would show where they were. She made no search, but went directly to where they were. She did not hesitate in the slightest.

Mullaly said he thought that the smaller of the two hatchets with handles had about the same appearance when found that it had now. It was clean and clear of dust. The two axes he found, and they were dusty.

In speaking of the broken-handled hatchet, witness said at the time Fleet found the hatchet in the box the handle had been broken, and he saw a piece of handle corresponding to the long part of the one broken off the light hatchet.

District Attorney Knowlton, on being asked for this extra piece of handle, said he did not have it, and this was the first time he had ever heard of it.

Mr. Fleet was recalled and asked about the broken-handled hatchet, where he found it and what else he found. He said he found nothing in the nature of a piece of wood with a new break in it. There was a decided sensation as Fleet stepped from the stand.

Charles H. Wilson, police officer of Fall River, says he went to the Borden house about 1 o'clock in the afternoon. Witness said he heard

159

the talk of Miss Borden and Mr. Fleet. Mr. Fleet asked her where her mother was and she answered that she saw her last in the guest chamber about 9 o'clock, and that she had received a note and gone out.

District Attorney Knowlton here called attention to his desire to have somebody sent to Fall River to the Borden house to see if that piece of wood referred to above was in the box; all he wanted was justice.

"That's all we want," said Ex-Gov. Robinson.

"Well, you haven't any objection to our sending an officer over there to see about it, have you?" asked Mr. Knowlton.

"No such question has arisen yet," said Mr. Robinson, "and we will pass it now unless the court rules against it."

The court decided it was not necessary to proceed any further just now.

Annie M. White, the court stenographer of Bristol County, was called to tell her story of what took place at the inquest in Fall River. Asked if there was some conversation between the District Attorney and Miss Borden, Mr. Robinson asked that the further examination of this witness be dispensed with until a full explanation could be made of the important question which the testimony, proposed to be submitted, brought up.

A lengthy consultation took place between the Chief Justice and senior counsel, while the junior counsel for the defense put their heads together to see when they could get to Fall River and examine the box referred to by Mullaly.

The result of the consultation was that Miss White got no further in her testimony, and George A. Pettes was called. On the 4th of August last he passed the Borden house between 9 and 10 a.m., but saw no one when he was going down. When he came back he saw Bridget nearly at the front door. She had a pail and brush.

"I was in Wade's store about 11 or after," continued witness, "when I heard of the trouble at the Borden house. When I got there I saw Mrs. Churchill and Bridget, Frank Wixon, and Dr. Bowen. I went into the room where Mr. Borden was. The blood was quite fresh, and I think I could detect a movement of the blood."

The witness described the position of Mrs. Borden about as the others did. He went to her head to raise it up or to see what condition it was in. He found the hair was dry and matted, and as he passed his hand over it no moisture came away on it. The blood on the floor was dry and shiny and he saw no fresh blood anywhere.

Witness said he had an opinion as to the priority of death, but the defense objected to using the witness as an expert. Witness was not used as an expert, the court ruled against it.

After some relatively unimportant testimony had been given by Andrew J. O'German and Mrs. Churchill, the court adjourned until 9

160

o'clock tomorrow. The first business tomorrow will be the presentation of arguments concerning the admissibility of Miss White's testimony.

Before dismissing the jurors Chief Justice Mason cautioned them against discussing the case and reminded them that, as they could hear but one part at a time, they must be careful about making up their minds as to the value of any of the evidence until it was all in and carefully weighed.

June 11, 1893

MORE TALK ABOUT HATCHETS

Another Contradiction by Witnesses in Borden Case.

Policemen Tell Different Stories About an Important Matter -- Testimony Tending to Show that Lizzie Borden Was Not in the Barn at the Time of the Murders -- Argument Upon the Admissibility of the Prisoner's Testimony Before the Inquest to Take Place Monday.

NEW-BEDFORD, MASS., June 10 -- The evidence in the Borden trial today was chiefly corroborative of prior testimony and not of great value to either side. One witness, however, was badly confused on cross-examination, and others admitted several facts of some importance to the defense.

The first thing was the testimony of Officers Edson and Mahoney that they tried last night to search the Borden cellar for the hatchet handle, about which Mullaly testified yesterday, but were not allowed to enter.

The officers would not have found the handle had they been allowed to enter the house and search the cellar. At least they would not have found it had they not been better searchers than Charles J. Holmes, one of the counsel for the defense. Mr. Holmes was at the Borden house last night looking for the hatchet handle -- was probably there while the officers were cooling their heels at the door. He didn't find what he was looking for.

Officer Edson had a good deal to say in his testimony about hatchets and so did all the other witnesses. There was direct contradiction between two of the witnesses relating to one of the hatchets.

Mr. Edson and Capt. Desmond each claimed that he wrapped up the hatchet in a newspaper. Capt. Desmond was closely cross-examined upon this point, but he stuck to his story.

When counsel for the defense gave him the hatchet and asked him to show how he had wrapped it up, he unhesitantly did what he was asked, and insisted that the original wrapping up was just like that shown to the jury.

161

This was rather startling in view of the fact that a half hour before Officer Edson had with great positiveness declared that it was he who did the wrapping.

The Captain was examined with great care as to his visit to the barn loft the day of the murders. It was considered important by the counsel for the State that he had found no tracks upon the dust-covered floor of the loft. The purpose of this testimony was evidently to impeach the statement of Miss Lizzie Borden that she was in the barn when the murders were committed.

There was considerable heard about the blue dress with the diamond spots which Lizzie Borden wore the morning of the murders. That dress is considered one of the great features of the trial.

Argument upon the admissibility of Miss Borden's testimony before the inquest was postponed until Monday, but counsel agreed upon a statement of facts which was submitted to the court. This statement will be the basis of the argument.

The underlying fact in the statement is the one referred to in today's *New-York Times* -- the fact that Miss Borden, while under suspicion and practically under arrest, was dragged before the Coroner's Jury and compelled to testify, her request being denied, that counsel be allowed to come before the jury and advise her.

Lieut. F. L. Edson of the Fall River police was the first witness of the day. He was examined at first relative to a visit he made to the Borden house last night. He was sent there to search for the piece of a hatchet handle which Officer Mullaly said he saw in the box where the hatchet with a broken handle was found.

"Did you go to the Borden house last night?" asked Assistant District Attorney Moody.

"I did," was the answer.

"Did you go up to the door and ring the bell?"

"I did."

"Who lives there now?"

"Miss Emma Borden."

"Whom did you see?"

"I saw a servant."

"Did you get into the house?"

"I did not."

"Did you use all persuasive means to ask a entrance?"

"I did, but I could not get in."

Witness was then inquired of about his visit to the Borden house the morning of August 5, the day after the murders.

"On the morning of the 5th of Aug.," said witness, "I took two wood axes, a hand axe, and a small shingle hatchet from the Borden house. The axes and hatchets were taken to the Central Police Station, and I haven't had anything to do with them since. When I was at the

162

house on the morning of the 5th I was talking with Emma, and Lizzie came in and asked Bridget whether she was sure the back cellar door was locked, and the answer was, 'Yes'.

"I took part in a search of the premises on the 8th. Desmond, Connors, Quigley, Medley, and an outsider, Mr. A. J. Jennings, and Inspector Hanscom were there also; they came there when we were searching. So far as I know, Hanscom was never associated with the police in any work."

On cross-examination witness said: "The morning of the 8th Officer Medley took away a hatchet head. He showed it to me. It was wrapped up in a paper. It had no handle and he had no handle in his possession; I saw no handle there. I don't know where he got this hatchet. During my search of the cellar I found nothing bearing upon this case, and at that time I was satisfied there was nothing. I was there as long as I wanted to be and had every opportunity to search that I wanted. Mr. Jennings never interferred; on the contrary, he said it was perfectly proper. Mr. Hanscom never interferred with us, and he went away in a short time after we went to work. They took away lead I think; I am not sure, but they were looking at it. While we were there Mr. Seaver and McHenry came. They looked about the place."

"Who is this Seaver?"

"He is a state detective."

"Who is McHenry?"

"He was a friend of Seaver's."

"What was he doing there?"

"Just looking around."

"Where does he belong?"

"He hails from Providence then."

"Where does he hail from now?"

"The last time I heard of him he was in New York."

"Still travelling?"

"I don't know."

"Still detecting?"

"I don't know."

"Did he ever help you officers?"

"Not that I know of."

"Has he been around police headquarters since?"

"Yes, Sir."

"How long has he been there?" (Objected to, but allowed.)

Witness said, continuing: "I don't recall having seen him prior to the tragedy. I don't know whether he was paid by the City for his service."

Other questions brought out the fact that nearly all the Fall River police prominent in this case have been promoted since the murder except Mullaly, who yesterday contradicted Fleet.

After Policeman Samuel F. Mahoney had given some unimportant testimony, William H. Medley, Inspector of Police, Fall River, was sworn. He reached the Borden house at 11:40 a.m. the day of the murder.

"I asked Lizzie," said witness, "where she was when this thing occurred, and she said she was in the barn. I asked her if she had any idea who did it, and she said she had not. I asked her where Bridget was, and she said she was upstairs. During this time the officers were arriving fast, and searching was going on all over the place.

"I went right out into the barn. The door was locked with a hasp. When I went to this door there were quite a number out there. After I went into the barn I went upstairs and I looked about, my view crossing the line of the barn floor. The dust was thick, and putting my hand down I brought away an impression of dust and left the mark plainly in the dust on the floor."

"And could you discern your finger marks?"

"I could."

"Did you see any other footsteps than your own up there in the barn?"

"I did not."

"Did you look for others?"

"I did."

Witness then told about the finding of the hatchet without a handle. Said he: "On the Monday following the murder I went to the house and took part in the search. I went into the cellar. On a block, I think a chopping block, I found a box, in which, besides the handless hatchet, was a lot of old rubbish. Desmond was nearby at the time, and I showed it to him. In consequence of what he told me I took it to the Marshal, and I haven't had possession of it since that time.

"I never had possession of any other part of the handle except that which was on the hatchet."

Here witness identified the small hatchet.

Continuing he said: "When I saw it first it was covered with dust, like the dust of ashes, which had blown over it. I noticed that the break in the handle was new, but did not notice any dust or ashes at the place of the fracture. I could not say whether the dust adhered or was loose."

On cross-examination, Medley said McHenry was engaged with him on the case. The prisoner leaned forward and anxiously watched the witness as he said that it was more than likely he consulted Marshal Hilliard about the case when McHenry was present.

Capt. Dennis Desmond of the Fall River police force came next:

"On Saturday following the 4th day of August," he said, "I made an examination of the dresses in the house. I saw nothing which attracted my attention in any of them. I saw none soiled with paint or spots of any sort. Upon the Monday following I was in command of a search party. Medley was in the squad.

"During the progress of the search in the cellar he showed me a small hatchet. I examined it closely at the time, and saw that it was all dirty and covered with dust of a coarse nature, not a sediment which might have fallen on it by long rest in one position. There were many spots on it, and the heaviest dust was on the sides of the blade. The break in the handle appeared much fresher than now. I handled the box from which the hatchet came. It sat on a larger one. The small box contained mostly old iron, nails and bolts. I didn't observe the rest of the articles with reference to dust in particular, only that there was a much lighter coat; the dust about the cellar was entirely different from that on the hatchet; it was much finer. In consequence of what I told Officer Medley he took the hatchet with him. I gave it to him wrapped up in a newspaper. I was not at the house on August 4 at all."

On cross-examination, referring to his visit of Saturday, witness said:

"We went into all the rooms in the attic and searched carefully. The doors were all opened for us. There was a trunk in the attic which bothered us about opening. We had to send downstairs for assistance to open it. I don't know whether it was Lizzie or Emma who showed us how to open it. There was nothing in it that we wanted.

"Then, after Assistant Marshal Fleet looked out over the roof we went down into Mrs. Borden's room. I guess that we gave it a thorough search, but we did not take the bed apart. In the room nearby, where the safe was, it seems to me there were both dresses and men's clothes. I did all I could to find something, but failed.

"I could find no blood, grease, or paint spots. We searched Lizzie's room and the little alcove and the bookcase and desk and closet, examined the carpet, and gave the place a thorough search. Then we went into Emma's room and examined it the same way. Then we went through the first floor the same way, making an absolute and unrestrained search of the premises."

After Desmond came George F. Seaver, State Detective. He said:

"I went to the Borden house August 4 arriving there about 5 o'clock. I took measurements with reference to blood spots, but this was later on. On Saturday, I was there during the search by Capt. Desmond and his men.

"That was the day I first saw the hatchet with the broken handle. The hatchet was in a box in the cellar. The box was lying at that time on or near the floor, perhaps a foot from the floor. I handled the hatchet and looked in the box to see if there was any handle to it, but I saw none. The sides of the hatchet were covered with coarse ashes. There was a piece of wood in the eye of the hatchet. It had the appearance of being freshly broken off.

"On Saturday I made, in connection with others, some search among the dresses. I examined some dresses in the large closet over the front hall. I went in and opened the blinds, and then I took the dresses from the hook and passed them to Capt. Fleet, all except a few heavy silk dresses which hung up in the corner. There was nothing on any of those dresses.

"I saw no light blue dress with diamond spots on it and soiled on the bottom. That was the only place I searched for dresses."

Witness was asked if he had made a sufficiently thorough examination to have discovered the blue dress described had it been there, but the defense objected and the answer was excluded.

On cross-examination, witness said:

"When I first saw that broken-handled hatchet, the piece now out was in, but I do not know how those chips were taken off the side."

Witness was asked to look at the piece of wood and tell when some little slivers had been taken off.

He said he should think recently -- quite recently. Asked if he had had any experience with wood, witness said he had been a carpenter by trade before he went into the State detective position.

"Well, then, what kind of wood is that?"

"I can't tell; it may be oak or ash."

"How long have those slivers been off?"

"I can't tell."

"As a carpenter, now?"

"I can't tell."

"When was the session of the Grand Jury held?"

"Last November."

"Mightn't they have been off six months?"

"I don't think so."

"From your knowledge of wood would you undertake to say, within three months, when those slivers were taken off?"

"No, sir."

"Mr. Fleet and I," said witness, turning to another subject, "were the only ones who examined those dresses in the closet that day. We looked into a trunk and I think two or three boxes. I think there were 12 or 15 dresses there at the time. Wasn't looking for a 'bell' skirt or a blouse waist or any particular color. Think I saw a black dress. I can't tell what kind of dresses there were there; I don't know whether it was challie, or alpaca, or cambric or bedford cord. I am not in that business, and I wouldn't swear whether there was a blue dress there or not. I recognize this dress shown in court, [blue, with running white sprigs.] and saw Lizzie with it on that day."

"What, when she was in the funeral?"

"Oh, no."

"What did she have on then?"

"I don't know."

"Didn't she have a bedford cord on?"

"I don't know."

"Can't you tell me now what the first dress was you took down?"

"I think it was a silk dress."

"The second one?"

"It was a black one."

"Did you see any blue dress there?"

"I don't know. Think I did, but if there was one there I didn't discover any blood or paint on it, but I cannot describe those dresses to you.

"I was in the house when the dress which Lizzie wore that morning was asked for. I don't recall where it came from and if it came from the second hook in that closet I don't remember."

Mr. Seaver was the last witness examined today. When he had finished his testimony the court adjourned until 9 o'clock Monday morning.

The following agreed statement relative to the admissibility of Miss Borden's evidence has been signed by her and by the District Attorney. This statement is to be the basis of the argument next Monday:

1. The declarations offered are the testimony under oath, of the accused in a judicial proceeding, namely, an inquest as to the cause of death of the two persons named in the indictment now on trial, duly notified and held by and before the District Court in Fall River, in accordance with the provisions of the public statutes.

2. The defendant was not then under arrest, but three days before the time of giving such testimony was notified by the City Marshal and Mayor of Fall River that she was suspected of committing the crimes charged in the indictment on trial, and the house and the inmates, including the defendant, were thereafter, until her arrest, under the constant observation of police officers of Fall River specially detailed for that purpose and stationed around the house.

3. That before she so testified she was duly summoned by a subpoena to attend said inquest and testify thereat.

4. That before she so testified she requested, through her counsel, A. J. Jennings, of the District Attorney and the Judge to preside and presiding at said inquest, the privilege to have her said counsel there present, which request was refused by both the District Attorney and the Judge, and said counsel was not present.

5. That when her testimony so given was concluded, she was not allowed to leave the Court House, and was thereupon placed under arrest upon a warrant issued upon the charge and accusation of having committed the crimes set forth in this indictment. Said warrant was issued upon a complaint sworn to by said City Marshal after the

conclusion of the testimony of the defendant at the inquest. Being the same complaint upon which the defendant was tried before said District Court and held to answer before the Grand Jury. Said City Marshal was present at the inquest when the defendant testified.

6. Prior to said inquest, to wit, on the next day before she was summoned as above stated, a complaint charging her with the murder of the two persons as to whose deaths the inquest was held was sworn to by said City Marshal. The City Marshal did not serve this warrant and the defendant was not informed of it. No action was taken on said warrant, but the same was returned after the conclusion of the defendant's testimony and before the issuance of the warrant upon which she was arrested.

7. That before giving her testimony as above, she was not cautioned by said court or said District Attorney that she was not obliged to testify to anything which might incriminate herself, but said counsel was informed that he could, before defendant testified, confer with her in relation thereto, and he did.

8. The nature and character of the testimony offered may be considered by the court in determining the question of its admissibility.

June 13, 1893

BIG GAIN FOR LIZZIE BORDEN

Her Testimony at the Inquest Not To Go To the Jury

Brilliant Argument in Her Behalf by Ex-Gov. Robinson -- Medical Examiner Dolan the Chief Witness Yesterday -- He Exhibits Plaster Casts of the Heads of Mr. and Mrs. Borden and Tells How They Were Hacked by a Hatchet -- Twenty-nine Wounds in All.

NEW-BEDFORD, MASS., June 12 -- The defense won a decided advantage today when the court excluded as evidence the testimony given by Lizzie Borden at the inquest heard soon after her father and stepmother were murdered in Fall River.

There have been several breaks in the prosecution's case, none so bad as the one made by the decision as to the prisoner's evidence at the inquest. The decision will go a great way toward making Lizzie Borden a free woman.

At the inquest, the defendant, then practically, though not nominally, under arrest for the killing of her father and stepmother, was plied with questions by District Attorney Knowlton. She was not allowed to have counsel, nor was she warned that testimony there given by her might tend to incriminate her at a later time.

The statements made by her at the inquest were of a contradictory character, extremely damaging to her interests, and if they could have been introduced at the present trial might have been hard to dispose of.

168

The prosecution argued that the statements made by the defendant at the inquest were under the law, voluntary and on this ground should be admitted as evidence, while the defense set forth that she was under police supervision and that a pocket warrant had already been issued for her arrest. The inquest, it was further set forth, was practically an examination to determine her guilt or innocence. The discussion and consideration of the question for the competency of this testimony occupied nearly all the morning.

This afternoon, Dr. Dolan, Medical Examiner of Fall River, took the stand and described minutely the character and extent of the wounds inflicted on the victims of the homicide. An autopsy was performed in the family cemetery after the burial of the bodies and the heads were both removed and prepared by Dr. Dolan.

They are now in his possession, but were not brought into court today, plaster casts being used to indicate the injuries inflicted.

It has been a hard day for the prisoner. She is far from well, and while the Presiding Justice was rendering the court's opinion relative to the competency of her testimony she showed signs of great agitation. After she learned that the decision was favorable she put her fan to her eyes and wept for some time.

Once in the day she was compelled to leave the courtroom because of illness.

On the opening of court the question of the admissibility of the defendant's declarations at the inquest, when under suspicion before her arrest, was argued, the jury having been sent out of the room.

Mr. Moody, for the State, argued that, according to authority, principle, and practice, the testimony was admissible. He said that the defendant's conduct and declarations showing consciousness of guilt would be admissible, even if the defense should claim that a confession would not be. He did not understand there was any claim that the inquest was made in violation of the laws of the Commonwealth. The inference from the statute was that an inquest might be of a strictly private nature or it might not, as the language was that any or all persons besides the one testifying might be excluded.

The evidence was not in the nature of a confession, but of a denial. There was a difference between a confession and statements which might be taken as evidence of guilt.

In the case of the Commonwealth vs. Piper the Government offered the testimony of the pastor of the Church in which the murder of Mabel Young took place. It appeared that the prisoner was induced to make statements which he might not have made otherwise. While under the effect of these inducements he had a conversation with the clergyman. There was a struggle over the admission of the testimony of the clergyman, but it was finally admitted, the court holding that the evidence was admissible.

The precise question was whether there was anything in the stipulation of the facts which took the Borden case out of the rule that declarations of the defendant were admissible.

There was another rule, Mr. Moody said, which declared that no person should be obliged to testify against himself, but this only applied to compulsory testimony and did not apply to voluntary admissions.

Mr. Moody said he might well leave the question upon the authority of the rules of the Supreme Court, but he would go further, though not to the English laws, which were poorly drawn and ill adapted to the present day, so no aid could be obtained from them. He did turn to the laws of the States. New York was the only one where the matter had been fully discussed. In People vs. Henderson, a New York case, the testimony offered was, as here, denial and not confession. In that case, as here, the accused was not under arrest nor under suspicion. Another case was where a man was informed that he was under suspicion and was cautioned about his evidence, and the court admitted his testimony.

The last case was one where the Court of Appeals held that the prisoner had been arrested without warrant, and that he was ignorant of English and his rights, and had not been cautioned. His evidence was not allowed. The one was drawn upon the question whether the prisoner was under arrest or not.

"If this Borden case was in the State of New York the evidence would be admissible," said Mr. Moody.

This question had also arisen in Maine, Mr. Moody said. There it had been held that, where admissions were made voluntarily and without compulsion, there was no reason for exclusion thereafter. The question has also arisen in the State of Wisconsin, where the only test was whether the declarations were made voluntarily or not.

The Chief Justice asked Mr. Moody whether in the Wisconsin case the defendant was present upon the stand at his own request, and Mr. Moody replied that that fact did not appear.

Mr. Moody held that where the defendant was the subject of the prosecution, unknown to himself, and made a statement of his knowledge of the case and was afterward placed under arrest, this previous evidence might be used, judging from outside authorities. He then called attention to several cases in this State, one where at a fire inquest a man had made a statement and was afterward arrested. That evidence was held to be competent to be used against him. Mr. Moody said that hardly a term of criminal court passed that testimony similar to Miss Borden's was not admitted. In view of the authority outside this State and the common practice all over this State and that, if any error had been committed, the defendant's rights were secure. Mr. Moody submitted that her testimony should be admitted.

Mr. Robinson, in reply, said it was not a question today whether in times past departures were taken, but whether they were taken wrongfully. He hoped the court would not take any chances resting upon passing notice of other courts. He stood today upon the rights of this defendant at this hour, no matter what had been done in the past.

"We must not lose sight of the facts in this case," said Mr. Robinson, and he then reviewed the case up to the time of the inquest. He said:

"The murder was committed Aug. 4. The defendant was placed under police guard, practically, Aug. 6, and there was no time when the eyes of the police were not on these people, and the defendant knew the police were around her. The defendant was summoned Aug. 9. Before testifying she requested that her counsel be present and the request was refused. She stood alone through days, confronted by the District Attorney, watched by the City Marshal, and at all times surrounded by the police.

"She was not cautioned at any time. She was summoned on or before Aug. 9, but the court will see that complaint was made out on the 8th of August; the complaint was in due form on that day, and she was brought into court practically under arrest. Complaint was made and a warrant issued for her arrest before the inquest. The City Marshal held the warrant during all the time she testified.

"Can any one say she had not been proceeded against? The City Marshal stood at her shoulder authorized to make an arrest at any moment. We must assume this was done under the direction of the District Attorney -- it was not done at random. When the evidence was concluded she was not allowed to depart, but was placed under arrest.

"And when she went before the District Court she went on another warrant, and the law officers of the county know it. It was an evasion of the law, and may operate to deprive her of her rights. She was placed in the custody of the City Marshal, he with his hands on her shoulder -- she a woman who could not run -- empowered to pick her up at any time, and that went on for three days. She was denied her counsel, and the District Court and the District Attorney neglected to tell her of her rights.

"If that is freedom, God save the Commonwealth of Massachusetts!"

"The inquest was not to discover whether a crime was committed or not, but its use and power was devoted to extorting from this defendant something which could be made useful. The Government knew these murders had been committed by somebody, possibly by the defendant, possibly by some one else. Was the District Attorney to determine by whom? Yes, but not by dragging from her facts in such a manner. She was not examined to find out whether she had committed these murders. Because they had already sworn she had committed

171

them. They put this paper in their pocket and said: 'If we get anything out of her, we'll put it away.' That was worse than burning a dress."

The various cases cited by Mr. Moody were disposed of by the assertion backed by argument that they had nothing to do with the case. They were not parallel cases.

"Lizzie Borden," said he, "stands on the Constitution of this Commonwealth, and when the bill of rights says no person shall testify against himself, she stands on that. The shield of the State and the shield of the Nation are her protection in this hour."

Mr. Moody took a short time for a reply, in which he reasserted his position. Mr. Robinson's argument, he said, was magnificent, but it was not law.

The Judges thought differently, for after consulting together for a little over an hour they decided to exclude the testimony. In announcing the decision Chief Justice Mason said:

"The propriety of examining the witness at the inquest is entirely distinct from the admissibility of her evidence. It is with the latter question the court had to deal. We are of the opinion that if the accused was at the time under arrest her statements were not voluntary and her evidence cannot be admitted.

"From the agreed facts it is plain that the prisoner was at the time of the inquest as much a prisoner as ever she has been, and the evidence is excluded."

The prisoner was visibly affected by the court's decision, and remained some minutes with her face covered with her fan.

The jury returned at 12:12 and Dr. Albert C. Dedrick was called. On the day of the murder he went to the Borden house after 2 o'clock. When he got there a number of officers were there, Dr. Dolan, Coughlin, and another.

"I examined the bodies," said the doctor, "and noticed the blood. That of Mrs. Borden was coagulated and ropy. Mr. Borden's was bright and fresh. Mrs. Borden's body was colder and stiffer. I think she died first. I should say several hours before."

The defense asked no questions.

Officer Joseph Hyde of Fall River testified next. Said he:

"I am a patrolman and was stationed about the Borden house on the night of Aug. 4. Miss Russell was in the house that night. I saw her and Lizzie coming out of the sitting room, the latter with a toilet pail, Miss Russell with a lamp. Lizzie went to the water closet in the cellar and then to the sink, and then I heard water running. Then both went up stairs. That was at 8:45.

"In a few minutes after Lizzie went down cellar again, alone. She had a lamp and put it down while she went to the sink and stooped down, but what she did I don't know. She was there but a few minutes.

It was ten or fifteen minutes between the time of the two visits to the cellar."

On cross-examination witness said he was under orders to watch the house and see whatever he could. He said that the women made no attempt at concealment when they came down stairs, but he was certain that Miss Russell was nervous.

"What, nervous?" demanded Mr. Robinson.

"Yes, Sir."

"How could you tell?"

"By her actions."

"Did she shriek or make a noise of any kind?"

"No."

"Well, how did you know she was nervous?"

"I saw her shake."

"What part of her shook?"

"She shook all over."

"Did her hand shake?"

"Yes."

"She had a lamp in her hand, didn't she?"

"Yes."

"Did the lamp smoke when she shook the lamp?"

"I didn't notice it."

"Break the chimney?"

"No."

Dr. William A. Dolan, a medical examiner for Bristol County, was the next witness. He was at the Borden house as early as 11:43 A.M. the day of the murder. He chanced to be passing the house and was called in soon after the murders were discovered.

"I had a little talk with Lizzie Borden that morning," said the doctor. "She was in her room. I asked her about that note, and she said Mrs. Borden had received a note to go and see somebody who was sick. I asked her what had become of it, and she said she supposed she had thrown it in the stove."

The doctor then gave the particulars of his examination of the bodies of Mr. and Mrs. Borden. He said that applying the thermometer to Mr. Borden he found his temperature high.

"I learned this," said he, "from the hands."

Going on, he said: "At that time the blood was dripping in two places down the head of the sofa. There was no blood on top of the carpet, but it had soaked in. I saw no coagulated blood on Mr. Borden. I touched the body of Mrs. Borden and it was much colder than Mr. Borden's.

"I made an examination of Mr. Borden's wounds, and found there seemed to be from eight to ten wounds."

173

Witness described the clothes of Mr. Borden and also what valuables he had about him. In his pocketbook he found $61.50 in money, the greater portion of it bills. The watch and chain were in their usual places. There was a ring on a finger.

Witness collected a sample of the morning's milk, in consequence of what was told him, and afterward analyzed it.

Continuing, witness said:

"Then I went into the cellar and found some axes and hatchets. I saw one, a claw hammer, which appeared to have been scraped. The hatchets, which are now here, I examined a day or two after, if not the first day, with a magnifying glass.

"I found two hairs, one on the blade of the claw hammer and one on the fibre of the wood near where it goes into the handle. I put those hairs into an envelope and gave them to Prof. Wood. I saw several spots on the handle and blade of the hatchet which looked like blood. There was something which looked like blood on one of the axes.

"I prepared the body of Mr. Borden for burial, opened and removed the stomach, put it into a clean jar and sealed it up, and did the same to the stomach of Mrs. Borden. I packed these jars with the milk jars and sent them to Prof. Wood.

"I had," said witness, "a dress skirt and waist to look at. I had also Miss Borden's shoes and stockings."

The dress and white skirt were handed to witness. He identified the dress and proceeded to hunt for a blood spot on the white skirt in order to identify it fully, but he could not find any. He thought, however, that that was the skirt. Here the attention of witness was called to a hole in the white skirt, which he said was not there when he examined it at the time of the murder, and said there was a blood spot then about where the hole was.

The doctor then spoke of the autopsy. Death was caused in each case by the wounds in the head, and in no other way. Plaster casts of the heads of Mr. and Mrs. Borden were shown witness and he described the wounds. Describing first Mr. Borden's wounds, he said:

"The first wound, starting near the nose, was four inches long. The next, starting at the angle of the eye or on down past the mouth and on the chin, four and one half inches long. The next, over the left eye, was glancing. The next ran into that, down through the eye, cutting the eye and through the cheek bone -- this was four and one-half inches long. A two-inch wound was next, over the eyebrow. The next was half an inch long. The others, back of these, went through the brain. The next was three inches long. The two directly in front of the ear were four and one-half and four inches in length.

"There were ten wounds altogether. These wounds all were vertical, more from the left to the right, although the two or three on the face were almost directly straight in.

"The wound in the back on Mrs. Borden," said the doctor, "was a flesh wound only, about two and a half inches long and in the lower part of the neck, practically a little to the left of the centre of the back of the neck. There were some contusions on the face, three of them, which might have been caused by falling.

"The right side of the head was crushed in, commencing near the ear, running zigzag, upward, four and a half or five inches. There were eighteen cuts on the head running from half an inch to five inches in length. As there were some marks on the skull where there were none in the flesh, the instrument may have gone twice into the same wound, pushing the flesh aside and cutting the bone."

Witness thought the wounds on both heads were made by some sharp instrument with a handle, and that they could have been inflicted by a woman of ordinary strength. Taking all the circumstances, he formed the opinion that Mrs. Borden had died at least one and one-half hours before Mr. Borden. The condition of the stomachs would tend to show this fact.

On cross-examination witness said he did not recall having said at the first hearing that the claw-headed hatchet would fit any of the wounds, and he now desired to change the expression. Still he thought the hatchet could have made the wounds on the heads.

He said he remembered marking on a china doll's head the dimensions of a crushing blow, which were slightly wrong, because he did not have the skulls then. He changed his opinion on this by saying he could not remember whether the skulls were ready or not, but he would say positively that he had not examined them at that time.

"Then I had not measured the hatchet, and it was merely an opinion," said witness.

"I had authority from the Mayor of Fall River to make the first autopsy, and permission from other authorities to make a second one. When I removed the heads I never gave notice to the daughters of the fact.

"When I made the second autopsy I discovered the cut on the back of Mrs. Borden. When that blow was given the assailant was standing at the rear; I discovered no other injury then that I did not discover at the house. There were but nineteen wounds altogether, counting the one in the back.

"When I got those hatchets I never said there was blood on them, but said there was something which looked like blood.

"I know now those hairs were not human hair which I found on the hatchets."

Dr. Dolan was the last witness of the day.

MR. BORDEN'S SKULL IN COURT

Experts Handle It As They Give Their Testimony

The Head of the "Handleless" Hatchet Fitted Into the Wounds -- Prof. Wood Testified as to Analyses of Contents of the Bordens' Stomachs and Examinations of Miss Borden's Clothing -- He Found Nothing Suspicious -- The Prisoner Retires from the Courtroom.

NEW-BEDFORD, MASS., June 13 -- The grinning skull of Andrew J. Borden was exhibited in the Court House at New-Bedford this afternoon. It was decided to keep this ghastly relic out of the case as long as possible, but to-day's events made it necessary that it should be produced.

At the autopsy held at Oak Grove Cemetery a week after the homicides, the bodies of both Mr. and Mrs. Borden were decapitated and the skulls were prepared for future examination by Dr. Dolan, Medical Examiner, of Fall River.

The prisoner was allowed to leave the courtroom while the skull was on exhibition and while other testimony of a harrowing nature was being given. She sat in the corridor without in charge of a Deputy Sheriff.

The prosecution showed by expert testimony that Mrs. Borden must have died at least an hour before her husband, and demonstrated that the wounds inflicted in the skull must have been made by a weapon with a cutting edge no greater than three and a half inches, nor less than three inches.

The handleless hatchet which has been produced by the Government exactly fits into the gashes of the skull of Mr. Borden. Dr. Wood, a professor of the Harvard Medical School, and Dr. Cheever, also on the Faculty of the Medical School, testified to these facts.

They, however, admitted that the assailant of the Bordens must have been pretty well spattered with blood after the completion of the murders.

Since the exclusion of Lizzie's testimony one question which is causing great interest is whether the defendant will be put on the stand. The general opinion is that the defense will not risk this, since her testimony at the inquest cannot be read against her.

Mrs. Borden's skull was not exhibited in the courtroom to-day and will probably not be submitted to the gaze of the curious.

The prosecution is nearing the end of its witnesses and will probably be concluded by Thursday night.

An incident of the trial to-day was the removal by force from the courtroom of a New-York newspaper artist who had persisted in making pictures after he had been warned to make no more.

At the opening of court, Medical Examiner Dolan took the stand and his cross-examination by Mr. Adams was resumed. He was called upon to explain, according to his theory, the position in which Mr. Borden lay when he was killed.

He placed an armchair against the wall, to be used as an illustration of how the head of the sofa was when Mr. Borden lay on it last, the door of the courtroom leading to the anteroom standing as the door of the dining room. He then placed two coats in the chair and upon these put the plaster cast of Mr. Borden, in the position in which the body is alleged to have been, with the exception that there was the additional height of a pillow under his head when lying on the sofa.

"Granting that the chair was against the wall," said the witness, "the chair is relatively in the same position as was the sofa at the time of the murder.

"Of the ten blows," continued witness, "four penetrated the skull. The second blow beginning at the nose on the left, was four and a half inches long and out through the bony formation of the substance beneath the eye and very slightly through both jaw bones. These bones are comparatively hard; the bones about the eyes are not strong. This four-and-a-half inch cut did not bisect the eye, but the one next to it did, and it was a clean cut, indicating a sharp-edged instrument.

"In my opinion the claw-headed hatchet could have made the cut, and the cut was made from left to right. The one over the eye was also from left to right; the latter was even more marked in its features. There were no others having a left-to-right tendency that I discovered.

"I have seen the handleless hatchet before; it was before the first hearing. It has a clean-cutting edge. When I first saw it there were white particles of ashes on it.

"In that sitting room at that time there was the usual furniture of such a room; there was a table about four feet away, nearer the centre of the room; there were books on it, but I saw no blood on them or on the table.

"I saw no spots on the carpet between the sofa and the parlor door, but there were some on the parlor door, on the panels and on the division of the panels, but I cannot tell exactly how high above the floor, perhaps five or six feet.

"Taking all the things in connection with this matter, I should say the blood spots came from different directions. In every instance the pear end showed the direction of the blood. The spots on the doors showed they had come over in a curve from the body; those on the wall near the body had the heavy spots down.

"In my opinion, the assailant stood between the parlor door and the head of the lounge. I don't think the assailant swung the instrument in the direction of that table, and this accounts for the lack of blood on it, even though the blows came from left to right. I think a one-handed blow would have done the work.

"Had the artery below the jaw been cut, there would have been a heavy flow of blood; but the assailant would not have necessarily been covered with blood from the spurts. The swinging of the hatchet would have been likely to cause scattering of blood on the assailant and on the victim."

Referring to witness's statement that the blows were struck from the right, Mr. Adams asked, "By a left-handed person?"

Witness arranged the cast of Mrs. Borden's head in the chair to show the relative position of the body when found. Then he said:

"As she lay all the cuts on her head were seen. When I first saw her, the wounds were open, gaping, and distinct. The cuts were clean and sharp, and they were all left-to-right blows except the blow on the top of the skull. I don't think a very heavy blow was necessary. I think that moderate force only was used in all the blows. The head of Mrs. Borden did not come as far up as the top of the pillow sham. The spots on that sham came from left to right. The spots on the side of the spread were nearest to where she lay."

Here the spread was stretched over the jury rail, the foreman holding the lower edge and Mr. Jennings holding the sham above it, to give the arrangement as nearly perfect as possible for the jury to see.

Then witness said: "I found a few spots on the marble of the dressing case or bureau and there were some on the molding of the baseboard. Beyond the bureau and near the north wall there were some on the molding and some on the wallpaper, about three feet up. There were no spots on the window.

"Taking the spots and the position of the body, in my opinion, the assailant was astride the body facing the east wall. I don't think the blow in the back was from left to right."

Witness was then questioned concerning the dress and skirt which he identified yesterday. He had just begun to exhibit the dress when Juror Hodges of Taunton was taken ill. It was necessary for the Court to take a recess and for Mr. Hodges to leave the room. He fainted before he was over his attack.

Resuming his testimony, Dr. Dolan said that when he looked at a pocket of the dress there was a spot on the pocket which resembled blood, but, although he had not heard any report to the contrary, as he looked at it now he didn't think it was blood.

He said he had the shoes and stockings brought to him that same day, and thought there was blood on the sole of one of the shoes. He found some on the stockings.

Answering a question concerning the hatchets, witness said, "The wounds varied in length, but the exterior length of the wounds would not indicate correctly the size of the instrument used, in respect to its length. There is nothing in the length of the wounds to show that they could not have been made by a three-and-a-half inch hatchet."

Edward S. Wood, Professor of Chemistry in the Harvard Medical School, was the next witness.

"My attention," said the doctor, "was first called to this matter on the 5th of August, when I received a box in which were four preserve jars, one of which was labeled 'Milk of Aug. 3', another 'Milk of the 4th', a third 'Stomach of A. B. Borden', and the fourth 'Stomach of Mrs. Borden.' The stomachs were removed and thoroughly examined. There was no evidence of the action of any irritant. There was nothing abnormal or irregular in the condition of the stomachs.

"Assuming that they both ate at the same time and of the same kind of food, the difference in the time of death, from the condition of the stomachs, would be about one and one-half hours. Digestion stops at death. I have heard all the evidence thus far, and, taking all these facts and the examination I made myself, the more important data to show the time of death are the condition of the blood and the condition of the stomach and the heat of the bodies.

"On Aug. 10 I went to the Borden house, but afterward received from Dr. Dolan the axes and the hatchets, the blue dress skirt and waist, the white skirt, the pieces of carpet, a piece of false hair, a lounge cover, three small envelopes containing hair of Mr. and Mrs. Borden and hair taken from the hatchet.

"The claw-headed hatchet had several stains on it, on the sides, the head, and the cutting edge. All were carefully tested by me chemically, with negative results.

"The two axes I examined in the same way, with negative results, so far as blood is concerned.

"The claw-headed hatchet could not have been washed quickly, because of the crevasses of the blade.

"The hair sent me was undoubtedly that of a cow; was not a human hair.

"The other envelope which I received, in which was a note that a hair was in a piece of paper there, contained nothing but a mucilage spot. I only saw one hair. I want to say, however, that I found some cotton and wool fibre on the lower edge of the claw-headed hatchet.

"On the blue dress I found a brownish smooch near the corner of the top of the pocket, which at first looked like blood, but it was found not to be blood. Another spot on the skirt was found not to be blood. There was no suspicion of a blood stain on the waist.

"The white skirt contained a small blood spot six inches from the bottom. It was about one-sixteenth of an inch in diameter and appeared plainer on the outside than on the inside. It was a real blood spot."

The shoes of Miss Borden and the stockings were shown by the witness. He said he had found no blood on them.

"On the 30th," witness continued, "in the courtroom at Fall River, I received the small hatchet and the two pieces of wood. The claw-headed hatchet, I should say, measured four and a half inches on the cutting edge. The small hatchet had no blood stains. When I received the small hatchet, the fractured end was in the lower end of the eye. The blade was rusty, as it is now. There were several spots on the head which were not blood spots. The fractured end of the handle was very white and some chips, which have since disappeared, were there when I had it. There was no dirt in the broken end of the handle. No blood had been removed from the handle.

"In my opinion, if that hatchet was used for inflicting the wounds described and afterward was subjected to a cleaning process, I could not have discovered the blood if it was done before the handle was broken. After the handle was broken it would have been impossible to have washed the blood out, quickly at least. The handle in the small hatchet fitted very tightly; that in the claw-hammer does not."

On cross-examination witness said that the spot of blood on the white skirt might have been caused in another way than by a spatter from the body of one of the murdered parents.

Witness said that he considered the assailant of the murdered people must have been spattered with blood.

Dr. Frank W. Draper of Boston, professor at the Harvard Medical College, followed Prof. Wood. He assisted at the autopsy. The doctor described the wounds.

Miss Borden retired when he began his description, not caring to listen to the recital.

Witness was sure of the priority of the death on the part of Mrs. Borden. He was confident that there was at least an hour between the deaths.

The skull of Mr. Borden was produced by Dr. Dolan so that Dr. Draper could make a more comprehensive statement as to the position of the wounds and their effect.

By examination of the skull the witness was enabled to assert positively that the cutting length of the instrument used on the skull was 3½ inches. He demonstrated this fact by a piece of stiff tin, which he inserted in several of the cuts. He said the small, handleless hatchet could have been used in making the wounds.

Witness considered the blows to have been produced by a hatchet or some sharp cutting instrument. In his opinion the blows could have been caused by a woman of ordinary strength.

In the opinion of witness the assailant of Mrs. Borden stood over her; the assailant of Mr. Borden stood behind him at the head of the sofa.

On cross-examination Mr. Adams handed witness a new hatchet with a blade 3⅜ inches on the cutting edge.

"Doctor," he said, "just put that hatchet in the fractures as the weapon went through when the blows were struck."

Dr. Draper took the hatchet in his right hand and picked up the skull and placed the blade in one of the openings in the skull. The blade would not go through. The doctor held it up before the jury and said:

"It does not appear on the other side."

Mr. Adams said nothing, but it was plain that the effect of this demonstration upon the jury was great.

Witness said that the assailant of Mrs. Borden must have been more or less spattered with blood in front, although some of the blood might have gone in the air and come down behind and that the face and hair might reasonably have received some blood spatters.

Upon his re-direct examination Dr. Draper offered an explanation why the new hatchet shown him by Mr. Adams did not fit the wound. It was because it had not been sharpened, he said.

Dr. Davis W. Cheever, Boston, physician and surgeon, of thirty-five years' experience, devoting most of his time to surgery, was the last witness of the day.

"On the 31st of May," said he, "I saw the skulls of Mr. and Mrs. Borden, and have since then studied them with a view of determining the character and effect of the blows. I have heard most of the medical testimony in the case and was present when the casts were marked. In my opinion, Mrs. Borden died first, the minimum time of difference being one hour, the maximum not more than two hours.

"The injuries on the bones were made by a heavy metallic instrument with a sharp edge, not more than 3½ inches, such as a hatchet.

"I have examined the handleless hatchet, and assuming it had a handle of ordinary length, it would make the wounds."

Witness understood the nature of the wounds, he said, and was of the opinion that a hatchet not much smaller than the previously described could, perhaps, have been used, but in no event could the maximum of 3½ inches have been exceeded.

Here the witness fitted the small hatchet into the wounds on Mr. Borden's skull. He thought nearly all the wounds on Mrs. Borden's body had been made when the body was lying flat on the floor on her face. The scalp wound on the side, he thought, was given when the assailant and assailed were face to face. The wounds on both persons could have been inflicted by a sharp cutting instrument of sufficient weight and leverage, not less than twelve or fourteen inches, and a woman of ordinary strength could have done it.

Some of the blows indicated plainly the direction of them; the one which smashed in Mr. Borden's skull, for instance, was from right to left; on Mrs. Borden's head the scalp wound might have been cut either way.

On his cross-examination witness said that an instrument of a cutting edge of three inches and possibly less might have made one of the wounds on Mrs. Borden's head.

Witness further said that when he performed an operation in surgery he usually changed his outward clothes partly to insure cleanliness and partly to protect his clothing. In performing surgical operations blood rarely struck his hair, but sometimes his beard and face received some, and it was not uncommon to have his shoes spattered. There was a temple artery in the head where two of the cuts in Mr. Borden's head were made. They, when cut, would throw spray, and the direction of the cut would determine the course of the spray. If Mr. Borden was lying on his right side and the artery was cut from behind the spurt would be backward; the other artery, nearer the ear, would spurt on a level with the body. A person standing behind and delivering the blow which would cut this artery, the spurt would come on the assailant. A person standing behind while delivering the blow would be apt to get blood on his face, hair, hands, and body.

Witness thought the assailant of Mrs. Borden stood face to face with her when the scalp wound was made, and the others were made when the assailant was astride of the victim. He thought the assailant must have been spattered from the waist up. If the assailant stood bestride the victim it was a question, he thought, whether the shoes would be spattered, because the dress would have a tendency to hide them.

At Mr. Adams's request witness gave a representation of the manner in which one of the blows was struck, using Mr. Adams's hatchet for a weapon and Mr. Adams's head for a target. A shudder went over the courtroom as he struck the blow, stopping just short of Mr. Adams's skull.

June 15, 1893

PRUSSIC ACID IN THE CASE

Effort To Show That Lizzie Borden Tried to Buy Some.

Counsel Engaged in an Argument as to Admissibility of Evidence -- Story Told of a Quarrel Between Accused and Her Sister Emma -- Witnesses Testify that They Saw Nobody Enter the Borden Yard at the Time of the Murders -- State to Close Its Case To-day.

NEW-BEDFORD, MASS., June 14 -- The question of interest in the Borden trial at present is whether prussic acid can be used, except scientifically and medicinally, for any but a deadly purpose.

This afternoon the prosecution offered to show that on the 3rd of August last the defendant made two distinct attempts to purchase this acid, and gave as her reason for desiring it that she was going to use it to clean furs.

Counsel for the defense objected to this testimony being admitted, and the question of its competency was argued at length by District Attorney Moody and ex-Gov. Robinson.

The Commonwealth lawyers claimed that the testimony was important as showing the intent of Lizzie Borden, but Mr. Robinson replied that this testimony was purely collateral and in no way bore on the statements set forth in the indictment. Numerous authorities were cited bearing on the point at issue, and then the presiding Justices retired to consider the question.

It is the opinion of the court that the testimony is competent, provided that the prosecution can show that the acid, when used for other than medical or scientific purposes, must necessarily be used to take life.

To-night the prosecution is consulting experts and preparing its case, and to-morrow morning a written statement will be submitted showing the scope of the testimony the State desires to submit and just what it intends to prove by it.

The sensation of the day was the testimony of Hannah Reagan, matron at the Fall River Police Station. She testified that while Lizzie Borden was under her charge she overheard a quarrel between the defendant and her sister, in which the former said, "Emma, you have given me away."

At the time of the alleged quarrel an attempt was made by the friends of the prisoner to obtain a statement from the Police Matron that the story of the quarrel was untrue. This, however, proved unsuccessful. It is understood that the defense is prepared to show that Mrs. Reagan stated to certain persons that the whole story was without foundation. The prosecution will probably rest its case to-morrow and on Friday the defense will open.

Lizzie Borden was unusually cheerful to-day, and at the conclusion of Mrs. Reagan's testimony laughed and seemed more amused than disturbed by it.

City Marshal Hilliard of Fall River was the first witness to-day. He reached the Borden house at 3 o'clock in the afternoon of the day of the murders, and made an examination of the premises. He was there again the following Saturday afternoon and again Saturday evening. In the evening there was a crowd in and about the house, 200 or 300 persons, perhaps.

"I sent for officers," said witness, "and had the crowd removed to the street. Then I went into the house, where I saw the prisoner, her sister, and Mr. Morse. There was a conversation, but Mayor Coughlin and the others did the talking. After we entered the parlor Mayor Coughlin asked that the family remain in the house for a few days. He said there was much excitement, and he thought it would be better that they should not go on the street. I think he told them that if they were annoyed by the people to send word to the City Marshal or himself and they should be protected. Mr. Morse asked about the mail, and he was told they had better send for it. Then Miss Lizzie asked:

"What! Is there anybody in this house suspected?"

"The Mayor said: 'Perhaps Mr. Morse could answer that from what occurred last night.'

"Lizzie then said: 'I want to know the truth,' and the Mayor said he was sorry to say it, but that she was suspected.

"Then Emma spoke up and said: 'We have tried to keep it from you as long as we could.'

"Then the Mayor asked Lizzie where she was when the affair happened, and she said in the barn for twenty minutes looking for lead sinkers.

"Lizzie said, after Emma spoke: 'Well, I am ready to go any time.' "

Witness then told of the search made of the Borden house by himself and officers of his command. He said defendant gave him all articles which he called for, and when called on for assistance rendered it. He said, too, that she talked frankly and earnestly with him concerning the suspicion that had arisen against her.

"I asked Miss Lizzie," said witness, "if she would be kind enough to hand me the shoes and stockings which she had on at the time of the murders, and she went up stairs, and I think it was Mrs. Brigham who brought them down to me. There was a dress pattern brought from the house, but I don't know where it is now."

The District Attorney said the dress had no significance, and the subject was dropped.

"In fact," queried counsel for defense, "as the doctors say, this search had a negative result only."

"They might call it that," answered the witness, "but I call it a thorough search."

The court smiled at the answer.

"I didn't tell Mr. Jennings," said witness, "that I suspected Miss Lizzie, but I did tell him that somebody did. That night when we went there it was the Mayor who did the talking and who advised them to stay in the house. I didn't have the warrant in my pocket then."

District Attorney Moody here said he desired to show that the statement of Mayor Coughlin to the household was in good faith as meaning protection, because the night before Mr. Morse had been subjected to violence or threats of violence while going to the Post Office. Gov. Robinson objected to this because it had not been shown

184

that Lizzie knew what had happened to Mr. Morse, and the answer was excluded.

Mayor Coughlin of Fall River was the next witness. He described his visit to the Borden house with Marshal Hilliard, and corroborated the Marshal's testimony as to the conversation with the defendant.

In the house the first person he saw was Miss Emma. Then he saw Lizzie and Mr. Morse.

"We all went into the parlor," said witness, "where I said: 'I have a request to make of the family, and that is that you remain in the house for a few days, since I think it would be best for you all.'

"Lizzie asked: 'Why, is there anybody in this house suspected?' and I said: 'Well, perhaps Mr. Morse can answer better, as his experience of last evening might tend to convince him that somebody in the house was suspected.'

"Then Miss Emma said: 'We have tried to keep it from her the best we could,' and Lizzie said:

" 'Well, if I am suspected I am ready to go at any time.'

"Then Miss Lizzie, in answer to my questions, told where she was when the murders occurred. Miss Emma then said she wanted us to do everything we could for them, after I had told them to call on me for any protection needed."

On cross-examination witness said:

"When Lizzie asked if anybody in the house was suspected she spoke excitedly. When she said she was ready to go if she was suspected she spoke without hesitation and earnestly."

Mrs. Hannah H. Gifford of Fall River, who next took the stand, said:

"I am a manufacturer of ladies' outside garments. I have made cloaks for the Bordens. I made a sack for Lizzie Borden last spring. I had a talk with her about the stepmother, I think in March, 1892."

Mr. Robinson objected to witness's telling the conversation, because it was too remote, but the question was put, exceptions being taken.

"I spoke," witness said, "and called Mrs. Borden 'Mother.'

"She said: 'Don't call her mother; she is only my stepmother, and she is a mean, hateful old thing.'

"I said: 'Oh, Lizzie, don't say that,' and then she said that she always kept apart from her and ate her meals alone."

Miss Anna B. Borden, the next witness, said: "I am not a relative of the prisoner. I have known her five years. I went abroad with her in 1890, and occupied the same cabin with her on the outward and homeward voyage."

Witness was asked to state whether she had had any conversation with Lizzie Borden about family matters on the voyage, and the defense objected.

The court, after deliberation, ordered the witness aside and the jury to retire, and then Mr. Moody stated that the evidence which the State was about to offer was in substance that the prisoner regretted returning home after she had passed such a happy and pleasant Summer, because the home to which she was returning was such an unhappy one.

He held this expressed better than anything else the permanent condition of things in that household, even though the talk occurred two years before the homicide. It was an expression of the state of feeling in the family by one member of that family.

Mr. Robinson said the statement was altogether too remote. The witness had been abroad, and as they were coming across this conversation occurred. There was only one thing to object to in what she said, and that was the statement about the happy home.

"There isn't a person who ever starts to return home from a pleasant trip," said Mr. Robinson, "who is not likely to say: 'I wish I wasn't going home; I've had such a pleasant time.'

"If she made that statement, the fact that she went home and lived there, showed that everything was all right."

Mr. Moody said it had been shown by the previous witness that the defendant most of the time or a large part of the time didn't sit at the same table with her parents, and this tended to show that the alienation had been continued after she arrived home.

The court was of the opinion that the language used was so susceptible of other inferences that it would be better to exclude it, the idea evidently being that it might refer to some other member of the family besides the stepmother.

Lucy Collet of Fall River said that on the morning of the murder she sat on Dr. Chagnon's piazza in view of the Borden fence from 10:45 to 11:45, and saw no one about the Borden place.

"I staid at the Chagnon house," said witness, "until 4 o'clock, when Dr. Chagnon's clerk came I was there to tend the door and telephone, but the door was locked and I did not get at the telephone. During that time I saw no one pass out of the Chagnon yard."

Cross-examined by Gov. Robinson, witness said: "There was a man came to see Dr. Chagnon while I was there, but I told him the doctor was not at home and he went away."

"Oh! there was a man came there, was there?"

"Yes, Sir."

"Ah! who was it, do you know?"

"Yes, Sir; it was Mr. Robinson."

"Oh; Mr. Robinson." (Laughter.)

"Yes, Sir; when I was there I didn't see anybody go through the yard, but I was not looking particularly. If there had been one coming down the driveway and another coming along the other side of the house,

186

I could not have seen both. The driveway is on the Borden side. I never saw any man getting upon the fence and walking along. I didn't see any man at all."

Thomas Boiles of Fall River, a hostler, testified:

"On the morning of the murder I was washing carriages in Mrs. Churchill's yard, where I could see the wellhouse in the Borden yard. I was only about fifteen minutes washing the carriage. Then I took it over to Mr. Hall's barn, and while I was there Mrs. Churchill called me. While I was washing the carriage I saw no one go into or come out of the Borden yard, or go through the one where I was."

On cross-examination witness said he couldn't see much of the Borden yard, because there was a barn, a wellhouse, and a big piece of lattice-work in the way.

Patrick McGowan of Fall River, a laborer, testified: "On the morning of the Borden murder I was in the Crowe yard at 10:08, and remained there until about 10:30. There were two men working in the yard. I was over as far as the Borden fence. While I was there in the yard I saw nobody in the Borden yard."

Joseph Des Rosier, the next witness, said he remembered the day Mr. Borden was killed. He was working in John Crowe's yard, sawing and splitting wood. About 10 o'clock a man came over to where he was and told him of the murder. Up to that time he had seen no one passing through his yard to or from the Borden yard.

On cross-examination witness was asked by an interpreter:

"Did you see anybody in the Crowe yard?"

"Only Pat, who was working there."

"Did you talk to Pat?"

"No, he is an Irishman and I can't make him understand me. I don't know Mr. Wixon, and there wasn't any man got over the fence and come to where I was during the morning. There was a man came in the front gate and told us of the murder."

John Denny, a stonecutter of Fall River, testified: "When the Borden murders occurred I was in the Crowe yard. I was at work there all the morning, and during that time I saw no one go into the Borden yard or come from it."

Hannah Reagan, matron at a police station at Fall River, was the next witness. She said the prisoner was in her charge at one time.

"On the 24th of August," said Mrs. Reagan, "Emma came in to see her in the morning. I was in the room cleaning up. Emma came at 8:40. She spoke with her sister, and I went into a toilet room and hearing loud talk looked out and saw Lizzie lying on her side and Emma bending down over her. Lizzie said:

" 'You have given me away, Emma, but I don't care. I won't give in one inch' -- measuring on her finger.

"Emma said: 'O Lizzie! I didn't,' at the same time sitting down.

187

"They sat there until nearly 11 o'clock, when Mr. Jennings came, but Lizzie made no talk at all with her sister after that -- never opened her mouth to her.

"When I first heard the noise of loud talking I was about four feet away in a closet.

"When Emma left that morning there was nothing said by either, and no 'good-bye' was exchanged."

A decided sensation was produced by this testimony.

Cross-examined by Mr. Jennings, witness said:

"Emma remained there in that room until you came, and when you came, you said to Emma, 'Have you told her all?' and Emma said she had told her all she had to tell. Emma came again in the afternoon, but I can't tell just when. Mr. Buck was there, I am quite sure. He came every day.

"I do remember something about an egg that same afternoon. I said an egg could be broken one way and not another, and I made a bet with Mrs. Brigham about it. Lizzie took the egg and tried to break it her way, and, failing, said this was the first thing she ever attempted to do and did not succeed.

"When I spoke of the affair between the sisters, I spoke of it as a 'quarrel.' This was before the first hearing. I don't know what day of the week the quarrel was on. I don't know whether the story of the quarrel was published in the morning papers. I was asked about it by reporters that very afternoon and also in the morning. I never told any reporter it was all a lie, that there wasn't a word of truth in it.

"Mr. Buck spoke to me about it in my room, but I never told him it was not true. I never said a word to Mrs. Holmes about it. There was a paper drawn up subsequently in relation to this story. It was brought to me by Mr. Buck."

The statement was read, in which it was set forth that there had not been a quarrel between the sisters. Witness said she never expressed a willingness to sign the paper.

Continuing, witness said: "Marshal Hilliard never said a word to me about signing the paper. He never said, to my remembrance, 'If you sign that paper, you sign it against my express orders.' Mr. Buck never asked me about signing the paper if the Marshal was willing. The Marshal told me to go to my room. There was no one in the room when I went back, for I had the door locked and the key in my pocket. I never said to the Marshal that I'd rather leave my place than have such lies told about me. I never had any conversation with Mrs. Holmes about this paper. I never said to Mrs. Holmes in referring to the story: 'You know they didn't quarrel, because you were here and we were talking about the egg.' "

On the re-direct examination witness said:

"The reporter to whom I told the story on the afternoon was Mr. Porter of the Fall River *Globe.* I never saw the contents of any paper, but Mr. Buck came to me and said he had heard of such a report, that he had seen it in a paper,*and I said: 'You can't always believe all you see in the papers.' He wanted me to sign the paper, and said that if I did all would be right between the sisters. I said we would go and see the Marshal about it. We went down to the Marshal's office, and he told me to go to my room, and told Mr. Buck to mind his own business and he would attend to his.

"The Marshal said then what story I had to tell I would tell in court. I don't remember your being in the Marshal's room, and I don't remember your conversation with him; I never heard you say to the Marshal: 'If you refuse to let this woman sign this paper, I'll publish you to the whole world.' "

After Dr. Dolan and Bridget Sullivan had been put upon the stand to complete their evidence, Eli Bunce, a Fall River drug clerk was called. The defense objecting to Mr. Bunce's testifying, the jury was sent out of the room, pending an argument by counsel.

Mr. Moody said it was proposed to show that prussic acid was an article of commercial use; that the witness never had a call for it until the 3rd of August, 1892; that it was not used for cleaning sealskin sacks, and that the prisoner went to witness's place and asked for some with which to clean a sealskin sack.

Mr. Robinson, for the defense, said he understood there was no evidence to show a sale; it appeared, he said, that examination of the stomachs of the deceased showed no symptoms of prussic acid, and prussic acid had no connection with the case.

"Miss Borden," said Mr. Robinson, "is charged with slaying or killing those people with some sharp instrument. Now here is an attempt to charge her with causing death by wholly different means. It can't be considered here now for the reason that this charge refers to Aug. 3 when the killing was on the 4th. There is no weight in this evidence to connect it with the crime charged.

"While this is not remote in time it is entirely remote and foreign to the question. It is in amount an attempt to buy an article for another object. It is an article which anybody may buy. Its sale is especially provided for in the statutes."

Mr. Moody argued at length upon the ground that any act committed or attempted at or near the time of an act committed for which a person was held should have some weight and bearing as upon the other case. He cited numerous cases to show that similar evidence had been admitted in other cases.

Mr. Robinson once again reviewed the case, and repeated that the evidence should not be allowed unless it went to prove the crime with which the defendant had been charged. He held that evidence might as well be introduced to show that defendant attempted to shoot Dr. Bowen the day before in order to show evil intention toward her parents.

At the conclusion of the arguments the Justices withdrew for consultation. Half an hour later it was announced that the evidence was competent, and would be admitted.

This appeared not to satisfy the counsel for the defense, and they went at once to the bench, where the other counsel joined them, and another long discussion followed. The jurymen were conducted to their seats again at 4:45 and put at once in charge of the Sheriffs, and court adjourned until to-morrow morning at 9 o'clock.

June 16, 1893

STATE RESTS, DEFENSE BEGINS

Lizzie Borden's Answer to the Charge of Double Murder.

The Government's Case to be Attacked at Every Point -- Opening Witnesses Contradict Previous Testimony -- One says that He Saw a Woman Coming from the Borden Barn About the time Defendant Says She was There -- Another Hatchet Has Been Found.

NEW-BEDFORD, MASS., June 15 -- The case of the Government against Lizzie Borden was concluded this morning after the District Attorney had received a most serious blow in the refusal of the Justices to allow the introduction of the prussic acid testimony.

It was announced from the bench last night that if there could be presented by the Government proof that prussic acid was used properly, only for medical and scientific purposes, the testimony would be admitted. In consequence of this there was a scurrying around New-Bedford last night, with the result that three alleged experts presented themselves for examination this morning.

They were altogether too light timber to face the shots which were fired at them by ex-Gov. Robinson, and when he had done with them their stories were worthless as far as evidencing the uses of prussic acid was concerned.

The Justices consulted and then declined to allow the submission of the evidence, the announcement creating a decided sensation in the courtroom. Mr. Knowlton was very anxious to place this prussic acid evidence before the jury, and his failure made a very flat ending to the Government's case.

Miss Borden's friends were, of course, jubilant. Her attorneys profess to be well pleased with the present condition of the case. On every legal point the prosecution has been defeated, and this has greatly lessened the strength of their case. They rely largely, however, on the summing up by Mr. Knowlton, who is also to cross-examine the witnesses for the defense.

After the decision of the Justices to-day, Mr. Jennings made his opening argument for the defense in a plain statement of facts, almost entirely devoid of oratorical effort. The introductory testimony of the defense was very weak, but as it proceeded it gained in strength, and the stories during the afternoon produced a marked effect.

Particularly effective was the recital of the Jewish peddler who saw a woman coming from the barn to the Borden house, and the statements by the two boys who went to the barn after the homicide. The boys' story was a direct contradiction to the elaborate story of Inspector Medley, who testified that he examined the dust in the barn and found it undisturbed by a footstep.

There is a prevalent feeling here that there will either be a disagreement, or that the result of the trial will be an acquittal.

Mr. Jennings opened for the defense. He said:

"One of the victims of this murder was a personal friend, and I had known him since a boy, and if I become more affected than would seem natural it must be ascribed to this feeling; a lawyer does not cease ever to be a man.

"The brutal character of the wounds were only equaled by the time and place of the murder. I don't propose to go into detail about the character of these wounds, but know what they were.

"The person who was arrested for doing the deed was the youngest daughter of one of the victims. Up to that time she was of spotless character and reputation, who had moved in and out of that house for twenty-one years with her mother and father and sister. We shall show you that this young woman had led a spotless life, interested in religious and charitable work, and yet for some reason the Government seemed to have fastened the crime upon her.

"There is always an outcry from somebody to be punished for such a crime, but we want the guilty punished, not the innocent.

"Our law, and it is the one which you have sworn to apply to this case, presumes every man to be innocent until he is proved guilty. The law is for the protection of the living.

"The law of Massachusetts to-day draws about the person of everybody the circle of innocence until the contrary is proved. I say this is a mysterious case, and every thinking man must say the same, but you are not here to say how it was committed, but to say by whom. You are simply to answer as to this defendant, to say you are satisfied beyond a reasonable doubt that she is guilty or innocent, and a reasonable doubt is a doubt for which you can furnish a good reason.

"There are two kinds of evidence, direct and circumstantial. The first is the testimony of persons who have seen and heard and felt; circumstantial evidence is entirely different.

"I want to say that there is not one particle of direct evidence against Lizzie Andrew Borden to connect her with this crime; it is

191

wholly and absolutely circumstantial. We know, of course, that almost everything occurs under natural laws. In circumstantial evidence it is simply an opinion from you, an inference on your part. In certain cases such evidence may be as sure as direct, but there is no class of evidence known that under certain circumstances is as dangerous as evidence of this nature.

"To illustrate, a man is shot. There was no evidence to connect any one with the murder, but in taking out the ball, a piece of paper came with it, a part of the wadding. It was a piece of a song, and in the pocket of the man arrested for the murder was found the rest of the paper containing the song, and both pieces fitted. This was strong circumstantial evidence.

"Take the case of the man who was pardoned out of a New-Jersey prison last August after seven years' incarceration. He had been convicted of manslaughter because a piece of his coat was found near the murdered person. The suspected man said he found the man dead and got some blood on a portion of his coat. He tore the piece off, left it, and fled. He was not believed, and after seven years' imprisonment the real murderer confessed on his dying bed. Here are two illustrations.

"It is not for you to unravel the mystery of how these people died, but to say whether this woman did the deed or not.

"Circumstantial evidence has often been likened to a chain, and every essential fact in that chain must be proved by a reasonable assumption. There must be no weak links. Unless by the evidence you can tie this woman to the bodies of the murdered persons you must let her go free.

"We contend that with the evidence thus far produced there is no motive shown for this woman to do the deed. But it may be said it isn't necessary to prove a motive. One of the persons killed was this girl's own father, and while a motive may be assumed by the Government you will find that a motive as one of the links in the chain becomes of tremendous importance. The Government's chain is that whoever killed one killed the other, and where they have assumed to show a motive for the killing of her stepmother there is none for the killing of her own father.

"In measuring the motive you have got to apply it in this case as between this girl and her own father.

"The blood which was shown on the axes has disappeared. The claw-head hatchet has disappeared from the case, and it didn't disappear until after Prof. Wood had said, on that -- to the defense -- most glorious morning in Fall River, that there could not have been blood on it to have been washed so quickly.

"The attempt has been made here to surround this house -- to completely shut it in -- but you have seen it and have heard the evidence in that matter. And there has not been a living soul in all these witnesses to testify that he saw Andrew J. Borden go down to the bank from this house. He was actually invisible.

"We shall show you there were others about that house. We shall show you that Medley's cakewalk in the barn existed in his own imagination and that people were in that barn and all over it before he went there.

"We shall show you that Lizzie was in the barn just as she said she was.

"We shall show you that this dress was soiled with paint, gotten on early in May; that it was burned there in broad daylight with windows and doors open, officers and other witnesses about.

"We shall show you that she had on the very dress she says she had on, the one I gave to the officer myself.

"We shall ask you to see that, in view of the presumption of innocence which the law says you shall consider, that no blood was found upon her, and to consider the relations between father and daughter."

During the opening Miss Borden covered her eyes with her handkerchief and wept.

The first witness called for the defense was Martha Chagnon of Fall River, who said:

"I am Dr. Chagnon's daughter. Our yard is at the rear of the Borden yard. There is a fence between the two yards and there is a corner there where there is a doghouse.

"On the night preceding the Borden murder I heard a noise which disturbed me. It was about 11 o'clock at night."

"Describe it."

"It was a kind of a pounding noise along the line of the Borden fence, and it continued four or five minutes."

Marion Chagnon, wife of Dr. Chagnon, testified: "I was at home the evening before the murders and heard a noise about 11 o'clock. It was a noise like the step on the sidewalk or the fence. The noise seemed to come from the direction of the doghouse."

John M. Gerard of Fall River, a painter, said: "I painted the house of Andrew J. Borden in May, 1892. I took the paint there the 9th of May. I saw Miss Borden the next morning early. She was in the backyard near the barn. The color was not satisfactory, so I made it to suit her. She was about where the paint was. The paint tube was near the south door. We commenced painting the house right away; a dark drab with darker trimmings."

Mary A. Durfee of Fall River was called to tell how in the Fall previous to the murders she saw an unknown man in altercation with Mr. Borden, but she was not allowed to tell her story, the court holding that the date of the occurrence was remote from the date of the crime.

Charles N. Gifford of Fall River, a clothing store clerk, living next to the house of Dr. Chagnon, said he was at his house about 11 o'clock the night before the murders.

"I saw a man on the side steps leading into the yard," said he; "the side step of my house, I mean. He weighed about 180 or 190 pounds. He sat on the steps with his hat on his face. I shook him and his hat fell on the walk. I lighted a match and found I didn't know who it was. I left him and went into the house. There was no smell of liquor about the man. I have never seen the man since. Afterward Mr. Kirby came home in a few minutes, and I heard something said by Mr. Kirby."

Uriah Kirby of Fall River, who was the next witness, said:

"I remember the night before the murders when I went home at 11 o'clock I found a man sitting on my steps. I spoke to him, but got no reply. His hat was pulled down over his eyes and I put my hand on top of his hat. I detected no signs of liquor about the man. Those steps were near the driveway of Dr. Chagnon's yard."

Mark Chase of Fall River, a hostler, formerly a policeman of the city, testified: "My place of business is at a barn on Second Street, opposite Dr. Kelley's house. I was at the barn on the morning Andrew J. Borden was murdered. About 11 o'clock I saw a carriage -- an open box buggy -- standing by a tree near the Borden house. There was a man in the carriage. I never saw the man nor the carriage before. This was shortly before 11 o'clock or 10:50. I have tried to find the man since, but have been unable to do so. I have never seen him since."

Dr. Benjamin H. Handy of Fall River testified:

"I know where the Borden house is. I went by there on the morning of the murders at 9 and 10:30. I saw a medium-sized young man, very pale in complexion, with his eyes fixed on the sidewalk, passing slowly toward the south. He was acting strangely. In consequence of his appearance I turned in my carriage to watch him as he went by; I have a faint idea that I had seen him before.

"He was agitated and seemed to be weak. He half stopped and walked on. He seemed to be mentally agitated, judging by the expression on his face."

Della Manley of Fall River said:

"I passed by the Borden house on the morning of the murder. About 9:40 I saw a man standing in the north gate dressed in light clothes. He was a young man. I did not look at him sufficiently to describe his features. It was not anybody I ever saw before. He was standing looking at us. We stopped to look at some pond lilies, and he seemed to be listening to what we were saying."

Jerome C. Borden, relative of the defendant, testified that the next day after the murders he entered the front door of the Borden house without ringing the bell. The door was shut, but not locked.

Walter P. Stevens, reporter of the Fall River *News,* said that before Officer Medley made his inspection of the barn which enabled him to testify that nobody had recently been in the barn loft, he was in the barn and saw three persons walking about in the loft.

Alfred Clarkson of Fall River corroborated the reporter's testimony. He was one of the three men who walked about in the loft, he said.

Simon Robinski, an ice-cream peddler of Fall River, was the next witness:

"I remember," said he, "the time of the Borden murders. I know now where the house is, but I didn't know then. I keep my team in Second Street. It is opposite the Borden house. I went by there in my team that morning. It was 11:03 when I left the stable.

"When I was going by, I saw a lady coming from the barn. She had on a dark-colored dress and nothing on her head. She was walking very slowly toward the house. I was on my team at the time. I had seen the servant a few weeks before and had sold her ice cream. This was not the servant."

District Attorney Knowlton made a heroic effort to tangle up the witness, who spoke English somewhat imperfectly, but without success.

Charles D. Gardner, a livery man, who boarded Robinski's horse, corroborated his testimony as to the time that he left the stables.

Everett Brown and Thomas C. Barlow testified to paying a visit to the Borden barn loft after the murders, and, as they believed, prior to the arrival of Officer Medley.

The last witness called was Joseph LeMay of Fall River, who lives on a farm four miles out of the city. He was called to tell how on Aug. 16 he had seen a man passing along the road near his farm whose clothing was bloody. The man talked about the Borden murders. Questions as to the admissibility of this testimony having arisen, the jury was excused and it was agreed to argue the matter to-morrow morning. The court then adjourned.

FALL RIVER, MASS., June 15 -- Last night a boy named Potter, son of C. C. Potter, clerk in the Fall River Water Works office, while looking for a ball, found a hatchet on the top of John Crowe's barn, which is situated just in the rear of the Borden property.

The boy this morning reported his find to the police, and also sought an interview with the counsel for defense, but was unable to find Mr. Jennings. He still has the hatchet in his possession, and describes it as an ordinary implement with a hammer head. The handle is weatherbeaten, and the blade is covered with rust.

Some of the particles of rust having been removed, a slight coloring of gilt is visible, which serves to indicate that the hatchet was quite new when lost or discarded.

EDITORIAL

June 17, 1893

WILL IT REMAIN A MYSTERY?

It is many a year since a criminal case in this country has excited such universal interest and been the subject of so much discussion as that of the Borden murder. It has all the fascination of a mystery about which there may be a thousand theories and upon which opinions may differ as variously as the idiosyncrasies of those who form them. There is so little absolute evidence that everybody can interpret the probabilities and the circumstantial indications to suit himself, and much will depend upon his general view of human nature and its capabilities. There seems to be little prospect that the mystery will be cleared up by the trial that is going on at New-Bedford. The verdict, if there shall be a verdict, will make little difference unless there is to be some disclosure of which there is yet no sign.

The whole case is a tangle of probabilities and improbabilities, with little that is certain except that a man and wife were murdered in their own home on a frequented city street in the middle of an August forenoon, with nobody about the premises, so far as has been shown, but the daughter and a servant girl. It was improbable enough that such a crime should be committed at such a time and place at all. That any one should enter the house from the outside and commit it and get away without being observed or leaving any trace behind was most improbable. But the officers of the law were unable to find any evidence that the crime was perpetrated by any one outside of the family and the testimony brought by the defense to show that it might have happened in that way has proved nothing as to the crime.

The utter absence of any other explanation was the sole support of the suspicion against the daughter. In spite of the circumstances that made it look dark for her, there was as complete a lack of direct evidence against her as of any kind of evidence against anybody else. If circumstantial evidence is a chain only as strong as its weakest link, we have presented here an attempt to make a chain out of wholly disconnected links, which has no continuity or binding strength at all. Almost as strong a case could be made out against anybody who had the misfortune to be in a house where murder was committed and not on the happiest terms with the victim. The utter absence of proof of anything except the fact of murder, and the lack of real evidence against anybody, is likely to leave this as a baffling mystery, unless a revelation should be made of which there is as yet no premonition.

June 19, 1893

LIZZIE BORDEN'S TRIUMPHS

A Week of Disaster For The Cause of the Prosecution

The Evidence Chiefly Relied on for Convicting the Prisoner Ruled Out by the Court -- The Case of the Commonwealth Weakened by Blow After Blow -- Lizzie's Friends Very Hopeful of an Acquittal, and Sure that the Jury Will Not Convict Her.

NEW-BEDFORD, MASS., June 18 -- The last week was an important one in the Borden trial. It was a week of triumph for the defense and of disaster for the prosecution. Blow after blow has fallen upon the cause of the Commonwealth, until to-night, with the evidence all in and the case nearly ready to be submitted to the jury, the friends of the accused are elated and confident, and the supporters of the prosecution are correspondingly discouraged.

It is the general opinion that Lizzie Borden can never be convicted on the evidence submitted against her, and though there is a belief that the jury will disagree, the defense feel almost certain of her ultimate freedom. On Monday came the first of the series of disasters which overtook the Commonwealth, when the presiding Justices unanimously decided that the testimony given by the defendant at the inquest in Fall River last August was not competent as evidence.

This testimony was of the most vital character to the interests of the prosecution. It was Lizzie's story of her whereabouts on the day of the homicides, and so conflicting and confused were the statements made by her that Judge Blaisdell decided at the preliminary hearing that that alone was sufficient to bind the defendant over to the Grand Jury. If this testimony had been admitted, Lizzie Borden would have been obliged to have taken the stand and undergo the sharp cross-examination of District Attorney Knowlton. As it was, the counsel for the defendant decided that it would be unwise to require the prisoner to testify in her own behalf.

The prosecution received another adverse ruling last Thursday, when the testimony of several drug clerks of Fall River was excluded. These witnesses were prepared to testify that on the day prior to the murders the defendant made two unsuccessful attempts to purchase prussic acid, giving as her reason for wishing the drug that she desired to clean sealskin furs. On Wednesday the testimony of Anna Borden, a friend of the accused, was ruled out. This witness was to testify that Lizzie, some three years ago, said that her home was an unhappy one, and that she did not desire to go back to it. This statement, it was alleged, was made by the defendant while she was on a trip to Europe.

The Government made its strongest point on the testimony of its experts. By them it showed that Mrs. Borden died at least an hour before her husband, and that the blade of the hatchet which the Commonwealth assume to have dealt the fatal blows exactly fitted into a wound in Andrew Borden's skull. It was, therefore, argued that the cutting edge of the death-dealing instrument must have been three and a half inches, the exact length of the blade of the handleless hatchet in evidence. The priority of the death of Mrs. Borden is one of the strong points in the Government's case, since it is assumed from this circumstance that Lizzie Borden must have been in the house at the time of the murder of her stepmother.

Hannah Reagan, the matron of the Fall River Police Head-quarters, told a story of a quarrel between Emma Borden and the defendant. It occurred, she said, while Lizzie was under the matron's charge in Fall River. The witness testified that, during a visit of Lizzie's sister to the jail, she heard the defendant say: "Emma, you have given me away." Emma denied the accusation, but Lizzie seemed very angry and did not speak to her sister for several hours.

The defense opened its case Thursday morning and rested on Friday afternoon. Witnesses were brought forward to show that Mrs. Reagan had absolutely denied the truth of the quarrel story on the day after the quarrel was alleged to have taken place. They showed that the police matron had made a mass of false statements, and set her testimony entirely at naught.

A strong point of the prosecution was that Lizzie had stated that she was in the barn loft for twenty minutes during the morning of the homicides. Officer Medley testified that immediately after his arrival at the Borden house, soon after the tragedy, he visited the barn loft and examined the heavy dust on the floor. There were no signs of footprints in this dust. The defense produced testimony to show that the police officer did not arrive at the Borden house until after the barn loft had been thoroughly searched by others, and that Lizzie was seen just before the discovery of the murders walking toward the house from the direction of the barn.

Other witnesses testified that the dress burned by the defendant was soiled and covered with paint. Lizzie's sister, Emma, took the stand on Friday to testify in the defendant's behalf. She said that the dress was burned at her own suggestion, since it was made unfit to wear because of its soiled condition, and that it had no trace of blood upon it. District Attorney Knowlton in cross-examination obtained from her the important statement that Lizzie had not called Mrs. Borden mother for several years prior to the homicides, and that the relations existing between the dead woman and the accused were not in all respects cordial.

The defense suffered one adverse ruling of the court by which the testimony of Joseph Lemaire was ruled out as incompetent. Lemaire would have testified that a few days after the murders he discovered a wild-appearing man in the woods. He was spotted with blood and brandished a hatchet, exclaiming from time to time, "Poor Mrs. Borden!"

Reviewing the Commonwealth's case, the only facts which remain absolutely untouched are that Mrs. Borden died some time before her husband; that a note which Lizzie alleged had been sent to her stepmother on the morning of the tragedy, requesting her to visit a sick friend, has never been traced, and that the handleless hatchet in evidence exactly fits into a wound in the skull of Andrew J. Borden.

To-morrow the pleas of the opposing counsel will be made. Ex-Gov. George D. Robinson will speak in behalf of the accused, and District Attorney Knowlton will sum up for the Commonwealth. The charge will be made on Tuesday morning by Associate Justice Dewey, and then the case will be given to the jury. The entire trial has been characterized by great promptness of action, and has been remarkably short considering the mystery of the murders and the number of witnesses who have taken the stand.

June 20, 1893

WILL GO TO THE JURY TO-DAY

Last Words For Lizzie Borden Spoken by Her Counsel

Ex.-Gov. Robinson Pleads in Her Behalf that the State's Case has Fallen to Pieces -- Many Disappointed in His Address, Which Is Almost Bare of Eloquence -- District Attorney Knowlton Started on a Powerful Argument for the Prosecution -- He will Finish This Morning.

NEW-BEDFORD, MASS., June 19 -- In the presence of an audience that so filled the courtroom that it would have been hard to squeeze in another person, ex-Gov. Robinson spoke the last words of the defense to the jury that is trying Lizzie Borden on a charge of murder. He spoke for four hours.

Many who heard him were disappointed. They had expected an eloquent address; what they heard was a calm analysis of the evidence. The argument was that the State had failed to prove its case, and that the defendant had established her innocence.

District Attorney Knowlton began his reply. He will finish it to-morrow morning. So far as he has gone he has spoken with great force and eloquence. It is expected that the case will go to the jury as early as 1 o'clock to-morrow afternoon.

Mr. Robinson began by characterizing the murders as one of the most dastardly and diabolical crimes ever committed in the State.

"A maniac, not a man of senses and heart, a lunatic, a devil.

"They were well directed blows which caused those deaths, not directed by a blunder; none going amiss. Surely we can say at the outset that this was not the careless, untrained doing of one unfamiliar with such work.

"As you begin to contemplate this crime you must say such acts are physically and morally impossible for this young woman. It is a wreck of human morals to say this of her."

Mr. Robinson disclaimed upon the part of the defendant any feelings that she had not been fairly treated by the District Attorney. That officer, he said, was not after blood, but was simply presenting to the jury the case which had been given to him by the Fall River police.

Referring to these men, Mr. Robinson said:

"I have not time to go into sarcasm and denunciation. The blue coat and brass buttons cover up what is inside. The officer is always magnifying this and minimizing that and looking for the one who committed the deed upon which he is at work. The witness stand brings out their weakness when they knock their own heads together, but after all they show themselves to be only men with human weakness."

Urging the jury to confine itself solely to the question of the guilt or innocence of the accused, Mr. Robinson said:

"It is not your business to unravel the mystery, but simply to say whether this woman is guilty -- that's all, and, though the real criminal shall never be found, better that than that you should find a wrong verdict. Not who did it, how could it have been done, but did she do it?

"You must not think for a moment that this defendant is set for the finding out of who did it. She is not a detective, and she has been in jail for nine months under constant control from the very day almost of the murders.

"Don't ask her to do impossible things, to do what she can't do; the Commonwealth doesn't want any victims, either; in olden days sacrifices were offered, but in these days we don't even hang witches in Massachusetts. I ask only that you be true to yourselves.

"Under the laws of this State the defendant is permitted to testify on the stand if she desires, but if she does not the statutes say no inference will be drawn as to her action, and the District Attorney will not insult this Court by referring to this in the slightest degree. The law holds that it is too great a strain to put on a defendant to put him on the stand in such cases, and you will not, as you go to your room, depart from this understanding. You must leave out rumors, reports, statements which you heard before the trial commenced, and leave out every single thing which Mr. Moody said he was going to prove unless he did it.

"They were going to prove that this young lady went out to buy poison, but it was not proved. It was not allowed, and I shall expect the District Attorney to get up and say so or I shall be disappointed in him.

200

"They were going to show you the defendant had contradicted herself, but the court said this was not proper.

"Now, you are not going to say, 'I rather think Messrs. Knowlton and Moody would not have offered this if they had not proof.' That won't do. Decide the case from the evidence on the witness stand and nothing else. So you will leave those things out. No poison, no instrument prepared, no statement made under oath by her that you know anything about, I don't care what you have read.

"It is for us to see whether the defendant or she and accomplices did the deed. There sits the defendant. She comes here under the presumption of innocence, and you must bind her to the axe before you can change this. The chain of direct proof only can show you that she is tied up to this thing.

"There is absolutely no direct evidence against her. Nobody saw, heard, or experienced anything to connect her with the tragedy. No knowledge or use of any instrument has been shown, and it is not shown that she ever touched one, knew of one, or bought one -- in fact, the testimony is that she did not know where such things were in the house.

"And the murders told no tale through her. Not a spot on her from her dress to her hair. Yes, there was one on the white skirt -- one as big as the head of a pin -- and that's every spot of blood that was found on her clothing, and that was on the back of her skirt, although the Government may say she turned her skirt around before she commenced. But nobody claims now that that flyspeck tells any tale.

"Then, there was some talk about a roll of burned paper. That was found by Mr. Harrington, and there were some dark insinuations floating around that Dr. Bowen knew something about it. We thought that the Government was going to claim that the hatchet handle was in that paper, and that the wood had all burned out and left the envelope, and we worried about this until Mullaly and Fleet got here together. Now we know the orphan handle is still flying in the air. For Heaven's sake, get the 125 policemen of Fall River to chase it up and put it where it belongs.

"Now," continued Mr. Robinson, "you are to conceive of the murderer standing over the woman on the floor, and you are to consider how Mr. Borden was slain. Now, what reason is there to consider this defendant guilty? What right have they to say she is?

"Well, first they say she was in the house. Well, that may be the wrong place for her to be, because it is her own home; perhaps it might be better for her to be traveling the streets, but I don't think so. She was in her room when they say Mrs. Borden's body was lying on the floor and that she must have seen the body, but you know you can't stand on the landing and look into the guest chamber.

"Then there is not the slightest evidence that the door was opened at that time, but there is evidence that it was opened later. She had no occasion to go into that spare room. You know that from the habits of the family.

"Now, you know that after the tragedy she told Bridget that Mrs. Borden had a note and had gone out. Now, Mr. Moody said in his opening that Lizzie told a lie about this, but Bridget told the fullest and clearest story about it, and holds it down to herself. There is no doubt she did have a note and she did go out. Now, a person may say, where is the note? We would be glad to see it. They say nobody has come forward to say where it went, but you will find men in the county now who don't know this trial is going on. This note may have been part of a scheme, a foul scheme. We don't know. But that Lizzie lied about it is not so.

"Now, did she go to the barn?" queried Mr. Robinson, coming to his next point. "There comes along an ice cream peddler. Not a distinguished lawyer nor a successful doctor, simply an ice cream peddler, but he knows the nature of an oath, and he saw this woman coming down the yard. He told this story on the 8th of August to the police, and they had it all in their possession. Mr. Mullaly, one of the knights of the handle, you know, says that the peddler said he went down there at 10:30, but Mullaly was contradicted by his own associate."

Mr. Robinson went on from this point to discuss the various allegations of the State as to his client's conduct just before and just after the discovery of the murders. He contended that in these times Miss Borden's behavior was that of an innocent person, and that no inference could be drawn from her acts, her speech, or her appearance favorable to the theory that she committed the murders.

"Then," said Mr. Robinson, "they say she burned the dress. The first thought is that when a person burns up anything in such a case as this an inference is drawn the wrong way as such. But you know the common way now is to burn rags, because you have got to pay the ragman something to take them away. Now the Government says, 'We want the Bedford cord and you have burned it; we want the dress you had on that morning and you have given us another one.'

"Now, there is a difference of opinion among the witnesses about the dress Lizzie wore on that morning. Bridget Sullivan had on a light blue dress that morning and the Government says Lizzie had on a light blue dress, but they were not looking for dress patterns then, and there is likely to have been a difference of opinion. You know that when the people came in at first they saw that she had not a drop of blood on her or about her anywhere.

"Now you start with a dress that every one says there was no blood on it. That dress was in that closet on the shelf, and there it remained until it was burned. Seaver and Fleet say they looked carefully in that place and could find no dress with blood on it. And Emma found that old dress there when she came home, taking up a place she wanted to use.

"But they found another dress and Dr. Dolan discovered the damning evidence, for there was blood on it. But when the dress went into the hands of a man who knew something, Prof. Wood, the dress came back, for there was no blood, and they wanted another one.

"Talk about burning an old dress! Why, it didn't cost altogether over $2. Then the police got everything they could and notified the family that they had got all through, and on Sunday morning, with the windows open, with people about, in broad daylight, she burns this old dress. Couldn't she have disposed of it more easily in a different and more secret manner?

"They will say she changed it, or that she put it under another. If she put on another, then she burned two dresses instead of one, and the Government only wants one. They will go another step in their theory and claim this woman was nude when she committed this crime."

Speaking of the shifting by the State from one hatchet to another, Mr. Robinson said:

"Fall River seems to be prolific of hatchets. If we wait a while we may find another. If we had gone to trial with the cow's hair theory when it was ripe last Fall, the prisoner might have been beyond our reach now. They have had her for ten months in irksome and wearisome and wearing control. She has been in the custody of the State, in a place to which her home was a palace by comparison. You think, gentlemen, you feel the hand of the old Commonwealth guiding you, but you do not; it is a fraud, a theory.

"Murder is bad enough, but murder at the hands of theorizing experts or practicing officers is worse."

Turning to the matter of "exclusive opportunity," Mr. Robinson said:

"They have had all sorts of theories and have abandoned them all. They say they will prove exclusive opportunity. But I say if they can lock up that house to the exclusion of everybody but the two girls, then I am willing to admit that there is strong evidence against the defendant, but it is not so.

"Let us see. The cellar door was locked, sure. The front door is said to have been locked by a bolt, a spring lock, and one other, but we don't know that. The side screen door was not locked -- that we are sure of, and there was a perfect entrance to that house by that side screen door. Bridget was outside talking with the Kelley girl and said frankly anybody could have gone in."

Mr. Robinson then took the jury through the house and detailed to them how easily a man could get into the house and secrete himself until such time as he chose to show himself. Admitting such a person was there for murder, there was no reason, he said, why he should allow a second person to interfere with him in his design. He contended that a person could have come in at the front door or the side door at various times that morning.

"The Government says nobody saw any one go in," he added. "That is true, but nobody saw Mr. Borden go out."

Recurring to the matter of the absence of blood from Miss Borden's clothing and person, Mr. Robinson said:

"A significant fact is that there was no blood on her hair, because since there was none found on her the efforts to remove it must have caused a great deal of trouble. It is assumed that she committed that first murder, and what had she to do when her father came in. Why, she must have washed herself and changed her clothes, so as to be all right when her father came, and she undoubtedly was all right when her father came.

"Bridget Sullivan, you remember, does not speak of any changes in dress all the morning, so you must have her come down in the blue dress, get out of it, get in it again, and make several changes in a very brief time.

"She would have to get the bloody dress off a second time, or else use the second bloody dress. But how is the theory of the Government to be accounted for, since there is no other dress missing but the one with the paint on it, and there was no blood on it?

"In order to fit in on the handleless hatchet theory she must go down, wash the handle, break it in two, and go beyond scientific work to get all the blood from the handle. Have I said too much when I say it was a moral and a physical impossibility for her to do all this work of hiding clues in so short a time?"

Mr. Robinson closed with the appeal to the jury to decide the case upon the evidence and deal fairly and justly by his client.

District Attorney Knowlton replied for the State. He said that the jury was trying a crime which would have been believed impossible, and was trying a woman who it would never have been believed would have been charged with the crime.

"But," said Mr. Knowlton, "it was found that these men over in Fall River who went wrong a few years ago were members of a church, and it was demonstrated that those who stand close to the sanctuary are not free from the taint of sin. It is not for me to sneer at Christians; they are all sons of Adam and are but human. They fall all the surer that their reputation has been spotless before. I don't say that because a person has led an honest and upright life therefore he or she is more susceptible to error.

"But she is a woman and it is hard to believe that women can be guilty of crime. It is not a pleasant thing to say, but they are human and no better or no worse than we. They make up for lack of strength in cunning, their hates are more undying, more unyielding, and their passions stronger. The foremost of the murderers of the early ages were women, and they have come down to these times even.

"Over those bodies we stand and we say to ourselves: Can it be possible? This is the most solemn duty of your lives."

Mr. Knowlton said that the distinguishing feature of the case was that the murdered persons did not meet their deaths at the same time.

"That," said he, "is the key of the case. It was the malice against Mrs. Borden that inspired this murder. It was the act of a person who spent the forenoon in that house, and this fact bears on this case from beginning to end."

Having made this premise, Mr. Knowlton coupled with it the assertion, which, he said, was backed by the evidence, that there was ill feeling between Lizzie Borden and her stepmother.

"There was one woman in the world," said he, "who believed that old woman stood between her father and herself. There was nothing in those blows but hatred, and a great strong man would have taken that hatchet and with one blow only would have made an end of it. The arm that wielded that hatchet was strong only in hatred.

"When that woman fell under the blows -- the 200-pound woman -- the fall must have been heard by whoever was in the house at the time. If Lizzie was down stairs she was in the passageway of the assassin; if she was up stairs she was on the same floor, quite near, and she could not have helped hearing it. No matter how craftily murder is planned there is always some point where the plans fail, and they failed her at a critical time.

"She was alone in the house with that murdered woman. She must have known it, and she knew that by and by there was coming into the house a stern and just man who would have noticed the absence of his beloved wife and who would have asked for her, and that question must be answered.

"He came in and she went to him and said: 'Mother has had a note and has gone out.' When Bridget got through her work Lizzie told her that she was going to lock the screen door, as Mrs. Borden had gone out and she might go out, too. Counsel on the other side said this statement was not a lie, but there was no note. There never was anybody sick, and the note story originated with Lizzie Borden. Bridget Sullivan said she never heard anybody come with a note. She never saw any note, and the first she heard of it was what Lizzie said."

Before Mr. Knowlton could elaborate his theory and connect the killing of Mr. Borden with that of Mrs. Borden court adjourned until to-morrow.

After the evidence had been submitted in the Borden case, the one remaining task for the court was to instruct the all-male jury on the applicable law of the Commonwealth. In the American justice system, where an accused exercises his or her right to a jury trial, the jurors are the sole finders of the facts; that is, the jury alone determines what *in fact* happened from listening to the testimony of witnesses and viewing tangible exhibits admitted into evidence during the trial. The jury applies the criminal law, as explained by the court, to the facts as they find them and arrives at a verdict of guilt or innocence. The judge is prohibited from invading this province of the jury by expressing personal opinion about the evidence or otherwise influencing the jury in their fact-finding mission.

In a criminal case it is the responsibility of the trial judge to instruct the jury that the burden of proving each element of the alleged crime, beyond a reasonable doubt, rests with the prosecution; that the accused is presumed innocent until his or her guilt is established beyond a reasonable doubt; and that the jurors are the sole judges of the credibility of the witnesses and the weight to be given to their testimony. If jurors find conflict in the testimony of the witnesses that they cannot reconcile, it is their province to choose whom to believe and whom not to believe. In weighing the evidence, the panel may consider the interests that any witness may have in the result of the trial, the witness's demeanor on the witness stand, the plausibility of his testimony, his means of knowing the things about which he testified, his relationship (if any) to the accused or other interested persons, and such other considerations as may appear right and proper in arriving at the truthfulness of each and every witness.

A major feature of the Borden case was the prosecution's need to rely only on circumstantial evidence. The prosecutor had no direct evidence or eyewitness testimony as to the identity of the guilty person. When a jury is asked to infer the existence of "B" from proof of "A", the court is also required to charge the jury that "every reasonable hypothesis of innocence" must be removed before the jury can convict the accused. And the judge is not permitted to speculate as to possible theories about the strength of the evidence.

It is in the light of these standards of judicial behavior that Judge Dewey's charge to the jury deserves close scrutiny. Clearly he departed from his role and went beyond the limits of judicial action prescribed by law. Dewey's expressions of opinion were sometimes subtle, sometimes direct. For example his phrase, "I understand," often preceded some statement in which Dewey seemed to cast doubt on the testimony of witnesses or the facts in the government's case.

Like the defense attorneys and the prosecution, Judge Dewey appealed to the social prejudices and beliefs of his hearers. Consider, for example, his cautionary instruction as to Mrs. Gifford's testimony: he urged jurors to view her (possibly damaging) account of Lizzie's words against her stepmother in light of the fact that her language was "the language of a young woman and not a philosopher or jurist." Judge Dewey's charge is replete with this kind of guidance to the jury and reveals the avenues by which ideas and beliefs as well as evidence might have shaped the jurors' judgments in the case.

Judge Dewey's instructions lasted one and one-half hours -- an unusually long charge. One might wonder if he saw posterity, as well as those seated in the courtroom, as his audience. The jury, after retiring, voted immediately and unanimously for acquittal, then waited an hour before returning to the courtroom with their verdict. To what extent the court's instructions swayed or otherwise influenced the jury in their findings is, of course, a matter of conjecture. One writer has described the charge as "a plea for the innocent."

Text of the Charge

Source: From *Commonwealth v. Lizzie A. Borden.* Text provided courtesy of the Boston Public Library. Published by permission of Chief Justice James P. Lynch, Jr., Superior Court, Commonwealth of Massachusetts (Boston).

A Note on the Text: This text is reprinted here exactly as it appears in the typewritten court record, including all errors and eccentricities of punctuation, spelling, grammar, and language.

Mr. Foreman and gentlemen of the Jury:

You have listened with attention to the evidence in this case, and to the arguments of the defendant's counsel and of the District Attorney. It now remains for me, acting in behalf of the court, to give you such aid towards a proper performance of your duty as I may be able to give within the limits for judicial action prescribed by law; and, to prevent any erroneous impression, it may be well for me to bring to your attention, at the outset, that it is provided by a statute of this State that the Court shall not charge juries with respect to matters of fact, but may state the testimony of the law.

Without attempting to define the exact scope of this statute, it is not to be doubted, in view of expositions made of it by our court of last resort, that it was intended to prevent the judge presiding at the trial from expressing any opinion as to the credibility of witnesses or the strength of evidence, while it does not preclude them from defining the degree of weight which the law attaches to a whole class of testimony, leaving it to the jury to apply the general rule to the circumstances of the case.

207

I may perhaps illustrate this distinction in the course of my remarks; but, speaking comprehensively, I may now say to you that it will be your duty, in considering and deciding the matters of fact necessary to rendering your verdict, not to allow your judgment to be affected by what you may suppose or believe to be the opinion of the Court upon such matters of fact.

The law places upon the Court the duty and responsibility of furnishing you with a correct statement of such rules and principles of law, applicable to the case, as you need to know; and places upon you, and you only, the distinct duty and responsibility of deciding all questions of fact involved in the issue between the Commonwealth and the defendant; and your decision can properly rest only on the law and the evidence given you, together with those matters of common knowledge and experience relating to the ordinary affairs of life, and the common qualities of human nature and motives of action, which are never proved in court, but which, as jurors, you are expected to bring with you to this investigation.

I will here add that nothing in the prior official proceedings in this case, neither the inquest nor the hearing or trial in the District Court at Fall River, nor the action of Grand Jury in finding the indictment can properly influence your judgment in this case. In connection with those proceedings, by the usual legal formalities, the case is brought before you for inquiry, and it is independently of any official action that has gone before. It is still more plain that neither the defendant's confinement in prison nor coming here in the custody of an officer, nor the legal restraint under which she manifestly is, raise against her any presumption of guilt. They are a part of that necessary discomfort which, under our laws as they now are, one is called to experience who is regularly charged with a capital crime. The defendant is being tried before you on a written accusation, termed an indictment, which contains two charges or counts; one count by the use of the usual legal language in substance charges her with the murder of Andrew J. Borden in Fall River in this county on August 4, 1892. Chapter 202 of the Public Statutes contains these sections: "Murder committed with deliberately premeditated malice aforethought, or in the commission of or attempt to commit a crime punishable with death or imprisonment for life, or committed with extreme atrocity or cruelty is murder in the first degree. Murder not appearing to be in the first degree, is murder in the second degree.

The degree of murder shall be found by the Jury," -- in connection with rendering their verdict, if they find against the defendant. The Government claims that the killing of Mr. and Mrs. Borden, by whomsoever done, was done with premeditated, deliberate malice aforethought within the meaning of the statute and it was murder in the first degree. The statute nowhere defines murder itself, and for such definition we must resort to the common law, and according to that law "murder is the unlawful killing of a human being with malice aforethought." A short explanation may be needed of these elements of murder in the first degree. The term malice as here used means more than personal hatred or ill-will. It means any unlawful motive, or it is sometimes said to denote a state of mind manifested by the wrongful act done intentionally without just cause or excuse. The words malice aforethought by themselves alone have been settled by our Supreme Court to imply purpose and design in contradistinction to accident or mischance. The words "deliberately premeditated" mean that the wrongful intention to kill must have been formed before the act of killing. The killing must be the result of a plan or purpose to kill unlawfully, formed without reflection and deliberation by the guilty party. The law does not require that this intention, plan or purpose to kill shall have existed for any considerable time before it is carried out. The time may be very short. It is enough if there was a clear intent to kill formed before the act of killing; and so the Government claims that you ought to be satisfied that the killing of Mr. and Mrs. Borden was wrongful and malicious, that is, without just cause or excuse, and that it was deliberately premeditated, -- that is, the design to do it was first formed and after that was carried out.

Although most of the evidence may relate to both counts in the indictment, the counts are distinct, and will require a separate finding by you.

The second main proposition in the case is that the killing of Mr. and Mrs. Borden was done by the defendant. In considering the evidence with regard to this issue, you will need to have certain legal principles in mind and to use them as guides. One such principle is the presumption of law that the defendant is innocent. This presumption begins with her at the outset of the trial, and continues with her through all its stages until you are compelled by the evidence to divest her of it. As one learned writer has expressed it, "This legal presumption of innocence is to be regarded by the jury in every case as matter of evidence to the benefit of which the party is entitled." This presumption of innocence operating in behalf of the defendant also operates in behalf of all of us, and as was declared in an important capital trial, it is a presumption founded on that universal beneficence of the law which says that every man does right till the contrary appear.

The law does not undertake to fix or measure the force of this presumption in this case by any formal or arbitrary rules, but leaves it to your just and intelligent judgment. It may vary in different cases, its force being strengthened amongst other things by the character and previous way of life of the defendant. I understand the government to concede that defendant's character has been good; that it has not been merely a negative and neutral one that nobody had heard anything against, but one of positive, of active benevolence in religious and charitable work. The question is whether the defendant, being such as she was, did the acts charged upon her. You are not inquiring into the action of some imaginary being, but into the action of a real person, the defendant, with her character, with her habits, with her education, with her ways of life as they have been disclosed in the case. Judging of this subject as reasonable men you have the right to take into consideration her character such as is admitted or apparent. In some cases it may not be esteemed of much importance. In other cases it may raise a reasonable doubt of a defendant's guilt even in the face of strongly criminating circumstances. What shall be its effect here rests in your reasonable discretion.

It is competent for the government to show that the defendant had motives to commit the crime with which she is charged, and evidence has been introduced from which you are asked to find that she had unpleasant relations with her stepmother, the deceased, and also that her father, Andrew Jackson Borden, left an estate of the value of from $250,000 to $300,000, and that so far as is known to the defendant, he died without having made a will. If his wife died before him, it is not disputed that he left the defendant and her sister as his only heirs. It appears that Mr. Borden was 69 years old, and Mrs. Borden more than 60 years of age at the time of their deaths. Taking the facts now as you find them to be established by the evidence, and taking the defendant as you find her to be, and judging according to general experience and observation, was the defendant under a real and actually operating motive to kill her father and his wife? An able writer on the criminal law says:

"In the affairs of life it is seldom a man does anything prompted by one motive alone to accomplish one end." Unless the child be destitute of natural affection, will the desire to come into possession of the inheritance be likely to constitute an active, efficient inducement for the child to take the parent's life?

If you find as a fact that the defendant was under an actually operating motive, pecuniary or any other, to destroy the life of her father and stepmother, then it becomes a matter proper to be considered. For, as one has said: "It may tend to repel the presumption which exists, in addition to the general presumption of innocence, that a person will not commit a crime without reason, inducement or temptation."

It is not necessary for the government to prove motive. It has been said that there can be no adequate motive for murder, but it is a part of the folly and sin of man that he will sometimes act contrary to the highest and strongest motive: by his perversity he will make a weak motive strong and then act upon it.

Imputing a motive to defendant does not prove that she had it. I understand the counsel for the government to claim that defendant had towards her stepmother a strong feeling of illwill, nearly if not quite amounting to hatred. And Mrs. Gifford's testimony as to a conversation with defendant in the early spring of 1892 is relied upon largely as a basis for that claim, supplemented by whatever evidence there is as to defendant's conduct towards her stepmother.

Now, gentlemen, in judging wisely of a case you need to keep all parts of it in their natural and proper proportion, and not to put on any particular piece of evidence a greater weight than it will reasonably bear, and not to magnify or intensify or depreciate and belittle any piece of evidence to meet an emergency. I shall say something before I have done on the caution to be used in considering testimony as to conversations. But take Mrs. Gifford's just as she gave it, and consider whether or not it will fairly amount to the significance attached to it, remembering that it is the language of a young woman and not of a philosopher or a jurist. What, according to common observation, is the habit of young women in the use of language? Is it not rather that of intense expression, whether that of admiration or dislike? Consider whether or not they do not often use words which, strictly taken, would go far beyond their real meaning. Would it be a just mode of reasoning to make use of the alleged subsequent murder to put enmity into the words and then use the words, thus charged with hostile meaning, as evidence that defendant committed the murder?

Again, every portion of the testimony should be estimated in the light of all the rest. What you wish, of course, is a true conception, -- a true conception of the state of the mind of the defendant towards her stepmother, not years ago, but later and nearer the time of the homicide; and to get such a true conception you must not separate Mrs. Gifford's testimony from all the rest, but consider also the evidence as to how they lived in the family: whether, as Mrs. Raymond, I believe, said, they sewed together on each other's dresses; whether they went to church together, sat together, returned together: in a word, the general tenor of their life. You will particularly recall the testimony of Bridget Sullivan and of defendant's sister Emma, bearing on the same subject. Weigh carefully all the testimony on the subject in connection with the suggestions of counsel, and then judge whether or not there is clearly proved such a permanent state of mind on the part of defendant towards her stepmother as to justify you in drawing against her upon that ground inferences unfavorable to her innocence.

Recall the evidence; reflect upon it; compare one part of it with another, and see whether you, as intelligent and reasonable men, desiring to approach the consideration of this case from a just and true standpoint, would be warranted upon the evidence in taking into your minds the conception and allowing that conception to operate upon all

211

your construction and estimation of the other evidence, -- the conception that at and about the time of these murders this defendant had towards her stepmother a feeling that could be properly called hatred. If that is not a just conception warranted by the evidence, then it should not enter and find lodgment in your minds as a controlling idea under the operation of which the evidence in this case is to be judged. Such a conception, if erroneous, may be more serious upon the operations of your mind and more liable to affect improperly your final conclusion than a mistake on any single portion of the evidence. Because, if it is a wrong conception, unwarranted by the evidence, unjust to the defendant, and you start out in the case with that, it colors and affects all the action of your minds till your verdict is rendered.

Now, gentlemen, the material charge in the first count of the indictment is that, at Fall River, in this County, the defendant killed Mrs. Borden, by striking, cutting, beating, and bruising her on the head with some sharp cutting instrument. In the second count the same charges are made in regard to Mr. Borden. And the Government claims that those acts were done with deliberately premeditated malice aforethought, and so were acts of murder in the first degree.

The law requires that before the defendant can be found guilty upon either count in the indictment every material allegation in it shall be proved beyond a reasonable doubt.

Now what do the words "beyond reasonable doubt" mean? Some courts do not favor an attempt to define them, thinking that the jury can judge as well without any suggestions. But I am unwilling to omit any further explanation, and I can in no way give you so accurate a description of their meaning, as by reading to you an extract from an opinion of the Court by whose views it is our duty to be governed. The Court says: "Proof beyond reasonable doubt, is not beyond all possible or imaginary doubt, but such proof as precludes every reasonable hypothesis or theory except that which it tends to support. It is proof to a moral certainty, as distinguished from an absolute certainty. As applied to a judicial trial for crime, the two phrases, beyond reasonable doubt, and to a moral certainty, are synonymous and equivalent. They mean the same thing. Each has been used by eminent judges to explain the other, and each signifies such proof as satisfies the judgment and conscience of the jury as reasonable men, and applying their reason to the evidence before them, that the crime charged has been committed by the defendant, and so satisfies them as to have no other reasonable conclusion possible. In other words, they must have as clear and strong a conviction in their own minds of the truth of that conclusion as they would require to have in the truth of a conclusion to be acted on by them in matters of the highest importance to themselves."

Now you observe, gentlemen, that the Government submits this case to you upon circumstantial evidence. No witness testifies to seeing the defendant in the act of doing the crime charged, but the Government seeks to establish by proof a body of facts and circumstances from which you are asked to infer or conclude that the defendant killed Mr. and Mrs. Borden.

This is a legal and not unusual way of proving a criminal case, and it is clearly competent for a jury to find a person guilty of murder upon circumstantial evidence alone. Indeed judges and juries have been somewhat divided in their views as to the comparative strength and value of circumstantial and direct evidence. In direct evidence witnesses testify that they have actual and immediate knowledge of the matter to be proved, so that the main thing to be determined is whether the witnesses are worthy of belief. The chief difficulty with this kind of evidence is that the witnesses may be false or mistaken, while the nature of the case may be such that there are no means of discovering the falsehood or mistake.

In circumstantial evidence the facts relied upon are usually various, and testified to by a large number of witnesses, as you have seen in this case. When the evidence comes from several witnesses and different sources, it is thought that there is more difficulty in arranging it so as to escape detection if it is false or founded on mistake. The principle that underlies circumstantial evidence we are constantly acting on in our business, namely, the inferring of one fact from other facts proved.

Sometimes the inference is direct, and almost certain. For instance, the noise of a pistol is heard from a certain room in a hotel. The door is unlocked or otherwise opened. A man is found, just dead, with a bullet hole in his temple. Near him is a revolver with one barrel discharged. In such a case, if no contradictory or controlling facts appeared, we should infer, with a very strong assurance, that the death was caused by the pistol. In other cases the facts from which the conclusion is sought to be drawn are numerous and complicated, and the conclusion not so closely connected with the facts or so easy to draw.

This is illustrated by the case on trial here. You have got to go through a long and careful investigation to ascertain what facts are proved. This is the same process essentially that you go through in dealing with direct evidence. Then after you have determined what specific facts are proved, you have remaining the important duty of deciding whether or not you are justified in drawing and will draw from these facts the conclusion of guilt. Here therefore is a two-fold liability to error, first in deciding upon the evidence what facts are proved, and second in deciding what inference or conclusion shall be drawn from the facts. This is often the critical or turning point in a case resting on circumstantial evidence. The law warrants you in acting firmly and with confidence on such evidence, but does require you to exercise a deliberate and sober judgment, and use great caution not to form a hasty or erroneous conclusion. You are allowed to deal with this matter with your minds untrammelled by any artificial or arbitrary rule of law. As a great judge has said, "The common law appeals to the plain dictates of common experience and sound judgment." The inference to be drawn from all the facts must be a reasonable and natural one, and to a moral certainty a certain one. It is not sufficient that it is probable only. It must be reasonably and morally certain.

In dealing with circumstantial evidence in such a case as this some special considerations need to be borne in mind. One of them is this. Inasmuch as the conclusion of guilt, if rendered at all, must be inferred or reached from other facts that are proved, every fact which in your judgment is so important and essential that without it the conclusion of guilt could not be reached must itself be proved beyond reasonable doubt, must be proved by the same weight and force of evidence as if it were the main fact in issue. But in seeking to establish a case by circumstantial evidence it may often happen that many facts are given in evidence, not because they are thought to be necessary to the conclusion sought to be proved, but to show that they are not inconsistent with that conclusion, but favorable to it, and have some tendency to rebut a contrary presumption.

If any facts of this second class should fail to be proved to your satisfaction, that would not prevent you from drawing the conclusion of guilt from the other facts, if they are sufficient to warrant it. In other words, failure to prove a fact essential to the conclusion of guilt, and without which that conclusion would not be reached, is fatal to the government's case, but failure to prove a helpful but not essential fact may not be fatal.

Now let me illustrate. Take an essential fact. All would admit that the necessity of establishing the presence of the defendant in the house, when, for instance, her father was killed, is a necessary fact. The government could not expect that you would find her guilty of the murder of her father by her own hand unless you are satisfied that she was where he was when he was murdered. And if the evidence left you in reasonable doubt as to that fact, so vital, so absolutely essential, the government must fail of its case, whatever may be the force and significance of other facts, that is, so far as it is claimed that she did the murder with her own hands.

Now, take the instance of a helpful fact. The question of the relation of this handleless hatchet to the murder. It may have an important bearing upon the case, upon your judgment of the relations of the defendant to these crimes, whether the crime was done by that particular hatchet or not, but it cannot be said, and is not claimed by the government that it bears the same essential and necessary relation to the case that the matter of her presence in the house does. It is not claimed by the government but what that killing might have been done with some other instrument. Take another illustration. I understand the government to claim substantially that the alleged fact that the defendant made a false statement in regard to her step-mother's having received a note or letter that morning bears an essential relation to the case, bears to the relation of an essential fact, not merely the relation of a useful fact.

And so the counsel in his opening referring to that matter charged deliberately upon the defendant that she had told a falsehood in regard to that note. In other words, that she had made statements about it which she knew at the time of making them were untrue, and the learned District Attorney, in his closing argument adopts and reaffirms that charge against the defendant.

Now what are the grounds on which the Government claims that that charge is false, knowingly false? There are these, as I understand them, -- one that the man who wrote it has not been found it, second that the party who brought it has not been found and third that no letter has been found, and substantially, if I understand the position correctly, upon these three grounds you are asked to find that an essential fact -- a deliberate falsehood on the part of the defendant has been established.

Now what answer or reply is made to this charge? First, that the defendant had time to think of it; she was not put in a position upon the evidence where she was compelled to make that statement without any opportunity for reflection. If, as the Government claims, she had killed her step-mother some little time before, she had a period in which she could turn over the matter in her mind. She must naturally anticipate, if she knew the facts, that the question at no remote period would be asked her where Mrs. Borden was, or if she knew where she was. She might reasonably and naturally expect that that question would arise. Again, it will be urged in her behalf, what motive had she to invent a story like this? What motive? Would it not have answered every purpose to have her say and would it not have been more natural for her to say simply that her step-mother had gone out on an errand or to make a call? What motive had she to take upon herself the responsibility of giving utterance to this distinct and independent fact of a letter or note received with which she might be confronted and which might afterwards find it difficult to explain, if she knew that no such thing was true? Was it a natural thing to say situated as they were, living as they did, taking the general tenor of their ordinary life, was it a natural thing for her to invent? But it is said no letter was found. Suppose you look at the case for a moment from her stand-point, contemplate the possibility of there being another assassin than herself, might it not be a part of the plan or scheme of such a person by such a document or paper to withdraw Mrs. Borden from the house? If he afterwards came in there, came upon her, killed her, might he not have found the letter

215

or note with her, if there was one already in the room? Might he not have a reasonable and natural wish to remove that as one possible link in tracing himself? Taking the suggestions on the one side and the other, judging the matter fairly, not assuming beforehand that the defendant is guilty, does the evidence satisfy you as reasonable men beyond any reasonable doubt that these statements of the defendant in regard to that note must necessarily be false? Sometimes able judges and writers in dealing with circumstantial evidence, have made use of illustrations. They have compared the indispensable facts to the several links in a chain. If one link of the chain breaks, the chain ceases to serve its purpose as a chain, no matter how strong the remaining links may be. So in the chain of circumstantial evidence, if one essential fact fails to be proved, the connection is broken, a gap arises in the process of proof and it cannot be legally affirmed that the conclusion aimed at is established beyond reasonable doubt.

Sometimes the process of proof by circumstances is compared to a rope cable and the several facts that may be material but not absolutely essential to the conclusion, are likened to the strands or cords in that cable. Some of the strands or cords may give way and yet the cable may not be broken, but may bear the strain put upon it. So in the process of proof by circumstantial evidence. Important but not absolutely essential facts may fail to be established, and the loss of them, while it may weaken, may not destroy the force of the remaining evidence. But I much doubt whether in ordinary life in reaching a solution and determination of problems that arise, the elements on which our decision depends assume either in the visible outward world or in our minds, the relation to each other of links in a chain or strands in a cable. Some of the facts may have a real connection with each other so that one may involve or imply the other; and they may thereby have additional weight and importance to us. Another fact may be independent of the rest, may have no connection with them in the real and outward world, the only connection being in our minds, and yet this separate fact may be decisive upon our conclusion. Let me illustrate: Suppose a gentleman already engaged in business is proposing to himself to start some kind of manufacturing business in this city. He inquires into the matter, the cost of his plant, the facilities for transportation, the cost of making the article intended, the probable demand for and price of the goods in the market, and all such other things as a prudent man would consider, and reaches the conclusion with a clear and strong assurance on which he is ready to act, that he will go forward with the enterprise. He then mentions his plan to his family physician. The physician at once says to him: This new enterprise may promise all that you think of it, but you must not undertake it. You are already carrying all the burden that your strength of body or mind will endure. If you take on another burden there is great danger that it will be disastrous to you. Having confidence in the skill and fidelity of his physician and believing the opinion given to be correct, he at once decides to relinquish the enterprise. Now we see a large body of facts leading to a certain conclusion are controlled by one separate fact opposed to that conclusion. Yet the body of facts and the separate fact have no connection with each other, save in the person's mind. This body of facts had nothing to do with cause, his state of health, and his state of health had nothing to do with the body of facts.

Hence it is a rule in the use of circumstantial evidence that as every real fact is connected with every other real fact, so every fact proved must be reasonably consistent with the main fact sought to be proved, -- namely in this case, the fact of the defendant's guilt. However numerous may be the facts in the Government's process of proof tending to show defendant's guilt, yet if there is a fact established -- whether in that line of proof or outside of it -- which cannot reasonably be reconciled with her guilt, then guilt cannot be said to be established. Now gentlemen, you know that I am expressing no opinion as to what is proved: I am only trying to illustrate principles and rules of law and evidence. Referring to the present case let me use this illustration: Suppose you were clearly satisfied upon the testimony that if defendant committed the homicides she could by no reasonable possibility have done so without receiving upon her person and clothing a considerable amount of blood stain; that when Bridget Sullivan came to her upon call and not long after some of the other women, she had no blood stains upon her person or clothing; that she had no sufficient opportunity either to remove the stain from her person or clothing, or to change her clothing. If these supposed facts should be found by you to be real facts, you could not say upon the evidence that defendant's guilt was to a moral certainty proved. So you see that in estimating the force of different facts, or portions of the evidence it is not enough to consider them as standing apart, for the force which they appear to have when looked at by themselves, may be controlled by some other single fact. In order to warrant a conviction on circumstantial evidence it is not necessary for the Government to show that by no possibility was it in the power of any other person than the defendant to commit the crimes; but the evidence must be such as to produce a conviction amounting to a reasonable and moral certainty that the defendant and no one else did commit them. The Government claims that you should be satisfied upon the evidence that defendant was so situated that she had an opportunity to perpetuate both the crimes charged upon her. Whether this claim is sustained is for your judgment. By itself alone the fact, if shown, that the defendant had the opportunity to commit the crimes would not justify a conviction; but this fact if established, becomes a matter for your consideration in connection with the other evidence. When was Mrs. Borden killed? At what time was Mr. Borden killed? Did the same person kill both of them? Was defendant in the house when Mrs. Borden was killed? Was she in the house when Mr. Borden was killed? In this connection you will carefully consider any statements and explanations of defendant put in evidence by the Government and shown to have been made by defendant at the time or afterwards, as to where she was when either of them was killed, and all other evidence tending to sustain or disprove the truth and accuracy of these statements. Did other persons, known or unknown, have an equal or a practical and available opportunity to commit these crimes? Is there reason to believe that any such person had any motive to commit them? Is there anything in the way and manner of doing the acts of killing, the weapon used, whatever it was, or the force applied, which is significant as to the sex and strength of the doer of the acts? For instance, the medical experts have testified as to the way in which they think the blows were inflicted on Mrs. Borden, and as to what they think was the position of the assailant. Are those views correct? If so, are they favorable to the contention that a person of defendant's sex and size was the assailant? Is it reasonable and credible that she could have killed Mrs. Borden at or about the time claimed by the Government, and then with the purpose in her mind to kill her father at a later hour, have gone about her household affairs with no change of manner to excite attention? As you have the right to reason from what you know of the laws and properties of matter, so you have a right to reason and judge from what you know of the laws and property of human nature and action; and if it is suggested that the killing of Mr. Borden was not a part of the original plan, that it was an incident arising afterwards, it will be for you to consider under all the circumstances, and upon all the evidence whether that suggestion seems to you to be reasonable and well founded.

Several witnesses called by the Government have testified to statements said to have been made by defendant in reply to questions asked, I believe in each instance, as to where she was when her father was killed, and considerable importance is attached by the Government to the language which it is claimed was used by her as showing that she professed not only to have been in the barn, but up stairs in the barn. And the Government further claims it is not worthy of belief that she was in the upper part of the barn, as she says, because of the extreme heat there and because one of the officers testifies that on examination they found no tracks in the dust on the stairs and flooring. Now what statements on the subject the defendant did make and their significance and effect is wholly for you upon the evidence, and there is no rule of law to control your judgment in weighing that evidence. But here, gentlemen, I may repeat to you the language of a thoughtful writer on the law, not as binding upon you, but as containing suggestions useful to be borne in mind in dealing with this class of evidence. He says, "with respect to all verbal admissions it may be observed that they ought to be received with great caution. The evidence, consisting as it does, in the mere repetition of oral statements, is subject to much imperfection and mistake, and the party himself either being misinformed, or not having clearly expressed his own meaning, or the witness having misunderstood him. It frequently happens also, that the witness, by unintentionally altering a few of the expressions really used, gives an effect to the statement completely at variance with what the party actually did say. But where the admission is deliberately made and precisely identified, the evidence it affords is often of the most satisfactory nature."

Gentlemen, it will be for you to judge whether that extract which I read, which I give to you in the way of suggestion and not as a binding authority, expresses a reasonable principle, a principle that is wise and safe and prudent to be acted upon in such a case as this -- whether there is not more danger of some misunderstanding, some inaccuracy, some error creeping into evidence when it relates to statements than there is when it relates to acts. Would you not hold that it was a just and reasonable view to take that if a party is to be held responsible in a case like this largely upon statements, that those statements should be most carefully and thoroughly proved?

Now the government has called as witnesses some gentlemen of scientific and medical knowledge and experience, who are termed experts, and there has been put into the case considerable testimony from them. Now, following a distinction which I have before pointed out, I think I may say to you that expert testimony constitutes a class of evidence which the law requires you to subject to careful scrutiny. It is a matter of frequent observation to see experts of good standing expressing conflicting and irreconcilable views upon questions arising at a trial. They sometimes manifest a strong bias or partisan spirit in favor of the party employing them. They often exhibit a disposition to put forward theories rather than to verify or establish or illustrate the facts. While they are supposed to testify on matters not the subject of common knowledge and experience, and in distinction from ordinary witnesses are allowed to express their opinions where the ordinary witness could not, yet when the jury pass judgment upon them and their testimony they have no peculiar privileges. The jury have the full right to consider them, their appearance, their candor or want of it, their apparent skill, the reasons they give in support of their view, the nature of any experiments which they have made, the consistency or otherwise of what they say with other proved facts or with the common knowledge and experience of the jury, and finally, acting under a due sense of their responsibilities, to give the testimony of the experts such value and weight as it seems to deserve. It often happens that experts testify to what is in substance a matter of fact rather than of opinion. A surveyor called to prove the distance between two points may express his opinions founded on his observation, or he may say, "I have actually applied my measuring chain and found the distance." So, for instance, Professor Wood may say, "There are in science tests of the presence of blood as fixed and certain as the surveyor's chain is of distance. I have applied those tests to supposed blood stains on a hatchet, and I find no blood;" or, "I have applied them to stains on a piece of board furnished, and I find it to be a blood stain." This testimony may be regarded as little a matter of opinion as the testimony of a surveyor. On the other hand, if Professor Wood shall be asked to testify as to the length of time between the deaths of Mr. and Mrs. Borden, from his examination of the contents of the stomachs, his testimony must perhaps be to some extent a matter of opinion, depending possibly on the health and vigor of the two persons and constitutional differences; upon whether they were physically active after eating, or at rest; upon whether one or the other was mentally worried and anxious, or otherwise. Now his knowledge and skill may enable him to form an opinion upon the subject with greater or less correctness; but the question to be dealt with is by its essential nature different from the other. If you should accept his testimony as correct and satisfactory on the first subject, it would not necessarily follow that you should on the second. So as to whether certain wounds in the skull were caused by a particular hatchet head or could have been caused by that hatchet head only, if you have the hatchet head and the skull you may think you can apply them to each other and judge as well as the expert. I call your attention to the subject in this way to make clear to you, first, that you are not concluded on any subject by the testimony of the experts, and, second, that it is important to apply to their testimony an intelligent and discriminating judgment. So doing, you may find that each person who has appeared as an expert has so testified as to warrant your confidence in his skill and knowledge, in his fairness, and in the correctness of his opinions.

Now, gentlemen, I have been asked by the counsel for the Commonwealth to give you instruction upon another view of this case, a view, so far as I remember, not suggested in the opening, or in the evidence, or hardly in the closing argument for the Commonwealth. And yet the evidence is of such a nature that it seems to us that, as a matter of law, the Government is entitled to have some instruction given you on this point; as a matter of fact, it would be entirely for you to consider whether the claim of the Government upon the matter to which I am now going to refer is consistent with claim which it has argued to you; whether the Government has not put this case to you, practically, upon the idea that the defendant did these acts with her own hands.

But it is a principle of law that a person may be indicted in just the form in which this defendant is indicted, that is, indicted as if she were charged with doing the act herself, and yet she may be convicted upon evidence which satisfies a jury beyond reasonable doubt that the act was done personally by another party, and that her relation to it was that of being present, aiding, abetting, sustaining, encouraging. If she stood in such a relation as that to the act, the act was done by some other person and she aided him, encouraged him, abetted him, was present somewhere, by virtue of an understanding with him, where she could render him assistance, and for the purpose of rendering assistance, then she would be a principal in the act just as much as the other party who might be acting.

But you notice the essential element. There must have been an understanding between her and this third party, if there was one, an agreement together for the commission of these crimes. She must have given her assent to it. She must have encouraged it. She must have been in a position where she could render assistance to the perpetrator, with his knowledge, by virtue of an understanding with him, and for the purpose of giving assistance either in the way of watching against some person's coming or furnishing him facilities for escape or in some other manner. The central idea of this proposition is that she must have been present by virtue of an agreement with the actor where she could render assistance of some kind, and for the purpose of rendering assistance. And if there was another party in this crime, and if she is proved beyond reasonable doubt to have sustained the relation to him in committing that crime which I have expressed to you, then she might be held under this indictment, because under such circumstances in the eye of the law, they both being in the sense of the law present, the act of one is the act of both.

Gentlemen, something has been said to you by counsel as to defendant's not testifying. I must speak to you on this subject. The constitution of our State in its Bill of Rights provides that "No subject shall be compelled to accuse or furnish evidence against himself." By the common law persons on trial for crime have no right to testify in their own defense. We have now a statute in these words, "In the trial of all indictments, complaints, and other proceedings against persons charged with the commission of crimes or offenses, a person so charged shall, at his own request, but not otherwise, be deemed a competent witness; and his neglect or refusal to testify shall not create any presumption against him." You will notice that guarded language of the statute. It recognizes and affirms the common law rule that the defendant in a criminal prosecution is an incompetent witness for himself, but it provides that on one condition only, namely, his own request, he shall be deemed competent. Till that request is made he remains incompetent. In this case the defendant has made no such request, and she stands before you, therefore, as a witness incompetent, and it is clearly your duty to consider this case and form your judgment upon it as if the defendant had no right whatever to testify.

The Supreme Court, speaking of a defendant's rights and protection under the constitution and statutes, uses these words, "Nor can any inference be drawn against him from his failure to testify." Therefore I say to you, and I mean all that my words express, any argument, any implication, any suggestion, any consideration in your minds, unfavorable to defendant based on her failure to testify is unwarranted in law.

Nor is defendant called upon to offer any explanation of her neglect to testify. If she were required to explain, others might think the explanation insufficient. Then she would lose the protection of the statute. It is a matter which the law submits to her own discretion, and to that alone. You can see, gentlemen, that there may be cases where this right to testify would be valuable to a defendant. It may be able to afford the jury some further information or give some explanation that would help the defense. In another case where there was no doubt that an offense had been committed by some one, he might have no knowledge as to how or by whom it was done, and could only affirm under oath his innocence, which is already presumed. The defendant may say, "I have already told to the officers all that I know about this case, and my statements have been put in evidence; whatever is mysterious to others is also a mystery to me. I have no knowledge more than others have. I have never professed to be able to explain how or by whom these homicides were committed."

There is another reason why defendant might not wish to testify. Now she is sacredly guarded by the law from all unfavorable inferences drawn from her silence. If she testifies she becomes a witness with less than the privileges of an ordinary witness. She is subject to cross-examination. She may be asked questions that are legally competent which she is not able to answer, or she may answer questions truly and yet it may be argued against her that her answers were untrue, and her neglect to answer perverse. Being a party she is exposed to peculiar danger of having her conduct on the stand and her testimony severely scrutinized and perhaps misjudged, of having her evidence claimed to be of little weight, if favorable to herself, and of great weight so far as any part of it shall admit of an adverse contruction. She is left free, therefore, to avoid such risks.

Gentlemen, we have given our attention to particular aspects of this case and of the evidence. Let us look at it broadly.

The government charges the defendant with the murder of Mr. and Mrs. Borden. The defendant denies the charges. The law puts on the government the burden of proving beyond reasonable doubt every fact necessary to establish guilt. The defendant is bound to

222

prove nothing. The law presumes she is innocent. The case is said to be mysterious. If so, the defendant cannot be required to clear up the mystery. There is no way, under the law, by which the burden of proof as to any essential matter can be transferred to her. The government offers evidence. She may rest on the insufficiency of that evidence to prove her guilt, or she may also offer evidence partially to meet or rebut it, or raise a reasonable doubt as to any part of the government's case. You are not to deal with the evidence in a captious spirit, but to allow it to produce on your minds its natural and proper effect. You are to think of it and reason upon it in the same way as you think and reason on other matters, only remembering the strict proof to which the government is held by the law.

In such a case as this, or in any case, you cannot be absolutely certain of the correctness of your conclusion. The law does not require you to be so. If, proceeding with due caution and observant of the principles which have been stated, you are convinced beyond reasonable doubt of the defendant's guilt, it will be your plain duty to declare that conviction by your verdict. If the evidence falls short of producing such conviction in your mind, although it may raise a suspicion of guilt, or even a strong probability of guilt, it would be your plain duty to return a verdict of not guilty. If not legally proved to be guilty, the defendant is entitled to a verdict of not guilty. The law contemplates no middle course.

You will be inquired of by the clerk as to each count of the indictment separately and in the same manner. If you find the defendant guilty of murder in the first degree, the Foreman, in reply to the inquiry of the clerk, will say, "Guilty of murder in the first degree," and so as to murder in the second degree, if you find that to be the degree of murder. As to the second count, if the finding is the same, the answer should be the same. If, on the other hand, your finding is "Not guilty," the Foreman should so reply to each inquiry.

Gentlemen, I want to refer at this point briefly to one or two matters, not in a connected way, where it seems proper to me that a brief suggestion should be made. Something was said in the arguments in regard to defendant's attitude towards the officers, and criticism made of the officers by the defendant's counsel, not by her.

Of course there are certain senses in which a party is represented in Court by his counsel or her counsel and bound by their action. But in a matter relating to the personal guilt of the defendant, where evidence is sought to establish that guilt, I do not understand that the law turns the attention of the Jury to any action of the Counsel. The action of the Counsel may affect her in some ways, may affect her legal rights, but the question is: Is she guilty? Has she done anything which, as a matter of evidence, should be reckoned against her?

And now take this question of her relations to the officers. Turn over the evidence, recall so far as you can, every portion of it, and do you recall any portion -- it will be for you to determine whether you do or not -- do you recall any portion of the evidence where it appears that at any time, at any place, under any circumstances she found any fault with the officers for asking her questions or for making searches? Something was said in the argument -- properly said because the Counsel charged with the duty of presenting the evidence to the Jury in such a light as they honestly think the evidence ought to be considered and weighed, --in regard to statements alleged to have been made by the defendant. The duty of Counsel for the Government is different from that of the Jury and different from that of the Court. Primarily it is, -- while they do not seek to do anything wrong or to mislead the Jury or to introduce any untrue evidence -- to present to the attention of the Jury those things that make for the side which they are sustaining or seeking to sustain. I said something was said in regard to the statements which there was evidence tending to show the defendant had made in regard to presentiments of some disaster to come upon the household; and as I understood the argument, you were asked to look upon those statements which were testified to by one of the witnesses, as evidence tending to show that the defendant might have been harboring in her mind purposes of evil with reference to the household, -- statements made only, I believe the day before this calamity fell on the household, only the day before the deed was done by the defendant, if she did it.

Now, in considering that evidence, you should not necessarily go off in your view of it upon the suggestion of counsel, but, so far as you deem it important, hold it before your minds, look at it in all its lights and bearings, and see whether it seems to you reasonable and probable that a person meditating the perpetration of a great crime, would, the day before, predict to a friend, either in form or in substance, the happening of that disaster. Should any different principle be applied to such a statement made by the defendant with reference to her own family than should be applied to the statement which one man might make to another man and his family?

Suppose some person in New Bedford contemplated the perpetration of a great crime upon the person or family of another citizen in New Bedford, contemplated doing it soon. Would he naturally, probably, predict, a day or two before hand, that anything of the nature of that crime would occur? Is the reasonable construction to be put upon that conversation that of evil premeditation, dwelt upon, intended, or only of evil fears and apprehensions?

Take this matter of the dress, of which so much as been said, that she had on that morning. Take all the evidence in this case, Bridget Sullivan's, the testimony of these ladies, Dr. Bowen's. Lay aside for the moment the question of the identification of this dress that is presented. Taking the evidence of these several witnesses, considering that evidence carefully, comparing part with part, can you gentlemen, extract from that testimony such a description of a dress as would enable you from the testimony to identify the dress? Is there such an agreement among these witnesses, to whom no wrong intention is imputed by anybody -- is there such an agreement in their account and in their memory and recollection, and in the description which they are able to give from the observation that they had in that time of confusion and excitement, that you could put their statements together, and from those statements say that any given dress was accurately described?

Then take, again, the matter of Mrs. Reagan's testimony. It is suggested that there has been no denial of that testimony, or, rather, that the persons who busied themselves about getting the certificate from Mrs. Reagan had no denial of it.

MR. KNOWLTON -- Not by me, sir. I admit it.

DEWEY, J. -- Admit what?

MR. KNOWLTON -- That she did deny it.

DEWEY, J. -- Mrs. Reagan?

MR. KNOWLTON -- Yes, sir.

DEWEY, J. -- Oh, no doubt about that. It is not claimed that Mrs. Reagan does not deny it. But I say it is suggested that the parties who represented the defendant in the matter, and who were seeking to get a certificate from Mrs. Reagan, were proceeding without having received any authority to get the certificate, and without having had any assurance from anybody that the statement was false and one that ought to be denied.

You have heard the statement of Miss Emma about it here; and it would be for you to judge, as reasonable men, whether such men as Mr. Holmes and the clergymen and the other parties who were interesting themselves in that matter, started off attempting to get a certificate from Mrs. Reagan contradicting that report, without first having taken any steps to satisfy themselves that it was a report that ought to be contradicted.

Gentlemen, I know not what views you may take of the case, but it is of the gravest importance that it should be decided. If decided at all it must be decided by a jury. I know of no reason to expect that any other jury could be supplied with more evidence or be better assisted by the efforts of counsel. The case on both sides has been conducted by counsel with great fairness, industry, and ability. You are to confer together; and this implies that each of you, in recollecting and weighing the evidence, may be aided by the memory and judgment of his associates. The law requires that the jury shall be unanimous in their verdict, and it is their duty to agree if they can conscientiously do so.

And now, gentlemen, the case is committed into your hands. The tragedy which has given rise to this investigation deeply excited public attention and feeling. The press has ministered to this excitement by publishing without moderation rumors and reports of all kinds. This makes it difficult to secure a trial free from prejudice. You have doubtless read, previous to the trial, more or less of the accounts and discussions in the newspapers. Some of you, when you were selected as jurors, said that you had formed impressions about the case, but thought that they would not prevent you from giving a candid judgment upon a full hearing of the testimony. Doubtless you were sincere in that declaration; but in this matter you will need great care and watchfulness, for we are often influenced in forming our judgments by what we have heard or read at some previous time, more than we are conscious of. You must guard so far as possible against all impressions derived from having read in the newspapers accounts relating to the question you have now to decide. You cannot consistently with your duty go into any discussion of those accounts or in any way use or refer to them. Your attention should be given to the evidence only, for the discovery of the facts; and any other course would be contrary to your duty.

And, entering on your deliberations with no pride of opinion, with impartial and thoughtful minds, seeking only for the truth, you will lift the case above the range of passion and prejudice and excited feeling, into the clear atmosphere of reason and law. If you shall be able to do this, we can hope that, in some high sense, this trial may be adopted into the order of Providence, and may express in its results somewhat of that justice with which God governs the world.

The Verdict

Not guilty, the jury found.

The jury seemed scarcely to deliberate, to assess the witnesses or weigh the evidence. Perhaps the prosecution simply failed to prove its case. But, in considering the verdict, the facts of Lizzie's family name, her wealth, and her sex ought not to be ignored.

The New York *Times* reported the verdict, Lizzie's response, and public reaction immediately. The editor of the *Times* also took the occasion to offer his own remarks on the case.

New York Times Reports and Editorial

June 21, 1893

LIZZIE BORDEN IS ACQUITTED

Jury Declares Her Guiltless of the Crime of Murder.

Verdict Reached After a Deliberation of Little More Than an Hour --
Great Rejoicing in the Courtroom at the Result of the Trial -- Miss
Borden Gives Herself Up to Tears -- She Proceeds to Her Home in Fall
River by an Evening Train.

NEW-BEDFORD, MASS., June 20 -- Tonight Lizzie Andrew
Borden sleeps in her old home at Fall River a free woman, innocent in
the eyes of the law of the awful crime with which she was charged nearly
a year ago.

At 4:30 o'clock this afternoon the jury came in with a verdict of
not guilty. It had been deliberating but little more than an hour.

During the absence of the jury Miss Borden's self-possession
never deserted her, but her face became livid, her lips were compressed,
and her eyes assumed a vacant look as she tottered to her feet and
looked at the jury in accordance with the instruction of the Clerk.

Then came the verdict and she sank to her chair, covered her face
in her hands, and wept such tears as she had not shed for months.

The closing scene in the trial was in direct contrast with those
which had preceded it. Heretofore all had been decorous and in
keeping with the dignity of the most dignified court in the country. But,
when the verdict of "Not guilty" was returned, a cheer went up which
might have been heard half a mile away through the open windows.

There was no attempt to check it. The stately Justice looked
straight ahead at the bare walls. Sheriff Wright was powerless to wield
the gavel, which lay ready for his use, and not once during the
tremendous excitement, which lasted fully a minute, did he make the
slightest sign of having heard it.

He never saw the people rising in their seats and waving their
handkerchiefs in unison with their voices, because his eyes were full of
tears and were completely blinded for the time.

Mr. Jennings was almost crying and his voice broke as he put his
hand out to Mr. Adams, who sat next to him, and said "Thank God,"
while Mr. Adams returned the pressure of the hand and seemed
incapable of speech.

Gov. Robinson turned to the rapidly-dissolving jury as they filed
out of their seats and gleamed on them with a fatherly interest in his
kindly eyes, and stood up as Mr. Knowlton and Mr. Moody came over
to shake hands with the counsel for the defense.

As soon as possible the room was cleared, although it was a hard task since everybody wanted to shake hands with Miss Borden. When the spectators had finally gone she was taken to the room of the Justices and allowed time to recover her composure with only the eyes of friends upon her. At the expiration of an hour she was placed in a carriage and driven to the station where she took the train for Fall River.

As she passed from the Court House the crowds without gave cheer upon cheer for the freed woman.

June 21, 1893

MISS BORDEN AT FALL RIVER

Crowds Surround Her Home -- Spends the Night at Mr. Holmes's.

FALL RIVER, MASS., June 20 -- The news of Lizzie Borden's acquittal was received with the greatest surprise in this city. Even her warmest friends and most ardent supporters dared not hope anything better than a disagreement after reading the District Attorney's forcible argument in behalf of the Government.

When it was flashed over the wires that the prisoner had been acquitted, the greatest excitement prevailed. Upon the streets the sole topic of conversation was the unlooked-for discharge of Lizzie Borden.

It had been stated that Miss Lizzie would ride over from New-Bedford in a carriage, and as the hour of coming was uncertain, a crowd of curious ones assembled early at the Borden homestead to get a glimpse of the woman who in the past ten months has gained such a world-wide reputation. But the hours passed and there were no signs of her coming.

The crowd increased to such an extent that it was necessary to detail a special squad of policemen to keep the street clear. Inside the house a light was brightly burning in the kitchen, where Bridget Sullivan, who, it is said, has resumed her former position, was preparing for the coming of Lizzie and her friends.

At 8:15 p.m., while the crowd was surging about the homestead on Second Street, a carriage stopped at the residence of Charles J. Holmes, 67 Pine Street. The first one to alight from it was Mr. Holmes, and he was followed by Lizzie Borden. Then came Emma and Miss Annie Holmes.

Miss Lizzie did not wait for Mr. Holmes's escort, but bounded up the steps and disappeared within the house. There was no one about the house at the time save a few reporters.

The United Press reporter entered the house and had an interview with Miss Lizzie. The party, which included Mr., Mrs., and Miss

Holmes, Emma and Lizzie Borden, Joseph A. Bowen, and Mrs. Jubb was seated in the drawing room.

Miss Lizzie said that she was "the happiest woman in the world." She did not care to dwell upon the subject of the trial, and said that the whole party had agreed not to discuss that subject. She said she would probably spend the night at Mr. Holmes's house. She intended to go home, but her friends advised her not to, on account of the great number of people assembled there.

Mr. Holmes's house was thrown open and many visitors were received, but few were allowed to talk with Miss Lizzie.

At the Borden homestead the crowd kept increasing until 10 o'clock, when there were over 2,000 people there. Just before 10 o'clock a band stopped in front of the house and played "Auld Lang Syne."

EDITORIAL

June 21, 1893

THE ACQUITTAL OF MISS BORDEN

It will be a certain relief to every right-minded man or woman who has followed the case to learn that the jury at New-Bedford has not only acquitted Miss Lizzie Borden of the atrocious crime with which she was charged, but has done so with a promptness that was very significant. The acquittal of the most unfortunate and cruelly persecuted woman was, by this promptness, in effect, a condemnation of the police authorities of Fall River and of the legal officers who secured the indictment and have conducted the trial. It was a declaration, not only that the prisoner was guiltless, but that there never was any serious reason to suppose that she was guilty. She has escaped the awful fate with which she was threatened, but the long imprisonment she has undergone, the intolerable suspense and anguish inflicted upon her, the outrageous injury to her feelings as a woman and as a daughter, are chargeable directly to the police and legal authorities. That she should have been subjected to these is a shame to Massachusetts which the good sense of the jury in acquitting her only in part removes.

The theory of the prosecution seems to have been that, if it were possible that Miss Borden murdered her father and his wife, it must be inferred that she did murder them. It was held, practically, that if she could not be proved innocent she must be taken to be guilty. We do not remember a case in a long time in which the prosecution has so completely broken down, or in which the evidence has shown so clearly, not merely that the prisoner should not be convicted, but that, there never should have been an indictment. We are not surprised that the Fall River police should have fastened their suspicions upon Miss

Borden. The town is not a large one. The police is of the usual inept and stupid and muddle-headed sort that such towns manage to get for themselves. There is nothing more merciless than the vanity of ignorant and untrained men charged with the detection of crime, in the face of a mystery that they cannot solve, and for the solution of which they feel themselves responsible. The Fall River police needed a victim whose sacrifice should purge their force of the contempt that they felt they would incur if the murderer of the Bordens was not discovered, and the daughter was the nearest and most helpless. They pounced upon her.

But the responsibility of the law officers was very different. They were men trained in the law, accustomed to analyze and weigh evidence. They knew what justice required in the way of proof of the crime of murder in the first degree. It is not easy to believe that they did not know that no such proof, and nothing like it, was in their possession. Indeed, they seem to have entered upon the trial without it, and to have groped along afterward in clumsy efforts to develop it. We cannot resist the feeling that their conduct in this matter was outrageous; that they were guilty of a barbarous wrong to an innocent woman and a gross injury to the community. And we hold it to be a misfortune that their victim has no legal recourse against them and no means of bringing them to account. Her acquittal is only a partial atonement for the wrong that she has suffered.

LAST SCENE
IN THE GREAT BORDEN TRIAL.

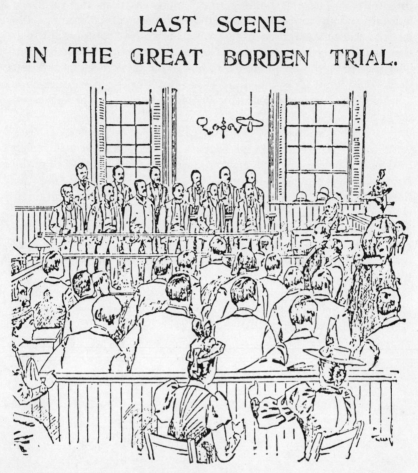

Clerk—Mr Foreman, look upon the prisoner; prisoner, look upon the Jury. What say you, Mr Foreman—   Foreman (interrupting)—Not guilty!

Cartoon from the Boston Globe

In the days before newspapers carried photographs, cartoons offered visual accompaniment to news stories. This drawing of the courtroom depicts Lizzie facing her all-male jury to hear their verdict -- that they had found the lady innocent.

Source: Boston *Daily Globe,* June 21, 1893.

IV
Lizzie After the Trial
Maplecroft

The house on Second Street, with its narrow, box-like appearance and its peculiar arrangements, was certainly a factor in the development of Lizzie Borden. She lived there for twenty-seven years, from the age of six to the age of thirty-two; its dark and inhospitable confines bore witness to most of her childhood and the formative years of her adulthood.

Since Mrs. Borden had died first, Lizzie and Emma were Andrew Borden's only heirs. Soon after the acquittal, Lizzie and Emma used part of their large inheritance to purchase a house on French Street, and Lizzie named the new house Maplecroft. Still standing solidly on the hill, Maplecroft is the only extant expression of what Lizzie wanted. She selected and furnished it, and its marked contrast with the house on Second Street provides considerable evidence both of Lizzie's own tastes and of her feelings about the parental home.*

Maplecroft is imposing. Some of Lizzie's biographers imply that the thirteen-room mansion is pretentious and tasteless. Victoria Lincoln, who wrote an astute analysis of Lizzie's background and personality in *A Private Disgrace,* described its exterior as "McKinley-Queen Anne." Perhaps so, but the interior is far from tasteless; it is, in fact, spacious, comfortable, and sometimes elegant.

---

*We are grateful to Frank Silvia, for many years the owner of Maplecroft, for his gracious hospitality. The following description of Maplecroft is based on the guided tour of the house which he generously gave in August, 1978.

The house sits on extensive grounds, but it is separated from the sidewalk only by a flight of steps. Lizzie had the name "Maplecroft" engraved on the top step, a small ostentation which did not conform to Fall River's precepts of good taste. The steps lead to a long, curving, glassed-in porch which opens into the large front entry hall. The back porch, also glass-enclosed, overlooks an attractive tree-filled garden. Lizzie ordered the construction of the stone wall that marks the back boundary of the property; it took workmen a year to build it.

The front hall and the entire first floor give a pleasing impression of spaciousness. The large rooms have many windows. The handsome living room has fine dark panelling and applied gold leaf molding. The dining room is, of all the rooms in the house, the least changed since Lizzie's day. The wallpaper is still there -- a delicate floral design; the heavy rose silk drapes were selected by Lizzie. On either side of the buffet are mother-of-pearl light fixtures. The dining room has a fireplace, as do most of the rooms in the house. The ceiling is covered in beige linen cloth. Such a pleasantly designed room is its own invitation to linger over coffee.

The house has a breakfast room and a well-equipped kitchen. Both are comfortable and well-lighted. A door from the kitchen leads to the outside. The glass in the upper half of this door has a subdued but definite letter "B" cut into it.

A stairway with rosewood bannisters curves upward from the front hall to the second floor. There Lizzie had two bedrooms -- one for winter and one for summer. The front (winter) bedroom extends the width of the house and has eight windows. Over the ornate fireplace a poem is carved in the wood:

> And old true friends, and twilight plays
> And starry nights, and sunny days
> Come trouping up the misty ways
> When my fire burns low.

There is also an over-sized closet with panelled walls and, just inside, a button to ring for servants. Such buttons are strategically located throughout the house. The summer bedroom, overlooking the garden at the back, is somewhat smaller, but still maintains a look of comfort. Each bedroom has an adjoining bathroom, and in each the bathtub is painted with delicate floral designs. The larger winter bedroom leads to a suite of rooms used for the extensive library Lizzie acquired.

There is a third bedroom on the second floor. It is a medium-sized room without special features of either comfort or beauty. It is fair to assume that Emma occupied this room in the years she lived at Maplecroft.

On the third floor are the servants' quarters and storage rooms. Although the servants' rooms have been partially panelled, some still bear the wallpaper chosen by Lizzie. Apparently in keeping with her taste, the patterns all have a romantic floral motif: small flowers, including appleblossoms, hovering butterflies, and birds.

Lizzie maintained several servants, including a housekeeper, maids, and a chauffeur, all of whom lived at Maplecroft. Carriages, and later automobiles, were housed in a garage set back from the house. It, too, is a large, handsome building, panelled and heated. In a small neighboring house, Lizzie installed her dressmaker conveniently nearby.

Lizzie's move to Maplecroft coincided with the new name which she adopted at this time and which she used for the rest of her life. After 1893, Lizzie Borden referred to herself as Lizbeth A. Borden. The new name and the beautiful new home could not, of course, change the past, nor could they alter Fall River's opinion of either the old Lizzie or the new Lizbeth.

Lizzie became almost completely self-sufficient within the confines of Maplecroft and its grounds. She even instituted a special system for the delivery of groceries to a designated box at the back of the house. To what degree this self-sufficiency was caused by Lizzie's ostracism by the townspeople of Fall River, and how far it was in keeping with her own personality and temperament, one cannot know.

Another Accusation

In February, 1897, Lizzie's name appeared in the newspapers again. This time it involved her alleged theft of two paintings from the firm of Tilden-Thurber, silversmiths and jewellers in Providence, Rhode Island. The news of the theft of the paintings, worth perhaps one hundred dollars, by a woman whose wealth could be counted in the hundreds of thousands, must have raised new questions about Lizzie's character. The Providence *Daily Journal* carried the story on February 16, 1897.

Providence Daily Journal Report

February 16, 1897

LIZZIE BORDEN AGAIN.

A Warrant for Her Arrest Issued from a Local Court.

TWO PAINTINGS MISSED FROM
TILDEN-THURBER CO.'S STORE.

Said to Have Been Traced to Miss Borden's Home in Fall River.

OFFICIALS LOATH TO FURNISH INFORMATION OF AFFAIR.

The Warrant Was Issued Some Time Ago and Has Not Been Served. --It is Understood That Miss Borden Claimed to Have Purchased the Articles and That She Retained Them.

It is but a brief period since notoriety attached itself to Miss Lizzie Borden, daughter of Andrew J. and Abby Borden of Fall River, who were found foully murdered at their home in that city a few years ago. Again is the name of the young woman before the public and this time in a less pleasant character than at the last time, when a story of her alleged engagement was current.

The information published in the Bulletin last evening to the effect that it was alleged that a warrant had been issued against her charging larceny of two paintings from the Tilden-Thurber Company of this city created a sensation. This warrant followed a complaint made against Miss Borden to the proper officials here.

The young woman has been a frequent visitor to this city and a customer of the Tilden-Thurber Company. It is alleged that a short time ago she visited the store and after her departure two paintings upon marble were missed. Investigation followed and the missing goods were tracked to the present residence of Miss Borden at Fall River. This was done after the members of the concern had consulted with officials.

Miss Borden was asked concerning the paintings and declared that she had purchased them in the Tilden-Thurber store. It is said, however, that there was no record of any such sale and it is also charged that the salesman in the department in which these goods were located knew nothing of the purchase claimed. There was some discussion regarding the matter and that members of the company were not satisfied with the statement of Miss Borden is evidenced by the fact that a request for a warrant was made to the local officials.

The alleged affair having occurred in this city the necessary legal documents in the case would have been issued in the Sixth District Court before Judge William H. Sweetland, upon the request of Chief of Police Baker. Being a criminal complaint, the head of the police department would draw the warrant and Judge Sweetland as presiding Judge of the Sixth District Court would place his signature upon it.

Chief of Police Baker will not make any statement concerning the affair. He will not deny, however, that a warrant charging Miss Lizzie Borden with larceny from the Tilden-Thurber Company was issued, and Judge Sweetland, being Judge of the District Court, does not care to make any statement concerning the swearing out of this particular warrant in the District Court.

In fact, Judge Sweetland never makes known the contents of the warrants taken before him by officers for issuance.

The ends of justice would be frustrated in many instances were he to make known the contents of legal papers placed before him for his signature.

In the present instance he will not deny that such a warrant as referred to is in existence.

Despite all this, however, it is known that the warrant was issued. It was never served and it is said that the two paintings are still in the possession of Miss Lizzie Borden. Whether a settlement has in the meanwhile been made or the exact reason for the withholding of service of the warrant is entirely a matter of speculation. While there has been no denial that the warrant was issued, officers of the Tilden-Thurber Company, speaking generally, say they either know nothing of the matter or refer inquiries to their associates.

It is said at the store that Miss Borden had been a large purchaser there. The two paintings which were missed and upon the loss of which the warrant was issued were jointly valued at about $100. Officers in this city were employed in the case and it is believed that the assistance of Fall River officials was also brought into the matter.

MR. JENNINGS HADN'T HEARD IT.

Andrew J. Jennings of Fall River who was engaged as counsel by Miss Borden when she was first suspected of murdering her father and mother, and who defended her in the Second District Court at the preliminary hearing of the case, would have nothing to say yesterday when informed that it was reported that a warrant has been issued for her arrest on a complaint charging his former client with shoplifting. That is, Mr. Jennings said nothing to indicate that he had the slightest knowledge of any such offence on Miss Borden's part, and intimated that he did not believe there was any foundation for the story.

Fall River authorities, including the Inspectors, who are usually detailed to assist officers from other cities in investigating matters of this kind, also stated that they were ignorant of any accusation of the kind. From other sources, however, it was learned that Detective Parker of Providence arrived in Fall River some little time ago and was heard to inquire of a man with whom he left the train where "she" was living at present.

The news printed in the Bulletin created a profound sensation, as does most news which recalls the remarkable assassination of Mr. and Mrs. Borden, and many tongues discussed the details of the crime once more.

A rumor going the rounds is that Detective Parker was in town last week, inquired for Marshal Hilliard, who did not happen to be in the city, and later called a well-known lawyer out of a place of amusement and disappeared with him.

A footnote:

In reply to the editors' query about the shoplifting story, the current president of the company, William H. Thurber, confirmed the accuracy of the account: "Everything you have read about Lizzie Borden is quite factual." The details of the theft were told to Mr. Thurber by his father, William G. Thurber, and his uncle, F. B. Thurber, co-owners of the store during Lizzie's era. (Source: Letters dated August 10, 1979, and June 26, 1980, from William H. Thurber to Joyce G. Williams.)

The Sisters Part

Although Lizzie lived in Fall River for the rest of her life, she visited Washington, New York, and Boston to shop and to go to the theater. She became acquainted with actress Nance O'Neil in Boston and entertained Miss O'Neil and her theatrical company at Maplecroft in 1905. This brought repercussions from the sedate townspeople of

Fall River and from her sister, Emma. Even Lizzie's domestic life became a subject of headlines.

Sunday Herald Report

Source: Sunday Herald news clipping from the files of the Fall River Historical Society.

LIZZIE BORDEN LEFT BY SISTER

Former Writing Play for Nance O'Neil --
Emma Borden Objects to Actress,
Entertainment of Theatrical People and to Coachman.

FALL RIVER, June 3, 1905. After repeated disagreements, Lizzie A. Borden and her sister, Emma Borden, have parted company. Several days ago Miss Emma packed up her belongings, called a moving wagon and shook the dust of the French street home, where they have lived together ever since the acquittal in the famous murder trial, from her feet. She is reported to have moved to Fairhaven. Ever since her departure the tongue of gossip has been wagging tremendously, even for Fall River, which is saying a great deal. All sorts of reasons for the quarrel between the sisters have been afloat, but the best founded ones involve the name of Miss Nance O'Neil, the actress, and also that of Miss Lizzie's coachman, Joseph Tetrault.

It is nothing new to learn that the sisters have not agreed; that has been known ever since the famous murder, and even during that cause celebre it came out that they had never agreed on many things. Miss Emma was sedate and retiring. Miss Lizzie was fond of good times and jolly company. . . . The stage was distasteful to Miss Emma's orthodox ideas and when Miss Lizzie came to entertain a whole dramatic company at midnight hours, it passed Miss Emma's limit. And right here comes in Miss Nance O'Neil, the well known actress. It appears that Miss Lizzie and Miss O'Neil are warm personal friends. The two women met at a summer resort near Lynn last year, while Miss Borden was passing the vacation period there. A mutual attraction led to the cementing of a close and hearty friendship.

When Miss O'Neil came to this city with her company early this season she was entertained by Miss Borden. Not only was Miss O'Neil most hospitably treated, but her whole company dined at Miss Borden's table. Later, when Miss O'Neil came here and gave an impersonation of "Queen Elizabeth," which startled most people, but pleased others, Miss Borden's carriage awaited her after the play and together they went to Miss Borden's home. Miss O'Neil was entertained there, and it was not long after the entertaining that Miss Emma and her sister broke. The efforts of the gossips to tie these two things together have developed a story of the quarrel.

The entertainment afforded Miss O'Neil is said, however, to have been of the quietest character, such as one friend might give another, Miss O'Neil on the last visit being ill from overwork. Miss Borden has never seen her performance in Fall River, but the reviews of her acting published in the local papers have pleased her greatly. Miss Borden has seen Miss O'Neil act in Boston and New York, and has been entertained by the actress in Boston at the Hotel Touraine.

Among the stories that are current is one that has exceptional interest. It is said by rumor that Miss Borden is to write a play and that Miss O'Neil is to act it. Of course, Miss Borden makes no pretensions to stage knowledge, but it is known that she has literary ability, and had passed much of her time in reading, writing and travelling. No hint is given as to what the new play will be based on.

A Boston Herald reporter called that afternoon upon Miss Borden. Miss Lizzie Borden herself came to the door. "May I see Miss Borden?" asked the correspondent.

"What do you wish to see her about?" The newspaper man told his story.

"I don't think Miss Borden will see you," was said. "She never sees newspaper men under any circumstances."

The Borden Case Continues In The News

Newspaper interest in the Borden case and Lizzie continued. The Fall River *Daily Globe* published an anniversary story about the Bordens each year. Some stories represented conventional reporting, while others made an attempt at dark humor. The two examples reprinted here suggest that suspicion, hostility, and resentment lingered in Fall River.

In 1913 Emma Borden broke her long-standing silence to grant an interview to the *Sunday Post*. In her frankness she revealed much about the relationship of the two sisters, and the interview offers a rare picture of the retiring Emma.

News Stories from the Daily Globe and the Sunday Post

A Note on the Text: As with other news accounts, the editors have corrected typographical errors but have allowed variant spelling, punctuation, and grammar to stand.

Source: Fall River *Daily Globe*.

A DOZEN YEARS

Since the Bordens Were Brutally Butchered,

And Yet the Horrible Crime Is Unpunished.

Perhaps Murderer, or Murderess, May Be in the City -- Who Can Tell?

A dozen years!

What a long time it seems, yet how quickly passed in this busy, practical world, where so few people have the time to devote to retrospect or reflection, on all the good, and all the evil that is encompassed in the historic chronicle of such a period of time.

Twelve years ago this morning, when God's radiant sunshine was dispelling its August warmth, and casting its brilliant reflection over all in this peaceful community, the just and the unjust, the rich and the poor, the contented and the envious, the pharisee and the publican, there sallied forth from the midsummer peace, on outrage bent, a demon in human form, whose quickly accomplished hellishness, was destined to make Fall River occupy a place in the centre of the stage under the entire country's observation, such as has been the misfortune of few civilized communities to stand in.

In the quietest and dullest hours of the forenoon, and in one of the most modest, and presumably -- only presumably, however, -- happy households on Second Street, on that fateful fourth of August, 1892, there was enacted a scene of carnage and red handed slaughter, that, never in all the years that have passed since the butchery was perpetrated, has been approached for horror, vileness, and unnatural and degenerate greed for gore and gain, by man or woman on murder bent, in this or any other country within the pale of so-called Christian civilization.

An old man, fast nearing the brink of that fateful precipice, which marks the dividing line between the present and the hereafter, was brutally and wickedly hastened to that end, which in the natural sequence of earthly things, he could have escaped but a few days more. And why? Was it because he had lingered longer in the control and possession of those worldly stores he set so much value upon, and the acquisition of which had been the all pervading passion of his prudent, industrious life? Who can tell?

Perhaps that incarnate fiend in human form, which crept up to the old-fashioned hair cloth sofa and rained cruel, vengeful, bloody blow upon blow, upon Andrew J. Borden's venerable head can answer. If he

240

-- or she -- has ever thus far, taken time or opportunity to dwell upon a remembrance of that frightful August day, and what its ensanguined sin meant in results for the slayer and his -- or her --victim. But that muscular, determined, wielder of the busy axe, nerved on, no doubt, by inspiration from Satan, the patron and protector of murderers, or strengthened by overpowering sentiments of avarice and cupidity, and hope of the enjoyment of long desired, but long denied pleasures, had but partially completed the mission he -- or she -- had undertaken to accomplish.

There was more work for that willing, wicked arm on the upper floor, where, in utter innocence of a suspicion of the nearness of her untimely end, one more unfortunate awaited the bloody coming of the destroyer. A quick though quiet cat like step, a second's pause before taking steady hold upon the hatchet helve, an earnest downward blow, and all was over, for the unfortunate creature, whose honorably worn gray hairs, would have been her ample protection against the barbarous onslaught of anything or anybody but the foulest type of monster known in the annals of contemporaneous crime.

Although one blow ended all connection with life for poor and inoffensive old Abby Borden, it was not enough to satiate the hate, the venom, and the vengeance of that daylight assassin, for he -- or she -- continued to rain crash after crash from the cruel weapon, upon the quivering and unconscious form of the victim, furnishing the best evidence known to students of human nature, that long pent up hatred, malice, and murder were linked together as inspiring motives and as co-partners in the base, sordid, and selfish mind of the butcher, and that they had been appeased and satisfied by the fast succeeding wounds of the iron messenger of murder upon that insensate form that lay prone and stark in the brook of blood which flowed across the chamber floor.

Who that recalls that sultry, sickening gruesome day of an even dozen of years ago, will ever forget the day or the deed?

Who that brings back to memory the abuse and the ignominy heaped upon those intelligent members of the police department, some now dead and some living who, inside of 48 hours, made up their minds correctly as to who the dastard, that sent two unprepared souls before their Maker, and dared to mention their suspicions?

Who can forget the "wild eyed man" and the empty pated prattlers, who tried to connect such phantom possibilities with the crime?

And the poor Portuguese farm laborer?

And the man who had a grudge against Andrew Borden?

And Lubinsky?

And Me and Brownie?

And the stains of paint on the wrapper which furnished food for the kitchen fire, when a kitchen fire meant suffering to all within range of it on such a day?

And Bridget Sullivan's strange spell of devotion to window washing?

And the sinkers in the barn loft, and all the rest of the rot and nonsense that ran riot through the disordered imagination of a prejudiced or a gullible public?

But why enumerate, and why discuss the whole unhappy incident at this late day, may be asked. Simply to establish and re-establish, and confirm, and emphasize in this community, that in Massachusetts, the grand old Bay State, the commonwealth of progress, the seat of a vaunted high type of judicial administration, there occurred one dozen years ago today, one of the most shocking, unnatural, base and mercenary crimes that ever befouled the pages of civilized history, and the demon that swung the axe which sent two souls into eternity at that time, has never yet been punished for his -- or her -- foul crime. That is the reason -- lest we forget -- and it is reason enough, why The Globe sees fit, annually, to call attention to this shocking affair, which was well called the crime of the century, and also to the shameful fact, that such a devilish deed should have gone unpunished of man, during all these years.

Who knows, even now, that the vile minded murderer may not be at large in the community walking, stalking, or driving about, in carriage or in car, seeking the opportunity to make new criminal history?

Perhaps the good people of Fall River may be daily meeting him -- or her -- in hall or store, or railroad train, and, oh, what a frightful contemplation there arises, if such be the fact, that it is due to the miscarriage of justice in the grand old State of Massachusetts, the cradle of liberty, of advancement, of just judges and of historic statesmen!

And what a saddening and solemn reflection it must be for those who were near and dear to the murdered pair in life, to think that they have never been called upon to pay out that $5000 reward for the detection of the murderer, when they would have been so happy to spend that small portion of his horded wealth in hunting down those who robbed them of their father and mother -- no, step-mother, please!

And how little occupation there would be in the world for the trained detectives, such as the Pinkerton agency sent here after the murder, if they were to determine all mysteries as quickly as they discovered who swung the axe, and who bought the prussic acid, in the Borden case!

And how very soon after the announcement of this determination as to the identity of the murderer -- or murderess -- they found themselves like Othello, with their occupation gone!

242

And how the good and kindly disposed people of the town were shocked to hear the people who knew what they were talking about, mention their suspicions as to the identity of the murderer -- or murderess!

And how few of those good and kindly people are shocked in the least if the same story is repeated now!

Oh, what a difference a few years make!

And what a lonely, uninhabited, and inexpensive institution the state prison in Charlestown would be, if it was as difficult to get straightforward, common sense evidence before the courts of the commonwealth, in all criminal cases, and capital crimes as it was once upon a time, say about 12 years ago!

And how many murderers would pay the penalties of their crimes if some sanctimonious old jurist, was to be convinced in advance that a man couldn't commit a crime because he was a man or a woman because she was a woman? Not many of them would be suffering much more in the way of penalty, if such were the prejudiced and perverted views of all the criminal court judges, than the midday butcher of the Bordens is, at present, and there is the best of reason for believing that he -- or she -- is enjoying at least the waking hours of daily life very much as the neighbors do, well fed, well dressed, well waited on, however the still hours of the night may be passed, whether in the solace of refreshing slumber, or in the viewing of phantom pictures of the hideous scenes of 12 years ago this morning. Who can tell?

Perhaps before another year rolls round, self-accusing conscience may have taken up the task laid down by the criminal law authorities of the state and the man -- or woman -- who shocked the people of two continents with one of the most ghastly, cruel, selfish, and brutal of double murders 12 years ago, deliver himself -- or herself -- into the hands of the avenging law, as an escaped criminal. Who can tell?

Unless, in the event of some such unexpected and improbable sequel as this, the butchery of the Bordens, -- legally speaking -- is likely to remain as big a mystery as it was 12 years ago, when the police finished their work upon the case, although "legally speaking," is the only sense in which the murderer or murderess have anything left of "mystery" for the men with memories that can stand a 12-year strain.

Source: Fall River *Daily Globe.*

August 4, 1905

GREAT WRONG

Is Righted After 13 Years of Misrepresentation.

No Murders Were Committed On Aug. 4th, 1892,

Despite the Belief That Andrew and Abby Borden
Died in That Manner.

THIRTEEN YEARS!
THIRTEEN YEARS AGO TODAY!!

How time does fly and how well that fact is comprehended when intelligent men and women if blessed with memory, recall that on the fourth day of August, 1892 -- thirteen years ago today, -- when the mid-summer sun was scorching and shrivelling up everything from dandelion boutonnieres to straw hats and peek-a-boo waists, the town was terribly shocked and startled by the false but frightful alarm of murder, which went forth at midday from the Second Street home of the late Andrew J. and Abbie Drew Borden!

How the intense excitement grew and the wonder, too, that on that peaceful August morning, there should have been human beings existing in this orderly community so lost to the manifold considerations of truth and honor, as to have given credence to the foul and baseless rumors of inhuman slaughter, that flashed through the city like wild-fire wherein it was alleged that a man -- or a woman -- had raised the blood-stained hand of brutal violence and cut off the mortal career of two unoffending and reputable members of society.

Perhaps the city and its reputation have never suffered more vindictive, unwarranted and libellous assaults upon their stainless honor, than by the unbridled tongues of such people, as at that time gave circulation to the vile calumny that an axe had been swung by the strong and vengeful arm of some demoniac man -- or woman -- bent on murder and with mercenary motive.

And why, it will be asked, were such calumnies circulated, and such monstrous stories told when there was neither shadow nor substance on which to base them?

Simply because unthinking and idle gossips had said that certain members of the family had not been able to enjoy a cottage at Newport, a private coachman and a personal check book, as was their long cherished hope and desire.

Simply because members of the family had grown tired, weary even to the point of digestive rebellion of a steady daily diet of frapped

244

mutton and stewed pears and fain would occasionally have had the provender provider of the household loosen up to the extent of a porterhouse steak, French fried potatoes, and mushrooms, as a wholesome, refreshing and welcome change.

Simply because it was said that certain members of that quiet, old-fashioned household had not been allowed to indulge their inclinations to receive, entertain and intermingle with society, as they desired, and that with a funeral or two carried out to successful consummation, life would become more endurable for those who remained, after a brief and not too painful season of mourning.

Simply because relations between certain members of that household had become so painfully and hopelessly strained that life was unbearable under the conditions, and any form of change would be preferable to a longer continuance of it.

Others there were who based their false theories of slaughter, on the presumption that Bridget Sullivan, poor, quiet, unsuspecting, non-listening Bridget, who had taken an overdose of morphine pills and could see or hear nothing while washing those outside windows, had suddenly become the victim of murderous hallucinations, as a result of the drug and wielded an axe with dire effect as well as her window mop.

Then there was the Portuguese farmer, the man who owed Andrew Borden for rent, the wild eyed man, Lubinsky, the ice cream man, the bogie man, any rags man, and all the other men who were said to have been at large that fateful August morning, when the police were at Rocky Point and the rest of the town was burning up in the fierce rays of the sun.

One member of the family was falsely accused of having been in the house, when the very best and strongest evidence in the world, evidence that passed muster before the superior bench of the sovereign state of Massachusetts, was produced showing that she was out in the barn lot where it was cool and comfortable with a temperature of only 98½ in the hay, rigging out sinkers and bait to catch clams, cranberries, and other odd fish in the forests and salt hay meadows of Marion.

Oh, it is certainly surprising, looked at in the light of 13 long years of reflection and recollection, to think of all the novel and singular suppositions on which people founded their faith in the delusion that a double murder had been perpetrated in that old fashioned Second Street domicile on that hot and memorable day in August 13 years ago!

But time -- thirteen years of it -- in its flight has in one way and another served to show to a progressive world how baseless were the suspicions, and how idle the rumors and opinions that any crime had been committed or any law violated on that dread and long past occasion of harrowing memory.

Murders?

Why, there were no murders!

Didn't the learned and solemn oracles of the law so decide after hearing all the evidence -- that is all they were willing to hear -- that was offered in the case? Why, certainly.

The trial was a long and tedious one, but with the remarkable strides that have been made in the character and reputation of the learned and progressive members of the bar as exemplified in the present day and generation, no doubt, in case the matter came up for trial now, an attempt might have been made to prove that Andrew Borden first committed suicide, and later was guilty of accidental homicide, and all the estate that was left on earth, would now have been in possession of the lawyers who proved these facts. There is the best of reason for believing that there has been a notable betterment of conditions, in the legal field of endeavor of late. The lawyers of the present day, that is those who have been most conspicuous recently in the great questions of jurisprudence heard by the local courts, seem to have a better faculty for absorbing things that formerly, a better grasp, so to speak, on such questions, and other things, as come their way, but it is doubtful if even one of these lawyers with a known and undeniable fame for research and a penchant for getting at the bottom of things, when things were worth getting at, could have succeeded in establishing the fact that any crime had been committed in the Borden residence on Aug. 4th, 1892.

It has been said too, that there may have possibly been a murder at that time, and that the detective forces of that day were not competent to cope with the craft and cunning of the man -- or woman -- who did the deed. . . . It is hardly fair or just to say that the detectives were to blame for not catching a murderer -- or murderess -- when there was no murder.

Does anybody suppose at this late day, that the reward of $5,000 offered by the bereaved and sorrowing family, would not have been all powerful in causing the capture and conviction of the murderer -- or murderess -- in case there had been a murder?

Why, of course, it would!

Does anybody suppose, either, that the bereaved and afflicted family would have stopped in its generous desire to punish crime at the giving of a paltry reward of $5,000 in case some unknown and wicked assassin was captured by the police and convicted of the murder?

Why, certainly not!

They would no doubt have made a strong effort, to spare five times that amount, in case a murder had been done, to bring any miscreant outside the family to justice.

But, there was no murder!

How could there have been, when the supreme and sovereign majesty of the law says that there wasn't?

Have any of the contingencies that it was said would have had a possible or probable influence in impelling any man -- or woman -- to commit murder, been fulfilled since?

Has the wild-eyed man ever been seen? No more than has been Charlie Ross.

Has Lubinsky ever come forward to confess? No he's never been heard of this side of Poland from that day to this.

Has anybody changed their mode of living from indulgence in cold mutton to more nourishing and appetizing and fashionable food?

Has anybody given up the buying of car tickets and taken to travel behind a coachman in a family carriage?

Has anybody been unrestricted as to choice of companions and selection of place of abode, as a result of the terrible accident and visitation of Providence of 13 years ago, which must no longer be erroneously classed as a mysterious murder?

Has anybody given any evidence of having been able to indulge a taste for travel and a desire for high art and rare jewels that were impossible before the passing of the old-fashioned people in whose lexicon of life there were no words but thrift, industry and acquisition?

Why, certainly not, forbid and perish the sinful thought, and it seems almost incredible, after all these years, that otherwise sane and conservative citizens of this community, when reminiscent or loquacious should still continue to talk of the "Borden murders," when there were no murders.

It is only just and righteous at this time, 13 years after the honored and infallible courts of the commonwealth have officially decreed that there was no crime, that the fullest and most sweeping statement in regard to the case, should be made for the benefit of the public which is now officially and positively informed that there were no Borden murders.

There was no cause for murder.

There was nobody who could profit by any such crime.

No man -- or woman -- has ever secured possession of a single cent as the result of the deaths. Not one.

No man -- or woman -- has had any more liberty of action, or freedom of conduct since that day in 1892 when the town was upset by the cruel, false and malicious stories of murder. Not one.

No man -- or woman -- has entered into the realms of swell society, or is likely to as a result of the passing from earth's troubles of the old fashioned home loving and plain mannered Bordens. Not one!

Hence, what becomes of all the misleading theories and irresponsible vagaries as to existing cause and impelling motive, which were so idly and freely circulated at the time when cruel suspicion had the hardihood and was prepared to fall upon any man -- or woman -- where fickle fancy led the way.

No, indeed, the 13 years that have moved on into the dim shadows of the past have fully served to remove all suspicion not only of the belief that there was any man -- or woman -- guilty of murdering the Bordens, but they have also conspired to convince, satisfy and prove to every thinking man and woman in the community, that they have for 13 years nursed and harbored a delusion as cruel as misleading to the effect that two of their innocent, inoffensive and industrious neighbors were foully slaughtered in the sacred precincts of their home, when nothing of the kind had ever occurred.

No, there were no murders because the law of the land has said so.

There were no murders because no one of the persons who had exclusive opportunity, had anything to gain financially by committing the crime.

And now in the general interests of justice, and in the lofty and noble exercise of that superlative degree of respect which all men should hold for the opinions and decisions of an erudite and unbiased court of high degree, and with the purpose of no longer holding up, subjecting and exposing to ignominy any man -- or woman -- who may have been thought of by a censorious public in connecting their names with a crime which was never committed, the Globe suggests that its readers forget the past with its cruel errors of judgment, and its suspicions of pure and lofty souls and remember just this one thing for all time:

THERE WERE NO BORDEN MURDERS!

BOTH THE VICTIMS OF 13 YEARS AGO DIED AS THE RESULT OF EXCESSIVE HEAT!

Source: Sunday Post. Clipping from the files of the Fall River Historical Society.

April 13, 1913

'GUILTY -- NO! NO!'

Lizzie Borden's Sister Breaks 20 Year Silence

Tells the Sunday Post of Past and Present Relations With Lizzie

By Edwin J. Maguire

"Queer? Yes, Lizzie was queer, but guilty on that terrible charge made against her -- no -- emphatically, No. Time and again she has avowed her innocence to me, and I believe her."

Never was the adage "Blood is thicker than water" more strikingly exemplified than in this defence of Lizzie Borden, Fall River's woman of tragedy, uttered by her sister, Emma Borden to the Sunday Post.

Though an estrangement has held a wall of silence between the two sisters for eight years, kinship's ties spurred white-haired, gentle-faced Emma Borden to serve notice on the public at large, through the medium of the Sunday Post, that she believed her sister to be innocent, as declared by a jury in 1893.

And her statement is the first declaration to the outside world that either sister has made regarding that most notable murder mystery -- a butchery on which the faintest light is yet to be shed.

For 20 years the Bordens have maintained a sphinx-like attitude toward the treatment accorded the acquitted woman by the world in general and Fall River in particular. Doors of old-time family friends were closed to her following her trial on the charge of murdering Andrew J. Borden, one of the city's wealthiest citizens, and his second wife.

ACQUITTAL GREETED COOLLY

A jury's declaration that she was guiltless sent no wave of jubilation over the community where Lizzie Borden was born, where she had been prominent in church and social affairs, and where she had spent her entire life. Congratulations were not showered upon her by those who had been her intimate acquaintances before the trial.

Instead, the frigidity of an Arctic temperature displaced the pleasantries she had formerly known from life-long friends.

Eight years ago, Emma Borden quit the spacious mansion in the French street section of the exclusive "hill district" where she and Lizzie Borden were residing, and established her home with friends. Her seeking, in this way, another home caused the estrangement between the sisters. Since Emma Borden's departure they have never met or communicated with each other. . . .

At first she was disinclined to talk of the subject. Then the Borden blood came into its own, and she cast aside the reserve of 20 years to take up the cudgels for Lizzie Borden.

DIFFERENCE BETWEEN SISTERS

And her doing so presented a forcible illustration of the contra-distinctive natures of the Borden sisters.

Previously, the Sunday Post reporter had visited the splendid 14-room house where Lizzie Borden lives with her four servants, two bull terriers and three cats of the ordinary back-fence variety.

Access to the house was not allowed. The shades were drawn in all of the windows of the stately structure, the massive oak doors both in the front and rear remained securely bolted and the atmosphere of the place was one of decided seclusion. Repeated ringing of front and rear bells and knocking the various doors brought no answer. The caller might as well have tried to gain response from a tomb.

The only signs of life came from two of Lizzie Borden's pet squirrels that were playing havoc with a pile of peanuts she had placed under a tree near the house.

Heads that quickly appeared at the windows of the sightly dwellings of the neighborhood gave indication of the interest taken in happenings in and around the Borden house.

But shortly after leaving the Borden estate, the Post man utilized the telephone. This time there came a response. The maid who answered summoned Lizzie Borden to the telephone.

"Nothing to say," exclaimed Miss Borden in a strong calm voice, after a request for an interview had been made.

On being urged further she fairly shouted: "Nothing, absolutely nothing to say." Then came a decisive "bang" as she slammed the receiver back on the hook. Thus ended the conversation.

But at the residence of the late Rev. E. A. Buck, where Miss Emma Borden is making her home with the Misses Buck, the reception of the Sunday Post man contrasted with the French street visit, just as the characters of the sisters are diametrically opposite.

Lizzie Borden is now 53 years of age and is regarded by some as a woman with iron will, whose apparent disregard for the none too pleasant attention paid her when she ventures abroad is due to her phlegmatic, impassive temperament. There came no sign of emotion from her during the trial. Fall River residents say she has not given any indication of overwrought nerves in the years that have followed.

GENTLE-MANNERED SISTER

But in Emma Borden the writer met a gentle-mannered woman, who unhesitatingly led the way from the front portal of the Buck residence to the quaint parlor at the left. She was courtesy and gentility personified.

Her tranquil face, sweet of expression and enhanced by a pink and white complexion that a debutante might well envy, was crowned with heavy, snow white hair, parted in the center and rippling to the side of the head in curly billows.

There was a look of sadness, even of resignation in Miss Borden's large brown eyes. They seemed to reflect the sorrow and grief that were part of the heritage she received through the untimely death of her father.

A gray dress, rich in material, but unostentatious in style, bespoke the quiet, retiring character of the woman. With its wide flaring skirt and old-fashioned lace trimmings, the costume impressed one as a refined rebuke to the hobble, and other "latest" modes of femininity.

250

The parlor in which the Post representative interviewed Miss Borden, seemed consecrated to the memory of the Rev. Mr. Buck, who was one of the most beloved clergymen in Fall River, and who, by Emma Borden's own statement, was "my best friend in the world, the one who advised me when matters reached such a pass that I could not stay longer in the same house with Lizzie."

On the walls of the room, which during the Rev. Mr. Buck's lifetime had served as his study, hung framed scriptural texts and religious paintings. One of the latter was "The Last Supper." Another art work dealt with angels and cherubs. On tables and shelves were religious volumes and pamphlets. The chairs and couch were in solid, old-fashioned type, whose faded buff covering did not detract one bit from a comfortable appearance.

LIKE A FRIGHTFUL DREAM

"The tragedy seems but yesterday, and many times I catch myself wondering whether it is not some frightful dream, after all," said Miss Borden. . . . "Often it had occurred to me how strange is the fact that no one save Lizzie was ever brought to trial for the killing of our father and our mother-in-law. [i.e., stepmother -- Eds.]

"Some persons have stated that for years they considered Lizzie's actions decidedly queer.

"But what if she did act queerly? Don't we all do something peculiar at some time or other?

"Queer? Yes, Lizzie is queer. But as for her being guilty, I say 'No,' and decidedly 'No.'

"The day the crime took place I was at Fairhaven on a visit to friends, I hurried home in response to a telegram, and one of the first persons I met was Lizzie. She was very much affected.

"Later, when veiled accusations began to be made, she came to me and said:

" 'Emma, it is awful for them to say that I killed poor father and our stepmother. You know that I would not dream of such an awful thing, Emma.'

"Later, after her arrest and during her trial, Lizzie many times reiterated her protest of innocence to me.

"And after her acquittal she declared her guiltlessness during conversations that we had at the French street mansion.

PROOF OF INNOCENCE

"Here is the strongest thing that has convinced me of Lizzie's innocence. The authorities never found the axe or whatever implement it was that figured in the killing.

"Lizzie, if she had done that deed, could never have hidden the instrument of death so that the police could not find it. Why, there was no hiding place in the old house that would serve for effectual concealment. Neither did she have the time.

"Another thing to be remembered is Lizzie's affection for dumb animals. She fairly dotes on the dogs, cats and squirrels that are at the French street mansion. She always was fond of pets. Now, any person with a heart like that could never have committed the awful act for which Lizzie was tried and of which she was acquitted.

"I did my duty at the trial when I sat with Lizzie day after day and then testified for her. And despite our estrangement, I am going to do my duty in answering the cruel slanders that have been made against her both in public print and by gossiping persons who seem to take delight in saying cruel things about her.

"The happenings at the French street house that caused me to leave I must refuse to talk about. I did not go until conditions became absolutely unbearable. Then, before taking action, I consulted the Rev. A. E. Buck. . . .

"After carefully listening to my story he said it was imperative that I should make my home elsewhere.

"Before going, I had an agreement drawn up by our lawyer so that no trouble could arise regarding the French street house.

"Although the general public believes that Lizzie owns that house, such is not the case. It is our joint property, and so is the land it stands on. Under the agreement we entered into, Lizzie is to occupy the house as long as she lives, and is to pay me rent for the use of my half of the estate. Lizzie is the sole owner of land she added to the original estate.

"I do not expect ever to set foot on the place while she lives.

MOTHER'S DYING REQUEST

"Perhaps people wondered why I stood so staunchly by Lizzie during the trial. I'll tell them why. Aside from my feeling as a sister, it was because I constantly had in mind our dear mother. She died when Lizzie was only 3 years of age, while I had reached 12 years.

"When my darling mother was on her deathbed she summoned me, and exacted a promise that I would always watch over 'baby Lizzie.'

"From childhood to womanhood and up to the time the murder occurred, I tried to safeguard Lizzie.

"And although it is not generally known, the obligation imposed on me by my mother impelled me to assume as a duty the payment of one-half the costs of that murder trial. Of course, the expenses of such a case were very heavy. I stipulated before the trial was entered upon that I should pay one-half the costs, and I insisted on fulfilling my promise, after everything was over.

"I did my duty at the time of the trial, and I am still going to do it in defending my sister even though circumstances have separated us.

"The vision of my dear mother always is bright in my mind. I want to feel that when Mother and I meet in the hereafter, she will tell me that I was faithful to her trust and that I looked after 'baby Lizzie' to the best of my ability."

At this point of the interview, the emotion which Miss Borden had plainly repressed at times by sheer will power would be denied no longer.

OVERCOME WITH GRIEF

Her soft even tones dropped almost to a moan. Then utterance was checked absolutely. Convulsive sobs shook the form of Lizzie Borden's "little mother."

Abruptly arising from her low rocking chair, Miss Borden slowly paced to and fro, while she pressed a black bordered handkerchief against her face.

For several minutes the paroxysm of grief continued. Then the little figure straightened slowly to dignified posture, the remaining traces of tears were removed by soft dabs of the handkerchief, and Miss Borden became quite herself once more.

"Yes," she resumed slowly, but with clear articulation. "I intend to defend Lizzie against the harsh public so that mother will say I have been faithful to my trust.

"I have been told of the unjust stories that have appeared in print. Right here in Fall River, is a newspaper that year after year, on the anniversary of the crime, publishes what I consider a most uncalled for review of the case. Just what the purpose of this practice is I do not know.

"One of the stories that has been going the rounds in connection with my sister deals with Nance O'Neil, the actress.

"This report is to the effect that Nance O'Neil met my sister in another city, became intimately acquainted with her, and maintained this friendliness until she discovered that the Lizbeth Borden she knew was none other than Lizzie Borden, the woman who had been tried on a charge of murder.

"I know such a tale to be absolutely unfounded. Nance O'Neil has for years been a close friend of Lizzie, and she holds that relation to this very day.

"Another wild rumor has to do with the family fortune. Someone, who knows more about the Borden estate than I and my sister do, has declared that our combined wealth would go over the million mark.

"Now here is the truth in respect to that. If all the property that we own jointly should, through our lawyers, be turned into cash, the total amount of our worldly possessions would not go beyond one-quarter of a million dollars. That is a large amount of money, but is certainly less than a million.

"Some of the neighbors in and around French street who have criticised Lizzie so freely have not treated her as fairly as they might in certain things -- matters of business, I mean.

"Some unkind persons have spread the report that my father, despite his great wealth was niggardly and that he refused to even give us sufficient to eat.

"That is a wicked lie. He was a plain-mannered man, but his table was always laden with the best that the market could afford.

"Every Memorial Day I carry flowers to father's grave. And Lizzie does not forget him. But she generally sends her tribute by a florist."

At this juncture, Miss Borden requested to be excused from further conversation.

As she slowly conducted the Post man to the door, she murmured, as if to herself:

"Yes, a jury declared Lizzie to be innocent, but an unkind world has unrelentingly persecuted her. I am still the little mother and though we must live as strangers, I will defend 'Baby Lizzie' against merciless tongues."

Lizzie's Death

In 1926 Lizzie entered the hospital for a gall bladder operation. She was admitted under the name of Emma Borden of the Hotel Biltmore, Providence, Rhode Island. The south corridor of one floor in the hospital was cleared for the pseudonymous guest, and she became the subject of discussion in the wards.* The nurses found her an uncooperative patient. They had difficulty keeping Lizzie, her bed, or her room in proper hospital order; she would not use a bedpan. Nor did Lizzie like hospital fare. Long ago, when imprisoned, she had had much of her food catered. This time her chauffeur brought food to the hospital daily from Laura Carr's in Providence, caterers of local renown. Orange sherbet was a favorite. Lizzie never fully recovered from the operation and died the following year.

The comparison of obituaries published in the New York *Times* and the Fall River *Daily Globe* is illuminating. Had her home town forgiven Lizzie at last?

---

*The information about Lizzie's hospital stay comes from a former resident of Fall River who was also in the hospital at this time. She had just given birth to her second daughter and Lizzie asked to see the infant. As Lizzie held her, nurses told the mother later, she remarked that this was the first baby she had ever held. (Source: Letter to editors from Ruth A. Waring, dated December 1, 1979, recounting the Fall River woman's story.)

Obituaries from the Daily Globe and the Times
Source: Fall River *Daily Globe.*

June 2, 1927

LISBETH BORDEN
DIES AFTER SHORT ILLNESS, AGE 68

Miss Lisbeth A. Borden died this morning at 306 French street, where she had made her home for about 30 years. She had been ill with pneumonia for about a week, although for some time she had been in failing health.

A member of one of the old Fall River families, having been the daughter of Andrew J. and Sarah (Anthony) Borden, she had lived here all of her life. With her two maids she lived a quiet, retired life, paying occasional visits to out-of-town friends and receiving a few callers, whose staunch friendship she valued highly.

Taking an intense pride in the surroundings in which she lived, she did much to improve the locality, purchasing adjoining property that the same refined atmosphere might be maintained. Greatly interested in nature, she was daily seen providing for the hundreds of birds that frequented the trees in her yard, taking care that the shallow box where they gathered was filled with crumbs, seeds and other foods that they favored. She had miniature houses erected in her trees, and in these, frivolous squirrels made their homes. Her figure as she visited with her wild callers, many of whom became so friendly that they never seemed to mind her approach, was a familiar one in that section.

Another pastime in which she greatly delighted was riding through the country roads and lanes. She made frequent trips about the town in her motor car, but was never so pleased as when winding through the shady country by-ways.

Surviving Miss Borden is a sister, Miss Emma Borden of New Hampshire, formerly of Providence.

The death of Miss Borden recalls to many one of the most famous murder trials in the history of the state. On the fourth of August, 1892, Andrew J. Borden and his wife, Abby D. Borden, were found murdered in their Second street home. After a preliminary investigation, Lisbeth Borden was arrested and formally charged with the murder of her father. After a hearing in Fall River she was indicted by the grand jury and in November, 1892, was tried and acquitted in New Bedford.

The trial attracted statewide interest. No further arrests were ever made and the murder has remained an unsolved mystery since. Following her acquittal, Miss Borden lived a rather retired life and

255

devoted much of her time to private charities of which the public knew but little.

Source: The New York *Times.*

June 3, 1927

LIZZIE BORDEN DIES;
HER TRIAL RECALLED

Acquitted Thirty-three Years Ago
of Murdering Wealthy Father and Stepmother.

MYSTERY NEVER SOLVED

Stoutly Defended by Her Sister,
Who Became Estranged From Her in Later Years.

FALL RIVER, MASS., June 2 (AP). -- Miss Lisbeth A. Borden, better known as Lizzie Borden, who was acquitted of the murder of her father and stepmother in 1893 after one of the most celebrated murder trials in New England, died at her home here last night at the age of 68.

Miss Borden, who had lived quietly in this city since her acquittal, underwent an operation about a year ago and never fully recovered.

During her later years she had lived virtually alone and had few if any close friends. So far as known she never discussed with any one the murder of her parents, and her lawyer said today that they knew of no will or statement which she might have left.

The country was shocked on Aug. 4, 1892, when the bodies of her father and stepmother were discovered in their home on Second Street, Fall River. They had been hacked to death.

Lizzie was arrested and charged with the crime. Some of the most famous lawyers of the day took part in the trial. The leading attorneys in the trial are now dead. Attorney General Hosea M. Knowlton represented the State and Andrew J. Jennings of Fall River was chief counsel for the defense.

Other persons connected with the trial also have died, except for a sister, Emma, and possibly Bridget Sullivan, a servant in the Borden home, who was a leading witness and returned to her home in Ireland later.

Andrew J. Borden was a retired cotton broker and owned much valuable real estate in this city. In the middle of the forenoon of Aug. 4, 1892, his daughter Lizzie rushed into the home of a woman neighbor and told her that she had found her father dead in the living room.

The neighbor returned with her and saw the body, then went upstairs and found the body of Mrs. Borden in a bedroom. The

256

autopsy showed that both had been killed with either an axe or a cleaver.

CASE BAFFLED AUTHORITIES

For several days the case baffled the authorities. Finally, building up a case of circumstantial evidence, they arrested Lizzie and brought her to trial in New Bedford. The State sought to show that, in view of the fact that Mrs. Borden was her stepmother, Lizzie feared that she would not get a liberal share of her father's estate upon his death and decided to do away with both father and stepmother, that she and her sister Emma might get the estate at once.

Miss Borden testified that she was not in the house at the time of the murders. She said that Mr. and Mrs. Borden were alive when she went out to the barn to look for some fishing tackle, and when she returned, she found them dead. Her sister, it was established, was away on an errand. Emma Borden stood by Lizzie, insisting that her sister could have had no possible motive for the crime.

There was testimony at the trial about a man, possibly a peddler, who had been seen in the vicinity of the house on the day of the murders, but his identity never was established.

SEEKS DISTRIBUTION OF PROPERTY.

In May, 1923, Lizzie Borden appeared in the Probate Court at Taunton, Mass., in an effort to obtain an equal distribution of the property known as the A. J. Borden block, in Fall River, which she owned jointly with her sister. This was her first known appearance in a court room since her acquittal thirty years before.

In April, 1913, Emma Borden broke a silence of twenty years and declared her positive belief in the innocence of her sister, Lizzie. She said in part: "Often it has occurred to me how strange is the fact that no one save Lizzie was ever brought to trial for the killing of our father and his wife. Lizzie is queer, but as for her being guilty I say 'no' and decidedly 'no.' Here is the strongest thing that has impressed me of Lizzie's innocence: The authorities never found the axe or the implement or whatever it was that figured in the killing. If Lizzie had done that deed, she could never have hidden the instrument of death so the police could never find it."

In 1905 Emma Borden left her sister and made her home with friends, the action causing an estrangement between the sisters. Of this, Emma Borden said: "The happenings in the French street house that caused me to leave I must refuse to talk about. I did not go until conditions became absolutely unbearable."

So far as known, Emma is the only surviving relative of Lizzie.

The Will of Lizzie/Lizbeth Borden

A will allows an individual to determine the distribution of his or her property after death. It is, in that sense, an exercise of that person's power over his private property and, indirectly, over surviving family and friends. The choices a person makes in the granting of bequests -- and in the withholding of gifts -- may tell us a great deal about that person's ideas. For example, we may learn about a person's notions of responsibility to surviving relatives and dependents, about what a person thinks are good deeds, about a person's relationships with family, friends, business associates, and servants. A will can be a particularly important document if no other records of a person's feelings and attitudes survive, and it may be a revealing piece of evidence if it contradicts other sources of information.

Lizzie made her will a year and a half before her death. She did not forget the people she felt had been loyal friends. In her last years her most faithful friends had been Helen Leighton, a librarian who came to Fall River after the murders, and a cousin, Grace Howe. Both these women had visited Lizzie regularly.

Servants who had been in her employ for at least five years received bequests. Charles Cook, who had managed some of Andrew Borden's property, continued to work for the Bordens; Lizzie entrusted her business affairs to his care. In later years she also put more personal matters into his hands, such as the hiring of her servants. He was rewarded handsomely.

One of Lizzie's largest bequests went not to people but to animals. The significance of humans' relationships with their pets is currently the subject of psychological research; the meaning of Lizzie's gift for neglected and abandoned animals may be illuminated by that research.

Lizzie apparently did not forget her friends; nor, apparently, did she forgive those who neglected her. The obvious beneficiary in Lizzie's will ought, in family terms, to have been Emma. Emma was, of course, wealthy in her own right. And Emma had left Maplecroft and Lizzie in 1905.

Finally, Lizzie left five hundred dollars for the perpetual care of her father's lot in Oak Grove Cemetery. Such a bequest may have reflected Lizzie's filial piety for the whole family is buried there. But it was also a provision for the care of her own grave.

Source: Courtesy of Edward Sullivan.

I, Lizzie A. Borden, otherwise known as Lizbeth A. Borden, of Fall River in the County of Bristol and Commonwealth of Massachusetts, do make this my last will and testament hereby revoking all other wills heretofore made by me.

After the payment of my just debts and funeral charges I give, devise and bequeath as follows:

1. To the City of Fall River the sum of five hundred dollars, the income derived therefrom to be used for the perpetual care of my father's lot in Oak Grove Cemetery in said Fall River.

2. To my housekeeper and to each one of the servants who shall have been with me for five years and shall be in my employ at the time of my death the sum of three thousand dollars.

3. To Charles C. Cook, of said Fall River and Tiverton, for his long and faithful services to me the sum of ten thousand dollars and my so-called Baker Lot on French Street, across from where I live.

4. To the Animal Rescue League of said Fall River the sum of thirty thousand dollars, also my shares of stock in the Stevens Manufacturing Company. I have been fond of animals and their need is great and there are so few who care for them.

5. To Miss Helen Leighton I give my three diamond rings and diamond and sapphire brooch, my inlaid mahogany desk and chairs in my library, also my library desk with the reading lamp, and I also direct that she shall have the first choice and may take any and all of my rugs, books, china, pictures and furniture that she may choose. I also give and devise to her one-half of my share in the A. J. Borden Building, in said Fall River, if she shall survive me, if not I give and devise my interest therein to Grace H. Howe, to her and her heirs, executors, administrators and assigns forever.

6. To my cousin, Mrs. Grace H. Howe, my diamond and amethyst ring and I direct that she shall have second choice of my rugs, books, china, pictures and furniture, and I also give to her the privilege, so far as I have the same, to use the Oak Grove Cemetery lot for burial purposes. I also give and devise to her one-half of my share in the A. J. Borden Building in said Fall River, to her, her heirs, executors, administrators and assigns forever.

7. To Mrs. Margaret L. Streeter, of Washington, District of Columbia, the sum of five thousand dollars with my diamond and sapphire ring with five stones which she always liked.

8. To Mrs. Minnie E. A. Lacombe, of Washington, D. C., the sum of five thousand dollars.

9. To S. Howard Lacombe, the son of said Minnie E. A. Lacombe, the sum of two thousand dollars.

10. To Catherine M. MacFarland, of said Fall River, the sum of five thousand dollars.

11. To Gertrude M. Baker, of said Fall River, the sum of one thousand dollars.

12. To Mrs. Mary L. Orters of Sharon, Massachusetts, the sum of five thousand dollars; if she shall not be living at my decease I give the same to her husband, Henry L. Orters.

13. To Winnifred F. French, of said Fall River, the sum of five thousand dollars; if she shall not be living at my decease I give the same to her sister, Sara H. French.

14. To Alice L. Soderman, of said Fall River, the sum of two thousand dollars, also my jeweled watch and chain.

15. To Elsie F. Carlisle, formerly of Fall River, now in California, the sum of one thousand dollars.

16. To Dr. Annie C. Macrae, of said Fall River, the sum of one thousand dollars.

17. To my old school mate, Lucy S. Macomber, of said Fall River, the sum of one thousand dollars.

18. To my old school mate, Adelaide B. Whipp, of said Fall River, the sum of one thousand dollars.

19. To my housekeeper, Ellen B. Miller always called Nellie, all the contents of her room if she wants them.

20. To Mrs. Ethel H. Engel, of Los Angeles, California, the sum of one thousand dollars.

21. To my cousin, George E. Robinson, of Swansea, Massachusetts, the sum of one thousand dollars.

22. To my cousin, Edson M. Robinson, of said Swansea, the sum of one thousand dollars.

23. To my cousin, Percy V. Robinson, of said Swansea, the sum of two thousand dollars.

24. To Grace L. Terry, daughter of my chauffeur, the sum of two thousand dollars.

25. To Ellen B. Terry, wife of my chauffeur, the sum of two thousand dollars.

26. To Ernest Alden Terry, Jr. the sum of two thousand dollars, with the so-called Belmont lot which is west of my home lot.

27. To Animal Rescue League, of Washington, D. C., the sum of two thousand dollars.

28. I have not given my sister, Emma L. Borden, anything as she had her share of her father's estate and is supposed to have enough to make her comfortable.

29. The rest and residue of my property of every description or wherever situated I give, devise and bequeath in equal shares to Helen Leighton and my cousin, Grace H. Howe, but if said Helen Leighton shall not survive me I give and devise all of said rest and residue to said Grace H. Howe, to her, her heirs, executors, administrators and assigns, forever.

I nominate Charles C. Cook to be executor of this my last will and testament and request that he may be exempt from giving sureties on his official bond to any Probate Court.

If said Charles C. Cook shall not be living at my decease I nominate Frederick E. Bemis, cashier of the Fall River National Bank, to be executor of this my last will and testament and request that he may be exempt from giving sureties on his official bond to any Probate Court.

In testimony whereof I hereunto set my hand and in the presence of three witnesses declare this to be my last will and testament this thirtieth day of January in the year nineteen hundred and twenty-six.

Lizbeth A. Borden [signed]

Lizzie A. Borden [signed]

On this thirtieth day of January A. D. 1926, Lizzie A. Borden otherwise known as Lizbeth A. Borden of Fall River, Massachusetts, signed the foregoing instrument in our presence, declaring it to be her last will and testament and as witnesses thereof we three do now, at her request, in her presence and in the presence of each other hereto subscribe our names.

Ellen R. Nottingham [signed]

Carl A. Terry [signed]

Charles L. Baker [signed]

Lizzie Remembered

Police reports, news accounts, and legal records form the major sources of our knowledge of Lizzie and the Borden case. Mrs. Florence Brigham, Curator of the Fall River Historical Society, has pointed out that the memories of townsfolk, too, form part of our store of knowledge of those events of 1892 and after.

The Borden case survives in the folk memory -- as well as the official records -- of Fall River. Rumor and recollection alike can contain further clues to the truths of Lizzie's life and personality and of the times in which she and her family lived. But in Fall River today there is often a reluctance to discuss Lizzie openly. The standard reply, both guarded and well-mannered, comes: "She was tried, found innocent, and we really don't like to talk about it." One charitable lady adds: "Let the poor girl rest in peace." A few, however, who have had some special connection with the case or its principal participants, are willing to share their knowledge and views. In so doing, they have made a contribution to the store of knowledge and, perhaps, our understanding of the case and the environment in which it took place.

Interviews and Letters (Excerpts, in all cases used by permission of the author or interviewee)

Mrs. Florence Brigham, Curator of Fall River Historical Society: her mother-in-law, Mary Brigham, was a character witness for Lizzie at her trial in 1893. (Interview, July 6, 1979)

261

What about motive?

"Andrew Borden was said to be stingy. If you were in your thirty-third year and your sister even older, and if you had no close relatives to take you in -- and if you felt that Andrew Borden's money might go to the stepmother and her relatives -- you might have felt that you faced the possibility of going to the poor farm. That would have been a disgrace in those days."

The Church's influence?

"I think the ministers at Central Church got people together and told them not to talk about the case anymore."

Do you think Bridget received money for her testimony in Lizzie's behalf?

"I think she was given money to go back to Ireland. She may have known more than she told. Maids in those days liked to gossip, and Lizzie wouldn't have wanted her around, telling how Lizzie and her stepmother never got along."

The stepmother?

"Apparently Lizzie had a dislike for her from the beginning."

Why did Emma leave?

"I think she either decided Lizzie was guilty although she always said she was innocent, or maybe she had spells (as Victoria Lincoln claims in the book) which frightened her."

Attitude of Fall River residents?

"I think that while Lizzie was in jail people didn't want her to get the death sentence. But after she was acquitted she was ostracized. My mother-in-law, Mary Brigham, who testified that she had always been a good person who worked in the church, had to give up going to see her because her friends were starting to leave her alone."

Was Dr. Bowen involved in a 'cover-up' for Lizzie?

"I have heard that some maintained that Dr. Bowen took the weapon home in his bag."

Alice Russell?

"Lovely white hair -- a gentle person -- not a vindictive person and would not have told the story about the burning of the dress if her conscience hadn't bothered her."

*　　*　　*　　*

Mr. Ellis A. Waring, of Swansea, has two links to the Borden story. His cousin, Dwight Waring, married Defense Attorney Jennings's daughter, and, as a child, Ellis Waring played in the garden at Maplecroft. (Interview, July 5, 1979)

Of Lizzie he recalled: "She used to yell, 'Get out of my yard!'"

"The grocery man was scared to go in -- he left groceries in the back.

"She owned a Packard automobile. Always had a chauffeur. Apparently, he had other duties as well. People said that he played the piano for Lizzie's entertainment.

"She always wore black in later years -- black dress, black coat, and black hat and veil. I just remember a lot of black coming out of the house."

* * * *

Mrs. Ellis A. (Ruth) Waring, related by marriage to Defense Attorney Jennings and a resident of Swansea, where Andrew Borden owned property. Mrs. Waring's neighbor, Calvin Gardner, was the son of Chester Gardner, whose father's farm adjoined Andrew Borden's property. (Interview, July 5, 1979)

"Chester Gardner, who was about sixteen at the time, told us that about three days before the murder, Lizzie came over to Swansea to get an axe sharpened so she could kill some chickens." [They did as she asked.]

* * * *

Mrs. Miriam Durfee Holman, member of the Central Congregational Church of Fall River. Her family's pew in the church was located near Lizzie Borden's, and she had opportunity to observe the reactions of church people. (Interview, July 6, 1979)

What do you recall of the Bordens?

"I was a young child when it happened. . . . For years no one would sit in that pew [Lizzie's]. I believe it was Pew No. 21. (Our family pew was No. 19, and Lizzie's was in front of ours.) She never came to church after the incident. Rev. Jubb was very much for her."

Were most of the people in the church for her?

"I cannot answer that, honestly."

"My mother always said Lizzie did it."

* * * *

Mrs. Vida Pearson Turner, active in church society in Fall River, had a rich contralto voice and was often called upon to sing at funerals. She remembers receiving a call from a friend of Lizzie's, asking her to come to the house on French Street to sing "In my Ain Countrie." (Interview, July 6, 1979)

"I was summoned to sing. The undertaker unlocked the door, let me in, and locked the door immediately. I was ushered into a room, sang the song, and was then ushered out. The undertaker told me, 'Go straight home and don't tell anyone where you have been.' And I kept that promise for many, many years." (Mrs. Turner was asked if she wished to see Lizzie's corpse. She declined.)

Of the case, she said, "It is a thing against Fall River. I wish it could be completely erased."

* * * *

263

Russell B. Lake was a neighbor of Lizzie's in Fall River. (Letter dated December 26, 1979)

"I am more than pleased to write you what I remember of the life and circumstances under which Miss Borden lived across the street from my family. She had a typical gay 90's home. She purchased this house after she was acquitted. It, of course, was not the house in which the murder was committed. The house, as well as my family's home, was located at that time in one of the better neighborhoods. My father built our home in 1894. I was born there in 1895 -- three years after the murders in 1892. Miss Borden, I feel, was not extremely wealthy, but what one might call at that time 'comfortably fixed.' She kept her place and house in perfect condition. She had a cook, a second maid and a coachman, or general man around the place. He kept up the grounds and drove her pair of horses and two-seater when she wished to go shopping or take friends for a ride.

"I have tried to write the above so that you might get a mental picture of the conditions and home life she lived when I knew her. I, of course, was a boy at that time. She came over to our house a great deal and I went across the street with my mother to visit very often. My mother and Miss Borden were very good friends and neighbors. To me, as a child and later as a young man, she was just as nice and kind an old lady as one could ask for. Knowing her so well, it has been impossible for me to believe such a nice old lady could have ever committed such a gruesome murder. Therefore, it is hard for me not to come to her defense whenever I discuss the case with my friends. All of my friends, even those in the neighborhood, seemed to feel she was guilty and did not hesitate to say so and act that way toward her.

"Therefore, if you will forgive me, I will just ramble on and write what I have told many friends and casual acquaintances of the unpleasant conditions she was forced to live under. I will not try to coordinate my statements, but just write down my thoughts and memories as they come to me. You can read this as a whole and draw your own conclusions. I will try not to be prejudiced.

"My first memories of Miss Borden were when I was only a child and of her coming to our house and my mother taking me across the street to visit. She made a big hit with me by being my best customer when I had a lemonade stand. Later on, when I left for boarding school, she gave me my first fifty cents. I was one of the privileged children who could run through her yard and climb over the stone wall to get away from the neighborhood bully. I could duck in the kitchen or the hostler would see that no harm came to me. Most other children reflected their parents' views and treated Miss Borden and her house like she was a witch or some person to fear and the house was haunted or a place to keep away from.

"Some of these facts regarding Miss Borden were told to me by my mother. Although my mother was a Baptist, she sent me to the Congregational Sunday School, where I played the violin with the son of the organist for the singing of the other children. My mother had many friends going to the Congregational Church. This was the church where Lizzy and her sister taught Sunday School before the murder. During this period, it was the custom for members of the Church to pay so much a year for a pew. After the trial and acquittal, Miss Borden went back to church to sit in the family pew. No one in the church would sit within three or four pews of the Borden pew. She was left alone, surrounded by empty pews. Naturally after this treatment, she gave up going to church and the social life that came with it.

"Miss Borden was a figure of curiosity and mystery to everyone in the country at this particular period. She could not go anywhere without being recognized and embarrassed by stares from gathering crowds. I remember going shopping with my mother. We went to the largest dry goods store on Main Street, E. S. Brown & Co., owned by Harry Brown, a neighbor and friend of our family. When we came out of the store, Miss Borden's carriage and coachman were at the curb. Someone had recognized her carriage. There were at least 25 or 30 curiosity seekers standing around, waiting for her to come out of the store, so that they might get a look and pass some remarks.

"Day after day, the hackers who met the trains from Boston would stand around calling out to the passengers -- 'Come and see the notorious Lizzy Borden home, where she now lives.' Many times, I have been on our veranda and seen one or two hackers pull up their rig, full of drummers from Boston, who had come to work Fall River for the day. The hacker would take his whip and point out the house and deliver a spiel on Miss Borden, the servants and the murder. For this side trip on the way to their customers, the drummers paid two bits extra.

"My mother told me that to get away from this environment, she shopped a good deal in Providence. She also went to New York and Washington, where my mother said she had friends. One of these friends mother said was the buxom actress Lillian Russell. Miss Borden gave my mother a typical large theatrical picture of Lillian Russell. It was around the house for many years. Whatever became of it, I don't know. You may not remember, but the famous gay '90s dessert, consisting of a half a musk melon with a scoop of vanilla ice cream was called a Lillian Russell. I also seem to remember mother and Miss Borden talking about Nance O'Neil.

"Let me depart a little from what I remember of our friendship and social life. My family was a great defender of Miss Borden. They firmly believed, as I do, that as kind and good a woman as Miss Borden, could never have committed such a gruesome murder and in such a

265

manner as it was done. It would have to be done by someone with a great hatred and absolutely furious at their victims to commit a crime in the manner this was done. Miss Borden was never that kind of person.

"I don't know if what I am going to write now was ever in any of the books about the trial. I have never read any of them thoroughly. However, I am sure my mother got it from Miss Borden. Mr. Borden, her father, was a scrooge. He owned a lot of tenement property, which he rented mostly to mill help. Each Saturday in his stove pipe hat and cane, he went out to collect the rent. If they did not have the rent money or did not pay, out on the street they went, regardless of sickness or any other family problems. The cotton mills, during this period, were just coming into their hey-day. In order to get sufficient help, the mill owners brought over many jichey English and low-class Portuguese and French. These were mostly his tenants. My mother told me he was well hated by his tenants.

"Returning to Miss Borden's personal life, I do not remember many friends coming to her house. However, she was very generous and kind to anyone who worked for her or was associated with her. A Mrs. McFarland was Miss Borden's dressmaker, as well as my mother's. I know that Miss Borden took her for many carriage rides, which was a treat in those days and also helped her out financially.

"Miss Borden also helped her coachman buy a house. Mother told me she also helped his children through college. As you probably know, when she died she left the Animal Rescue League of Fall River and the one in Boston well endowed. From what I have written, you can see why she left her money to animals.

"As I grew older, I still continued to go across the street to visit with Miss Borden whenever I came home from boarding school. When I went tautoe fishing, I knew that tautoe (the local Indian name for the east coast black fish) was Miss Borden's favorite fish, so I always cleaned a couple and brought them over to her.

"I do not remember as much about her as I grew into my teens as I did when I was a child. I am sure that what has kept my memory fresh about her is that when anyone found out I came from Fall River and knew Lizzy Borden, I had to answer many questions and I told them what I have written you."

*   *   *   *

Mrs. Edith Coolidge Hart, a former newspaper reporter and long-time resident of Fall River, responded to the editors' request for her thoughts on the Borden case. Following are selections from her letters dated July 31, August 28, September 16, and December 16, 1979, and March 8, 1980:

"There is little doubt in my mind that Lizzie was indeed a mental case and her living conditions were not conducive to normality. Lizzie's daily companion was an immigrant Irish maid and a bromidic sister. Even her ministers were not scholars and they dropped her as soon as the trial was over.

"It doesn't need close analysis to learn that Lizzie grew up in a household utterly devoid of affection. Her sister, who was close to her, seemed governed by fear rather than love. Living in a home that had limited facilities and no affection, almost anyone would be a little queer. Lizzie was only three when her own mother died. Her sister ten years older was the substitute maternal influence. Hatred of a physically unattractive stepmother must have first been built up in her subconscious mind, nurtured to deep dislike and hatred. I feel sure that the stepmother was blamed for every neglect of the father. . . .

"Did Lizzie Borden have friends before and after the murder trial? It is safe to say that in that era there were very few, if any, laissez-faire friendships. There were certain 'crushes' that caused a great deal of talk but in good society parents kept a close watch and restricted intimacies. It is difficult to picture the restraints of that era unless you have lived through it.

". . . I never heard the words homosexual or lesbian until after my college days. It may be difficult to believe but even the written words, the theater, all social life was more or less restrained. It is an absolute fact that in the late 1890's an actress was arrested because she was carried upstairs on the stage in the arms of a man to what everyone knew was a bedroom. As you know, we kept our thoughts clothed as we did our bodies. A difficult thing to imagine in this era. . . . .

"Alice Russell was mentioned in all reports of the murders. She was a neighbor and not a friend. There was no camaraderie. She was a very quiet maiden lady of no great education. She lived across the street. . . .

"Maybe my point of view is not quite normal, but I find the most distressing years of Lizzie's life were those after she was acquitted. Her quick change of living atmosphere -- up on the hill she went into a spacious house in a good neighborhood. Many times I saw her in her horse-driven carriage and later in her automobile, driving around Fall River. Her face was always set in a glum unhappy pattern. I don't blame her for taking the bull by the horns and getting something out of life, even if she had to pay for it. . . . .

"Lizzie did what a great many people with money do. She tried to buy friendship and the good times she never had. She became interested in theatre and attended it in Boston and the one-night stands in Fall River. She entertained the casts at her home after the night performance and became involved with one actress in particular, Nance O'Neil. Lizzie's sister did not think the parties were 'seemly' considering the cloud under which they had lived. She left and went to New Hampshire and, strangely, died very soon after Lizzie, although she was ten years older. None of the town's people attended the parties and probably were not invited. Sister Emma was a dour person much like her father and probably could not condone her sister's type of entertainment. . . . .

"In that period it was difficult for people in any stratum of society to cultivate intimate friendships. There were afternoon teas, formal dances, dignified theatre parties, but none of the devil-may-care attitude of modern life in every stratum. . . . Society was vindictive in that day. There was little show of friendship for any family associated with the slightest 'sin' against established ethical rules. . . . .

"I haven't done a very good job of expressing the stiff spirit that pervaded Fall River in that era. People from foreign countries were coming in to the mills and were completely isolated in their own particular section of the city. . . . .

"The sister was a colorless personality. She evidently had no ambition, no particular interests. If she felt any resentment, it was not evident. Perhaps she took after the colorless mother who died. The same atmosphere evidently bred resentment in the much younger Lizzie.

"Self-preservation is a basic law even with the lowest animals. I believe it was the reason she murdered her father. With little education or the simple rules of living she did not have the capacity to cover the tracks of the first murder. I have great sympathy for Lizzie, a victim of an impossible social climate. . . . ."

Sources And Further Reading

The editors have benefitted from the work of previous students of the Borden case. The stream of works -- factual, fictional, and dramatic -- began shortly after the trial had ended. Edwin Henry Porter's *The Fall River Tragedy, A History of the Borden Murders* (1893) was the first book published about the Borden case. Written by the Fall River *Globe's* crime reporter, it offers a complete account of the case from the day of the murder until Lizzie was set free. The presentation makes a devastating case for Lizzie's guilt. The fact that Lizzie bought all the copies she could find suggests that she thought so, too. Only a few copies escaped her net: one is in the Library of Congress and another is in the Fall River Public Library.

Edmund Pearson wrote more books about Lizzie Borden than any other author. Pearson's private correspondence (now at the Lilly Library, Indiana University) indicates that from the time of his first book about the Bordens, *Studies in Murder* (1924), he grew increasingly attached to Miss Borden, referring to her as "my beloved Lizzie" (Letter dated February 6, 1936). Pearson became famous as a writer of true-crime literature and prospered professionally with Lizzie as a cherished companion.

Pearson's *Studies in Murder* describes five celebrated murder cases. The Borden case takes up nearly half the book and is told with irony and humor. A reviewer from the New York *World* judged that, to a mystery fan, every murder is a pretty good murder: "Some are better than others, and Mr. Pearson's are excellent." In *Murder at Smutty Nose* (1926) Pearson supplements his *Studies* by examining twelve murders, again including the Borden case, and brings to each a philosophical and psychological interpretation.

In 1937 Pearson published *The Trial of Lizzie Borden,* which contains the trial proceedings, cross examinations, and summaries from bar and bench. After more than a decade of writing about the Bordens, Pearson had become the acknowledged authority on the case, and his comments and narrative are illuminating.

In *Three Rousing Cheers* (1938) Elizabeth Porter, a reporter for the New York *World,* devotes a chapter to "Lizzie Borden and the Murders." Although Porter covered the trial for the *World,* her material about the murders and the trial is far from accurate, but her impressions of events and people ring true. She found Lizzie as aloof from the terrible ordeal of the trial as a Buddha image in its temple. And although Miss Porter believed Lizzie to be innocent, she felt that "Miss Borden was not the type of woman to confess anything to anybody."

Marie Belloc Lowndes, in *Lizzie Borden: A Study in Conjecture* (1939), observes that knowing the facts about the Borden case does not help solve the crime. She calls for conjecture, particularly on the question of motive. Belloc Lowndes posits the motive of romantic love. Lizzie, she speculates, had a lover. When her stepmother discovered his existence, she threatened to tell Mr. Borden. Lizzie murdered to keep her secret from Mr. Borden, but, after the murders, she decided never to see her suitor again. Belloc Lowndes offers a sympathetic, humanized picture of Lizzie. Love, she seems to suggest, is a better motive for murder than money.

In 1959 Edward Rowe Snow published *Piracy, Mutiny and Murder,* a collection of sixteen true stories of violence set mainly in New England. He includes a section on Lizzie Borden and recounts, for the first time, the story of Lizzie's shoplifting in 1897. He reports that Lizzie signed a murder confession in exchange for the dropping of the shoplifting charges.

Edward Radin, author of *Lizzie Borden: The Untold Story* (1961) attempts to prove that the jury was right -- that Lizzie was innocent. He argues further that Bridget, the maid, was guilty. He constructs an elaborate timetable of the day of the murders to prove his point, and his first-class detective work on this case makes it a must for crime buffs. His weakest point seems to be motive: why would a seemingly amiable maid kill her employers if she had no prospect of gain by their deaths?

One of the finest books to appear on the Borden case is Victoria Lincoln's *A Private Disgrace: Lizzie Borden by Daylight* (1967). An accomplished novelist, Victoria Lincoln has an advantage over other authors: she is a native of Fall River and as a child knew Lizzie Borden, then in her later years at Maplecroft. As an insider she knows the code, the way of life, the tensions within the first families of Fall River. She puts forward the fascinating thesis that Lizzie suffered from epilepsy of the temporal lobe and that she was subject to attacks during her menstrual periods. Lincoln believes that Lizzie wanted money and freedom and that she intended to kill Mr. and Mrs. Borden by poison. On the morning of the murders, however, she had a seizure and killed them with an axe.

A Pictorial History of the World's Great Trials, from Socrates to Eichmann, by Brandt Aymar and Edward Sagarin (1967) describes thirty-one trials. A twenty-page section devoted to the Borden trial is augmented by many pictures and drawings, including a seldom-seen photograph of Lizzie, looking carefree and almost happy.

Choreographer Agnes de Mille has produced one of the most unusual books about Lizzie Borden. While creating a ballet based on the Borden story, she also wrote *Lizzie Borden: A Dance of Death* (1968). The book is written in two parts: first, a straightforward account of the events in Fall River, and second, a description of the process of producing the ballet that would tell Lizzie's story. Miss de Mille gathered materials in Fall River with the help of famed lawyer Joseph

Welch. Two excellent minds, focused on the murders, has resulted in a clear, often innovative account of crimes and motives.

Colin Wilson, a British connoisseur of true crime, has written *A Casebook of Murder* (1969), in which he describes the changing patterns of murder in western society from the fifteenth century to the present day. Wilson's interest in murder is philosophical rather than scientific, and his work is a valuable contribution to the study of murder. The book contains a brief analysis of the Borden case. Wilson does not believe that modern forensic methods could shed any light on the case after the lapse of so many years but points out that, if modern methods had been available at the time, the crime would have been solved within hours.

Goodbye Lizzie Borden, written by Robert Sullivan (1974) is a legally-oriented presentation of the Borden murders. A former Justice of the Massachusetts Superior Court, Sullivan brought his experience and knowledge to the thousands of pages of trial records. Sullivan has no doubt of Lizzie's guilt, and his evidence is persuasively presented.

The Borden story has found its way into the writing of dramatists as well as that of historians, reporters, and crime writers. In their play, *Nine Pine Street* (1934), John Colton and Carlton Miles use basic facts of the Borden story, thinly disguised, together with their own hypotheses. The Holden family of New Bedford, Massachusetts, is comprised of father, stepmother, and two unmarried daughters. One of the daughters kills her parents, partly out of greed and partly for revenge, for the second Mrs. Holden had murdered the daughters' natural mother. Lillian Gish played the role of murderous daughter, and the play was well received.

Another play, *Goodbye Miss Lizzie Borden: A Sinister Play in One Act* (1947) by Lillian de la Torre, gives the story a new twist. Emma, not away visiting as she claimed, is the guilty daughter, but Lizzie takes the blame.

Tom Covel's unpublished play *Lizbeth* (1978) deals with a period untouched by other playwrights -- Lizzie's life after she moved to Maplecroft. Covel introduces material about the murders through dialogue between Lizzie and Emma. The plays shows, in Covel's words, "Lizzie's increasing isolation broken by a relationship with the actress, Nance O'Neil." According to Covel, Emma left Maplecroft because of Lizzie's involvement with Miss O'Neil. The play intimates that their friendship may have had lesbian overtones. Covel's accompanying bibliography demonstrates imaginative research on the Bordens and Nance O'Neil.

The editors have drawn on the following works in their treatment of the social environment of the crime and recommend these materials for further reading.

History:

Nugent, Walter T.K., *Modern America.* Boston: Houghton Mifflin, 1973.

Wiebe, Robert H., *The Search for Order, 1877-1920.* New York: Hill and Wang, 1967. (The Making of America Series, David Donald, General Editor.)

The Family:

Special Issue on "The History of the Family in American Urban Society," *Journal of Urban History,* I:3(May 1975). See especially articles by T.K. Hareven and Laurence A. Glasco.

Bridges, William E., "Family Patterns and Social Values in America, 1825-75," in: *Education in American History. Readings on the Social Issues,* ed. Michael B. Katz. New York: Praeger, 1973.

Clark, Clifford E., Jr., "American Protestantism's Teachings to Young Men," in: *The American Experience in Education,* ed. John Barnard and David Burner. New York: New Viewpoints, 1975.

Gordon, Michael, ed. *The American Family in Social-Historical Perspective.* New York: St. Martin's Press, 1973.

Sicherman, Barbara, "The Paradox of Prudence: Mental Health in the Gilded Age," *Journal of American History,* LXII:4 (March 1976), 890-912.

Women:

Barker-Benfield, Graham J., *The Horrors of the Half-Known Life. Male Attitudes toward Women and Sexuality in Nineteenth-Century America.* New York: Harper & Row, 1976.

Hartman, Mary, and Lois W. Banner, eds., *Clio's Consciousness Raised. New Perspectives on the History of Women.* New York: Harper Torchbooks, 1974.

Rosenberg, Charles, "Sexuality, Class and Role in 19th-Century America," *American Quarterly,* XXV (May 1973), 131-53.

Smith-Rosenberg, Carroll, "The Hysterical Woman: Sex Roles and Role Conflict in 19th-Century America," *Social Research,* 39 (Winter 1972), 652-78.

Welter, Barbara, "The Cult of True Womanhood: 1820-1860," *American Quarterly,* XVIII (Summer 1966), 151-74. Reprinted in: *The Underside of American History: Other Readings,* Vol. I: *To 1877,* ed. Thomas R. Frazier. New York: Harcourt Brace Jovanovich, 1974.